Karatedo Quantum Leap

空手道 クォンタム リープ

KARATEDO QUANTUM LEAP

空手道 クォンタム リープ

ADVANCING YOUR KARATE UNDERSTANDING TO THE NEXT LEVEL

KOUSAKU YOKOTA

横田耕作

ISBN: 978-0-9982236-3-6

This book was printed in the United States of America.

To order additional copies of this book, contact:
Azami Press
1-765-242-7988
www.AzamiPress.com
Info@AzamiPress.com

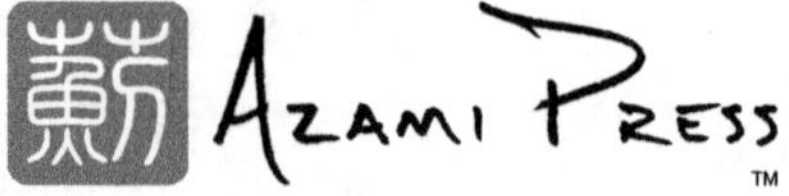

Dedication
奉納

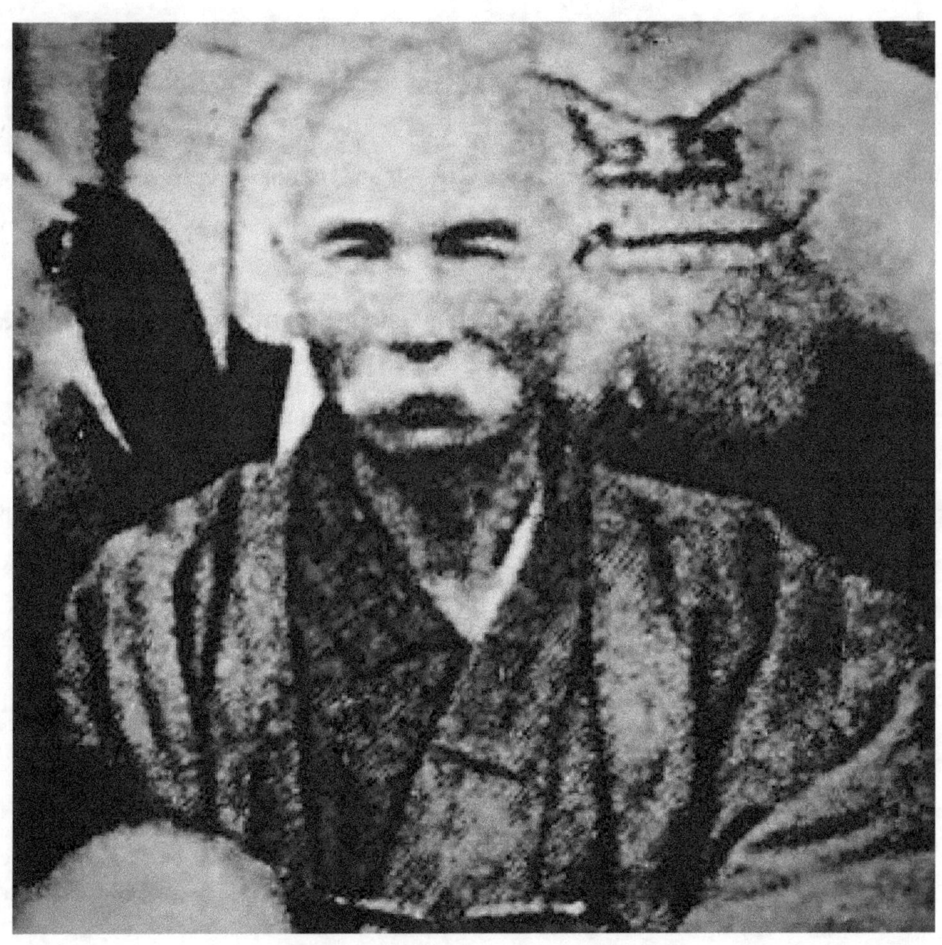

I wish to dedicate this book to Anko Itosu (糸洲安恒, 1831–1915). I feel he has not received the credit and exposure that he deserves. Therefore, I wish to introduce him and share some basic information about him in this dedication.

Gichin Funakoshi is known as the founder of the Shotokan style. In addition, he is also known among all karate practitioners as the father of modern karate since he spread Okinawan *te* to mainland Japan. We must remember that Itosu was sensei not only to Funakoshi but also to many of the Okinawan karate masters we know and credit with the shaping of modern karate. His impressive list of students includes Choki Motobu, Kenwa Mabuni, Chojun Miyagi, Kentsu Yabu, Chomo Hanashiro, Moden Yabiku, Kanken Toyama, Shinpan Gusukuma, Anbun Tokuda, Choshin Chibana, and more.

Itosu served as secretary to the last king of the Ryukyu Kingdom until the Japanese government abolished the native monarchy in 1879, after the Meiji Restoration. In the early twentieth century, he was instrumental in getting karate introduced into the public schools of Okinawa and also developed a systematic method of teaching karate techniques.

We must not forget that Itosu created the Heian/Pin'an *kata* for schoolchildren to learn. He is also credited with breaking the long Tekki/Naihanchi *kata* into three separate forms for easier learning. In 1908, he wrote the influential *Tode Kokoroe Jukkajo* (唐手心得十ヶ條, 'Ten Precepts of Karate'). If you wish to learn more about this important teaching, you can find it in Chapter 17: "Itosu's Ten Precepts of Karate" of my book *Karatedo Paradigm Shift*. Maybe Itosu was the true father of modern day karate.

Kousaku Yokota Biography
経歴

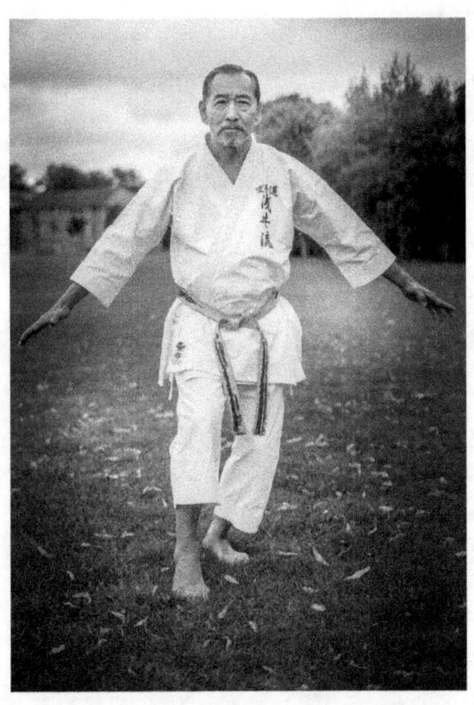

Shihan Kousaku Yokota (横田耕作), eighth *dan*, was born in Kobe, Japan, in 1947 and currently resides in California, U.S.A. He is a professional *karateka* with extensive experience in various martial arts. With over fifty-four years of training in Shotokan karate (松濤館空手), he specializes in Asai Ryu Bujutsu karate (浅井流武術空手). His wide range of experience includes training in *kobudo* (*nanasetsuben* and nunchaku), in the art of ki, and in the breathing method by Nishino Ryu Kikojutsu (西野流気功術).

He was a member of the JKA for forty years and then joined the JKS for seven years. In 2013, he founded his organization, ASAI (Asai Shotokan Association International [www.asaikarate.com]), to honor Master Tetsuhiko Asai (浅井哲彦). Shihan Yokota travels extensively around the world to share the knowledge and techniques of Asai Ryu karate.

He is the author of *Shotokan Myths* (Azami Press, 2010), *Shotokan Mysteries* (Azami Press, 2013), *Shotokan Transcendence* (Azami Press, 2015) and *Karatedo Paradigm Shift* (Azami Press, 2017), which are all available on *Amazon*. You can also read many of his articles, which cover a wide range of topics on the martial arts and Japanese philosophy, on his blog at the following URL: www.asaikarate.com/blog.

Acknowledgments
感謝の言葉

I must say that many people are responsible for making the creation of this book, *Karatedo Quantum Leap*, possible. I want to extend my gratitude to all those who have so generously contributed their time and experience to the creation of this book and to all those who have purchased it.

I must not forget to give thanks to all my instructors in different martial arts, past and present, for giving me the knowledge and understanding of not only Shotokan but also the way of *karatedo*. Master Gichin Funakoshi, the founder of Shotokan, said, "Karate training is a lifetime endeavor." Master Tetsuhiko Asai was the karate master who made the greatest impact on my karate. I consider him to be a karate genius, and he taught me to train every day by demonstrating his own daily training.

In the past, I learned from my sensei and my *senpai*. Today, though my sensei have passed, my students and other *karateka* are my new teachers. Without all of you, my karate would not be where it is today, and this book would probably not have materialized.

Last but not least, I want to thank you, the reader of this book. I hope you enjoy reading it as much as I have enjoyed writing it.

From the bottom of my heart, I want to say, "Thank you very much to all of you."

皆様に心より御礼申し上げます。
Minasama ni kokoro yori orei mōshiagemasu.

Foreword

By Alpa Khatri

Yondan, Asai Ryu

Mumbai, India

Yokota Shihan's new book, *Karatedo Quantum Leap*, revolves around a variety of vital concepts in the sphere of karate. It is a long, informative journey that is enlightening to the core. It begins by explaining the important but rarely addressed *budo* concept of *suemono ni suru* and then goes on to answer many other important questions and address other interesting and varied topics like *kuse*, the spiral fist, and *hado*.

The book also drops hints and truths about certain involved subjects and goes on to explain them like never before. It has just the right balance between effectiveness and terseness. It tells the true objective of team *kata*, gives five improvement hints for senior practitioners, and rethinks the karate fist.

Yokota Shihan is a man of deep knowledge and endless light. He has been a source of endless knowledge and rejuvenation coupled with ample support for everyone he is associated with. He has been the reason behind an enormous change in my perspective. It is under his guidance that I came home to *budo* karate. Life seemed to take an entirely different turn for me after that. This not only strengthened my roots in karate but also showed me a different face to it. I have been an ardent follower of *budo* karate ever since.

Yokota Shihan is a never-failing dawn. It is not just his books that spread the good word around; he is a constant practitioner himself. It is well said that actions speak more loudly than words. Several of his other books also prove to be mind changers as they shift the world in your brain. Reading them will nourish you with dedication, will, and stability. While *Shotokan Mysteries* reveals the forbidden answers to the mysteries of Shotokan karate, *Shotokan Transcendence* brings to life knowledge beyond the stealth and riddles of Funakoshi karate.

It is thoughtworthy how certain people can challenge your mind and make you a better human. Yokota Shihan has been that person. He has shown a never-waning strength, both mental and physical, accompanied by a blessed heart and a wish to pass on his humble learning to as many people as possible. It is a proud feeling to merely cross paths with a human like him. It is noteworthy how he takes time out to pay timely visits to India, where we are sanctified with the happiness of meeting him and are tiny rivulets in his course of spreading knowledge.

In the contemporary world, where we all lack time, this book is a must-have for your shelves. It will alter your way of going about life. It will make you want to spread the art to people yourself and will also make you want to be a part of the mystic journey.

We all come across necessary things in life; only delivering them in the right way makes them acceptable as necessary. This book is a nurturing journey that makes its way through your mind and soul. It does not support one particular ideology. Rather, it gives the reader a vantage point from which to just stand and look forward at the beautiful and transforming truth of this art.

Shotokan karate is so deeply rooted into me now that it is not just a simple portion of my life. Instead, it is the way I lead my life. Karate, in my belief, should not be restricted to being viewed as a martial art; it needs to be understood as a way of life. It needs to be seen as an art of the utmost importance that makes up our vital veins. It needs to be discerned as essential, a pleasant complement that clings to our existence.

This book will serve as a delight for all those who are associated with karate and as a mental shift and savior for all those who are not. It will be a prolific exploration of the world of martial arts and of our own selves.

FOREWORD

By Peace Emezue
Shodan, World Shotokan Karate Federation
Federal Capita Territory, Abuja-Nigeria

My foray into karate started several years ago, when I was struggling to overcome excess weight and protracted obesity. I had made dietary changes and supported this with aerobic activities but wanted a system of mind-body discipline to further drive my objective. This was when I met my karate sensei, who, in spite of my obvious struggles, took me on and taught me karate up to first *dan*.

Having trained as a female karate practitioner for about half a decade now, I have come to realize that karate is more than just a sporting exercise; it is a way of life that is embedded in deep philosophical foundations. I recall several discussions with my sensei on the issue of living the way. Much of this didn't make much sense to me until I traveled to China in 2015 and trained at the Shaolin Temple for about three months. At some point during the training, I had issues with my legs but had to adapt other parts of my body to forge on. Later, I also had the opportunity to travel to Japan in 2017 to attend the World Shotokan Karate Federation Championship. Through these separate yet similar experiences, I came to the realization that most classical martial arts have common denominators in terms of philosophical components and structure. I was very pleased to attend the seminar and championship under Kasuya Sensei in Japan in 2017. I was privileged to learn more things about Shotokan karate.

I was, therefore, excited when I met Yokota Kousaku Sensei online and eventually had the privilege of reading his book *Karatedo Paradigm Shift*. This book, by my assessment, answers several questions and proffers insights into many areas for any consummate karate practitioner. It clarifies the content and purpose of both competitive and *budo* karate while, at the same time, acknowledging the need for the evolution of Shotokan karate. This is clearly conveyed in the thematic undertones of the concepts of *shingitai* and *shuhari*, respectively.

I am particularly thrilled about Yokota Sensei's new book, *Karatedo Quantum*

Leap, as he throws more light on germane topics like *tanden* breathing methods, moving vs. using the body, and internal vs. external systems, to mention a few. Fortunately, I have been privileged to pick up some of these rudiments from my sensei, who is an enthusiast, a great admirer of Asai Tetsuhiko Shihan's legacy, and also a practitioner of aikido, yoga, and tai chi.

It is my belief that Yokota Sensei's book *Karatedo Quantum Leap* will not only build on the knowledge base of his previous works but further consolidate the narrative of the functional evolution and development of karate. I, therefore, have no doubt whatsoever that this new book will enrich the minds as well as the practice of martial artists under any style.

Foreword

By Olayinka Adetona Ayeni
Legal Practitioner & Shotokan Karateka
Agege, Lagos State, Nigeria

One of the most important aspects of our life is having good health and a sound mind, which we can only achieve through the togetherness of our body, soul, and spirit. Martial arts, such as aikido, kung fu, and karate, deal with the training of our body for developing stamina, fitness, self-defense, and a sound mind. This helps to sharpen our physical, mental, and spiritual being.

Karatedo Quantum Leap is an eighteen-chapter book in which Yokota Kousaku Shihan has provided individuals with a veritable, impeccable, idea-filled, rich compilation of relevant karate techniques on an international scale. I say, "relevant," because the book talks about traditional karate, that is, karate from its source. The style he has adopted in his work is simple and easy to learn through true individual commitment.

The reader can use the ideas stated in this book to improve his knowledge in karate in the form of a big jump (quantum leap). Yokota Shihan has truly done a great service to martial artists all over the world. Apart from his books, I watch his videos and learn some moves every morning and night despite my busy schedule as a legal practitioner. Everyone all over the world will surely read this book with much profit and gratitude.

The learned author has indeed succeeded in producing a handy reference book that provides a practical guide to karate. I congratulate Yokota Shihan on his selfless, valuable contribution to the attainment of excellence in the practice of the martial arts.

Preface
初めに

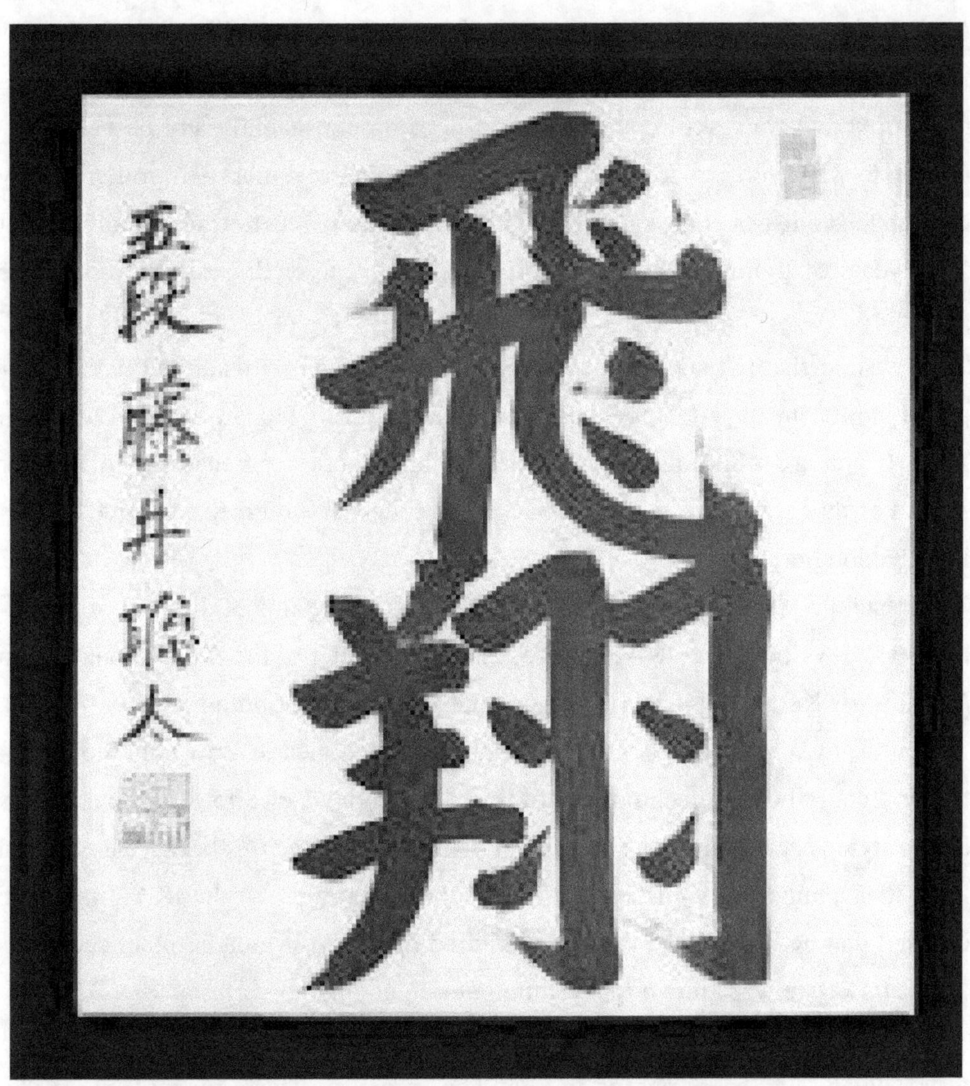

Calligraphic characters reading *hisho* (飛翔, ‘soar’ or ‘fly away’) by sixteen-year-old chess master Sota Fujii (藤井聡太, 2002–)

I want to thank the reader for selecting this book. I hope you enjoy reading it, but I also hope some, if not all, of the information is helpful and beneficial to your karate training.

The title of this book is *Karatedo Quantum Leap*. The definition of *quantum leap*, as found in *Merriam-Webster's Collegiate Dictionary, Eleventh Edition*, is "an abrupt change, sudden increase, or dramatic advance." It is true that improvement in your karate skill comes only if you train consistently and pay close attention to what you are doing. It is also true that improvement—if you are lucky enough to see it—is always gradual. This is the way it was for me during my first forty years of training. However, abrupt changes and/or dramatic advances are possible.

I wish to share my experience with a quantum leap in my karate life that happened in just one day. It happened at a seminar featuring the late Tetsuhiko Asai in 2001. If you are a Shotokan practitioner, no introduction is necessary for Master Asai. For those who are not Shotokan practitioners, I would like to give a short introduction here.

Tetsuhiko Asai (浅井哲彦, 1935–2006) was the technical director of the Japan Karate Association (JKA). He was also the founder of the International Japan Martial Arts Karate Asai-ryu (IJKA) and the Japan Karate Shoto Federation (JKS). He trained in White Crane kung fu when he was stationed in Taiwan in the seventies and combined the techniques of kung fu with those of Shotokan, making his karate style very unique and exciting. I call him a *karate genius* because he created more than a hundred new training *kata* to supplement those of the JKA. In fact, he claimed that he knew more than one hundred fifty *kata*, which he practiced regularly. His karate was known to be smooth, circular, and powerful.

When I participated in Master Asai's seminar, I was fifty-three or fifty-four years old and had been training in Shotokan karate for nearly forty years. At that time, I was at a critical moment in my karate life. In fact, I was debating whether or not I should give up on my karate training because I felt (erroneously, of course) that I had learned everything there was to know about Shotokan karate. I had learned and mastered all twenty-six JKA *kata* and felt that I was on a plateau, which took the joy out of training.

At that moment, I experienced Asai karate. Master Asai was sixty-six years old but moved like a teenager. Many of his techniques were totally new to me. On top of that, he introduced a few of his *kata*, which had many new techniques that blew my mind as I thought I knew all the *kata* of Shotokan. Master Asai demonstrated how nimble, flexible, and powerful a sixty-six-year-old *karateka* could be. He showed us how much more we needed to learn and practice before we could be considered masters.

In a way, the goal was daunting as it was so far away, but, at the same time, it gave me such hope and such a clear path to follow. Even though I did not experience a dramatic advance, I certainly did have an abrupt change in my mind-set and expectations. Indeed, meeting Master Asai saved my karate life.

I am no Tetsuhiko Asai, and my book does not offer enlightenment; however, I have selected some topics that may be new and unique to the reader. I have also added some concrete suggestions as to what senior practitioners can do to improve their karate. I hope you will open your mind and keep it flexible so that you can appreciate the ideas and concepts written in this book. If even one reader experiences an abrupt change in his thinking by reading this book, then I will consider the effort of writing it to have been well invested, and nothing would make me happier than that.

Contents

Dedication....vii
Kousaku Yokota Biography....ix
Acknowledgments....xi
Forewords....xiii
Preface....xix

Chapter 1 The Forgotten Secret Teaching of "Suemono ni Suru"....1
Chapter 2 Kumite Tempo....11
Chapter 3 What Is Meotode?....23
Chapter 4 What Is the True Objective of Team Kata?....37
Chapter 5 Five Practical Training Ideas to Improve Kata and Kumite....47
Chapter 6 The Truth about Foot Stomping....71
Chapter 7 Internal Systems vs. External Systems....79
Chapter 8 Eight Striking and Eight Nonstriking Points....87
Chapter 9 Ip Man's Wing Chun Rules of Conduct....97
Chapter 10 Bruce Lee's One-Inch Punch Examined....105
Chapter 11 What Is Ueshiba's Teaching of San Go Ichi?....115
Chapter 12 Do Not Explain in Karate Training....133
Chapter 13 Kuse: the Greatest Enemy of Improvement....145
Chapter 14 Rethinking the Karate Fist....157
Chapter 15 What Is a Spiral Fist?....173
Chapter 16 Moving the Body vs. Using the Body....181
Chapter 17 Can Karate Be Mastered by Practicing Only Kata?....193
Chapter 18 What Is Hado?....207

Chapter One
第一章

The Forgotten Secret Teaching of "Suemono ni Suru"
忘却された秘伝「据え物にする」

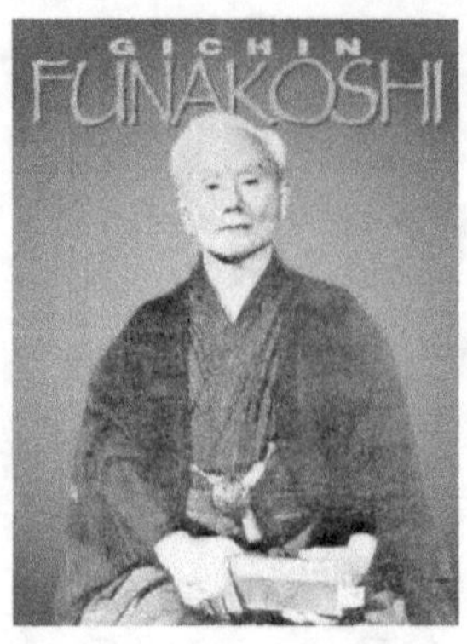

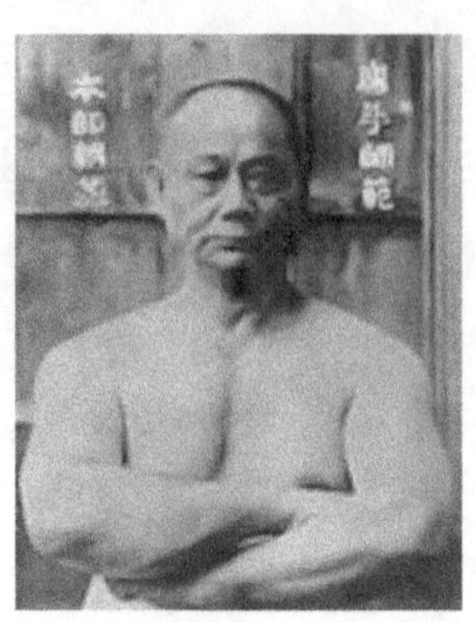

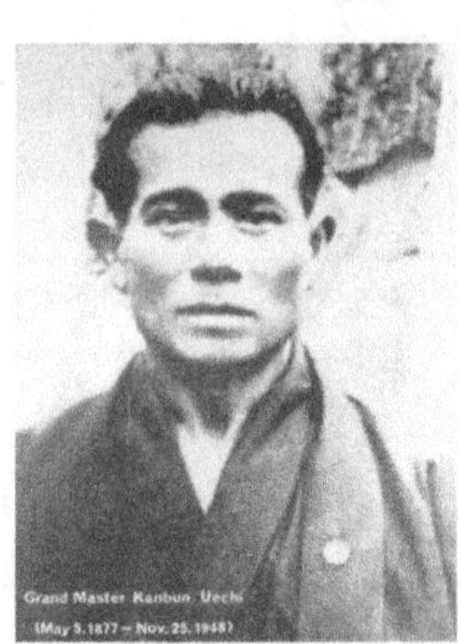

It is well known that Okinawan karate, or *te* (手), was formally introduced into mainland Japan in 1922, almost one hundred years ago, by Gichin Funakoshi (船越義珍, 1868–1957 [photo above left]). Though other Okinawan masters, such as Choki Motobu (本部朝基, 1870–1944 [photo above center]) and Kanbun Uechi (上地完文, 1877–1948 [photo above right]), came to Japan in the same period, their activities did not bear fruit mainly because they did not promote their karate in Tokyo. Funakoshi, on the other hand, migrated to Tokyo and promoted his art to university students as he could speak standard Japanese. Thus, he is remembered as the father of modern karate.

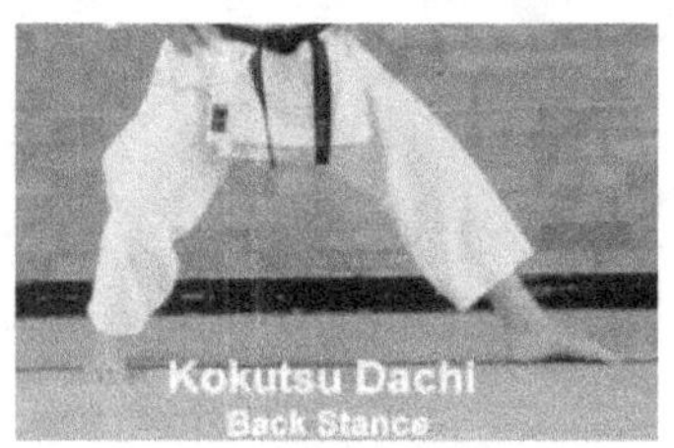

When Funakoshi introduced Okinawa Te (沖縄手) in the early twentieth century, he made many changes, such as replacing the original names of the *kata*, which made little sense to the Japanese, with names that did make sense to them. He changed some of the techniques, such as de-emphasizing *neko ashi dachi* (猫足立ち) and creating *kokutsu dachi* (後屈立ち). He also changed some of the *mae geri* (前蹴り) techniques to *yoko geri keage* (横蹴り蹴上げ) techniques in many *kata*. He created the *karategi* (空手着, 'karate uniform') and *obi* (帯, 'belt') with which we are now very familiar. There were many other changes, but I will address only one here. If you are interested in the other

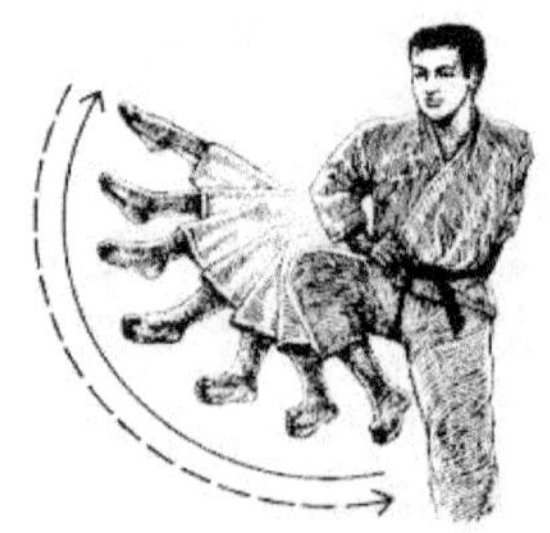

changes, I have already written a few chapters on this subject, which can be found in my books. One is Chapter 1: "New Techniques by Funakoshi?" of my book *Shotokan Mysteries*.

OK, enough of the introduction. Here I would like to bring up one very important karate concept that is almost forgotten by karate practitioners. The concept is *aite o suemono ni suru* (相手を据え物にする). Let me explain. The first word, *aite* (相手), means 'opponent'. The next word, *o* (を), is simply a grammatical particle that marks the object of the sentence. The third term is the key word: *suemono* (据え物). One of the most popular meanings of this word is used in iaido (居合道), where it refers to a roll of straw that a practitioner cuts with a katana (刀) to check his cutting ability (photo right). The original use of this word came from the time of the samurai (侍). It referred to a dead body or a condemned criminal (instead of a roll of straw) that was to be cut by the samurai to check the cutting ability of their swords or to execute the criminal (illustration left). As you can see, the body was tied down firmly so that it would not move when it was being cut. This is the key point in understanding the concept. The last two words, *ni suru* (にする), mean 'to make into' or 'to turn into'. So, all together, the sentence means 'to turn the opponent into a still target'.

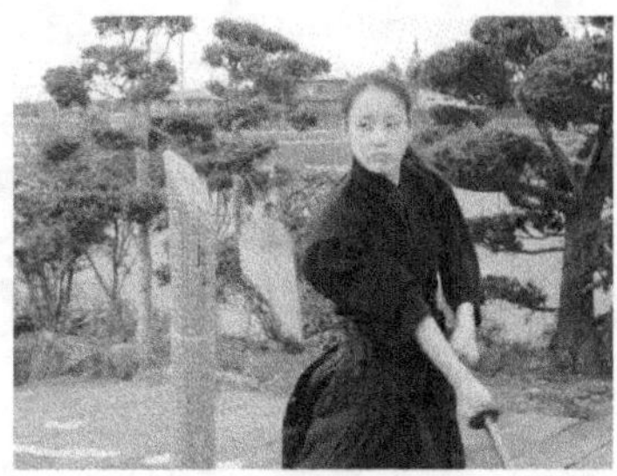

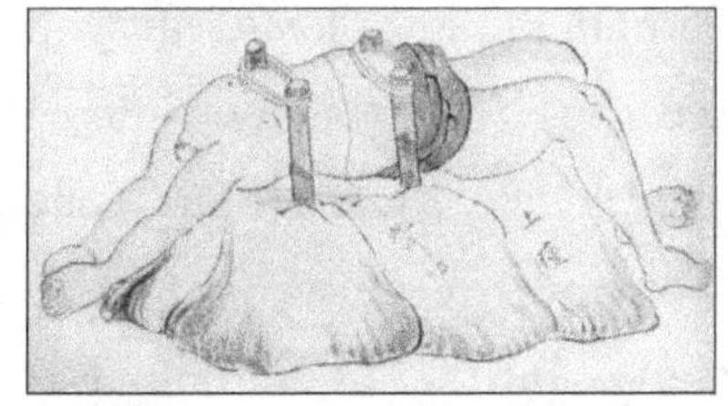

Now you understand the meaning of the Japanese sentence, but I suspect that you are not sure exactly what it means unless you have learned about this in the past. In order to understand this sentence, we need to look at a short history of karate over the past sixty years or so.

I assume most readers know that the original *te* was a *budo* (武道, 'martial art'). That was what Funakoshi and the other Okinawan masters took to Japan nearly a century ago. I cannot say what the other masters thought about introducing the *shiai* (試合, 'tournament') concept into karate, but I can at least say that Fu-

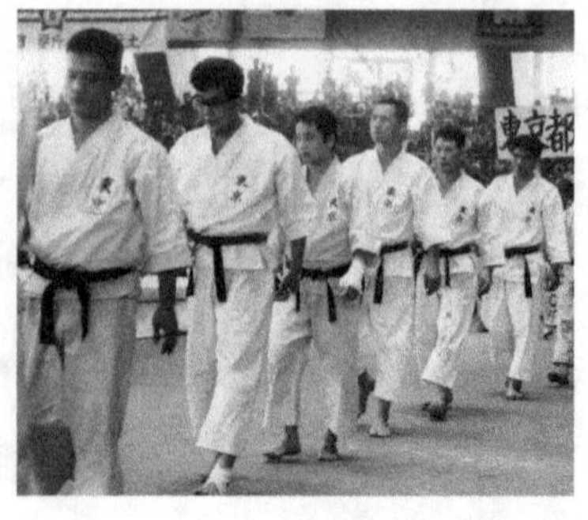

nakoshi was firmly against it until his death. It is true that there were many informal *shiai* (i.e., *shiai* that were not approved) among the karate clubs of the universities located in Tokyo. They did not call them *shiai* but rather *koryukai* (交流会, 'friendship meetings'). The formal tournament, the All Japan Championship, hosted by the Japan Karate Association (日本空手協会 [JKA]) had to wait until 1957, the year Funakoshi passed.

Since *shiai* karate (or sport karate) has become so popular these days, we are so accustomed to the *kumite* (組手, 'sparring') style that we mistakenly believe the "killing" techniques seen in matches are the only real and effective techniques. If you have been in a street fight in the past, you are well aware that the real situation is very different from what is seen in *shiai kumite* matches. First of all, the distance is completely different in most cases. There are no "Hajime!" (始め, 'begin') or "Yame!" (止め, 'stop') commands. You may have multiple opponents, and you may not know if they have weapons. This is why *zanshin* (残心, 'remaining mind') is extremely important in martial arts. In addition, the Okinawan masters knew one secret technique, which is what I am sharing with you now.

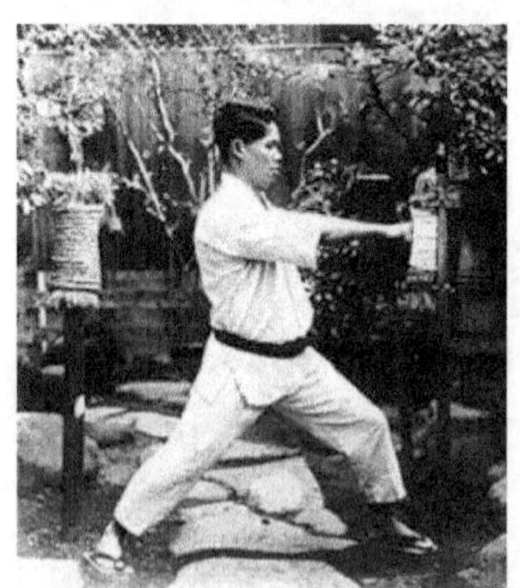

It is well known that *makiwara* (巻藁) training is considered to be a very important item in the training menu. Interestingly, I know that some Western-style boxers have criticized the punching of a stationary target for having little worth in boxing. They say that their opponent is always moving, so it is better to practice punching a moving target. They also do not need to toughen their fists as they wear gloves. I understand why they would say this, and it makes sense when you watch how *kumite* matches are conducted and see that the competitors are moving around almost all the time.

If this is the case, why did the ancient Okinawan masters mention the *suemo-*

no? Did Okinawan people fight without moving? Were Okinawan fighters unable to move fast? I do not think so and am sure the reader will agree with me. Some readers may know that Choki Motobu's nickname was *Saru* (猿, 'Monkey') as he could easily climb fences and rooftops. If that is the case, I hardly believe he was only able to move slowly. Once you understand the true meaning behind this concept, you will be impressed with the fantastic knowledge of the Okinawan masters.

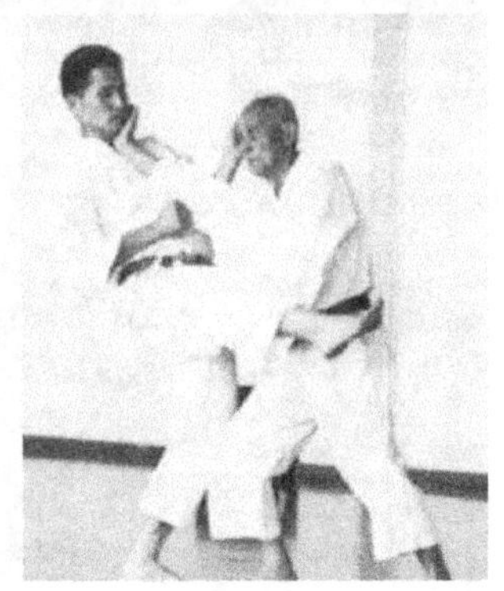

So, let me explain in detail. The masters knew that it was not very easy to knock down an opponent, especially another *karateka* (空手家), with one punch, even though the saying *ikken hissatsu* (一拳必殺, 'one punch, certain kill') was in use then. It is difficult simply because the opponent is constantly moving. The effect of punching and kicking is reduced significantly if the target moves in closer or backs away from the spot where you assume him to be. So, they developed techniques such as *deai* (出会い) and *irimi* (入り身), which are techniques where the defender moves in when the attacker is stepping in. In this situation, a high level of skill is required, and the counterattack can have a great impact upon the opponent as he moves in.

Other techniques are the *tsukami* (掴み, 'grabbing') and *hikiyose* (引き寄せ, 'pulling in') techniques. We know what *hikite* (引き手, 'drawing hand') is, and most of the time practitioners think it is a movement used only to pull their hand back as they deliver a technique with the other hand. However, in *kata*, many of the *hikite* techniques are in fact movements used for grabbing and pulling the opponent in. A good example is found in Tekki (鉄騎), or Naihanchi (ナイハンチ).

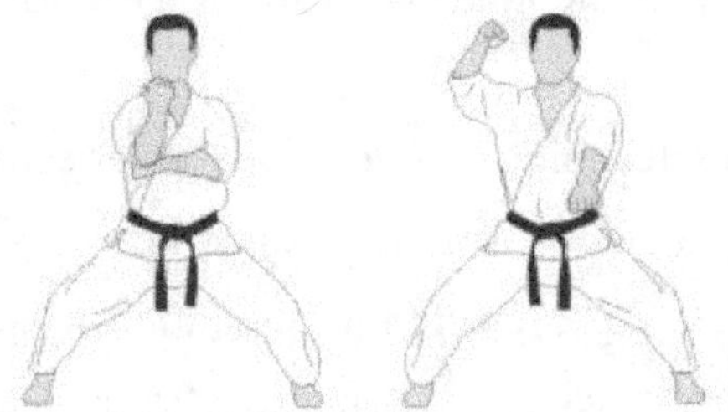

When you execute *jodan ura zuki* (上段裏突き), you are expected to grab the opponent and pull him in with the other hand (illustration left).

It is much more difficult to catch an opponent who is moving away from you. You may need to possess the skill of being able to reach farther than what the opponent would expect, and some people have developed the skill of being able to cover a much greater distance than what the average practitioner can. This technique is called *shukuchiho* (縮地法), which literally means 'distance-shortening method', but I will not go into an explanation of that in this chapter.

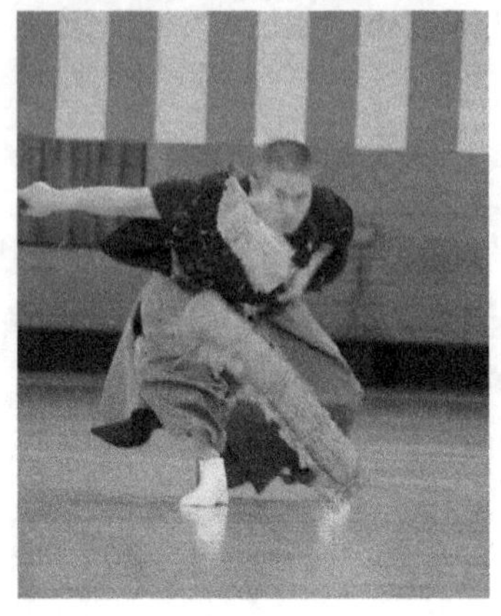

These are excellent techniques against a moving target, but the Okinawan masters came up with another brilliant idea, which is *suemono ni suru*, or the stop-the-opponent technique. The *suemono* is the fixed target, such as the roll of straw or the dead body, so this means that the technique makes your opponent stop or get into a fixed state momentarily. We all agree that it is much easier to punch or kick the opponent if he is fixed in one spot. In iaido, of course, the *suemono* is a roll of straw that does not move. In the time of the samurai, the body was tied down at the wrists and ankles so that it would not move. In karate, however, the opponent is completely free.

What is very interesting and brilliant is that this *suemono* technique in karate not only makes the opponent stay in one spot but also puts him into a mental state that doesn't expect what is coming. Have you ever experienced a situation where you were going down a staircase and thought you had completed all the steps, but there was one more step? What had happened to you? I bet you either lost your footing or at least felt a big shock in the stepping leg and almost fell down. This comes from having a mind that does not expect what is coming. It happens in a dark house at night or when you are looking at something else while you are going down the stairs.

OK, you understand in general that this technique can produce an effective result. But, the opponent is constantly moving, so you want to know how this is done. There are a few methods that can be used to create this situation. In fact, the *tsukami waza* that I mentioned earlier can keep the opponent at a constant

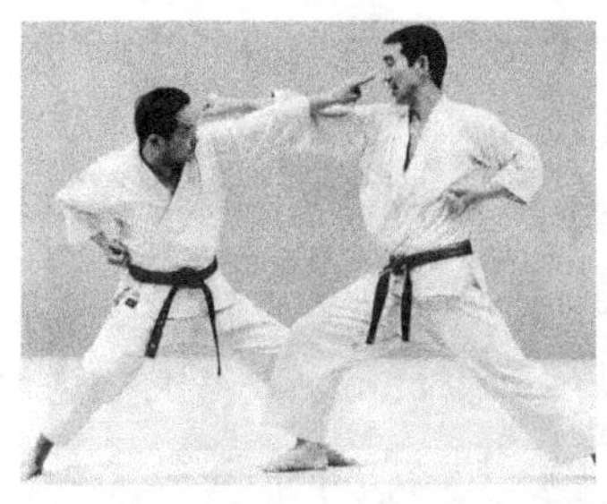

distance. However, he can see what is happening, so he can also use this constant distance as an opportunity to fight against you. Therefore, the most popular method within the *suemono* technique is *metsubushi* (目潰し, 'eye jabbing'), which is a direct method of making the opponent close his eyes. You typically use the fingertips of your open hand to either jab or swipe at the eyes.

Is this technique used in *kata*? Of course, you can find an obvious *metsubushi* technique in some *kata*, such as Chinte (珍手), in which it is done with *nihon nukite* (二本貫手, 'two-finger spear hand'). But, some techniques may not be so obvious. A good example is in Enpi (燕飛), where you find a *metsubushi* technique after the *jodan age zuki* (上段挙げ突き [photo right]). After this technique, you open your punching hand and then jump in to execute *gedan zuki* (下段突き). That open hand is used to blind the eyes.

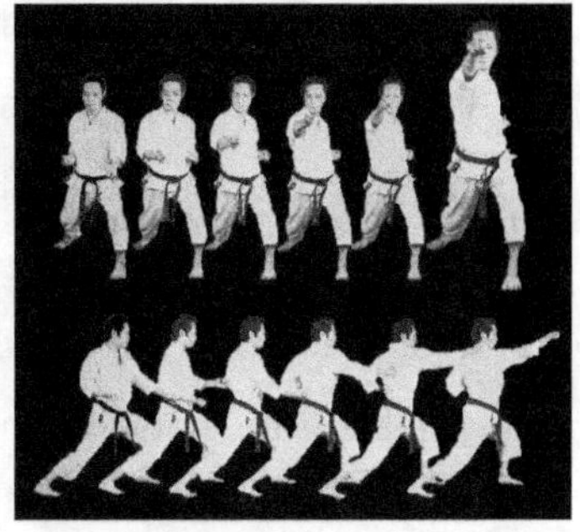

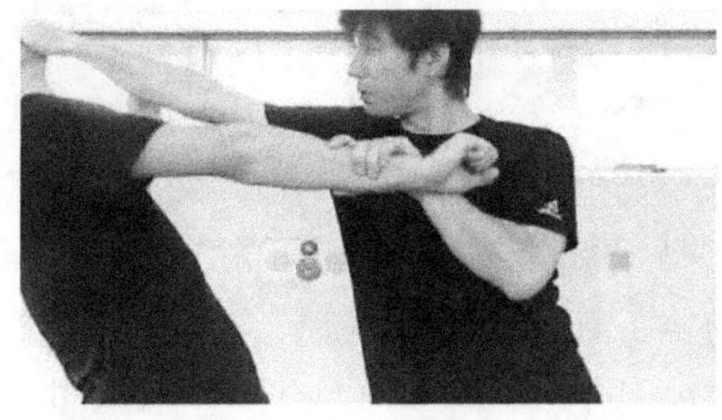

To the left is a photo of Tatsuya Naka (中達也, 1964–) of the JKA demonstrating the eye attack in Enpi. After the *jodan age zuki* (most likely to the opponent's chin), you open your hand and place it over the opponent's face with the *teisho* (底掌, 'palm heel') placed at the chin. Just spread your hand, and you will realize that the fingertips naturally reach the eyes. Pushing the whole hand forward will easily push the opponent back as you jump in to execute the *gedan zuki*. By the way, the other forearm goes to the other side of the head and looks like *jodan nagashi uke* (上段流し受け). This interpretation is not incorrect, but this can also be a *tsukami waza* or a *hikiyose waza*.

Another example of a not-so-obvious *metsubushi* technique is the last two

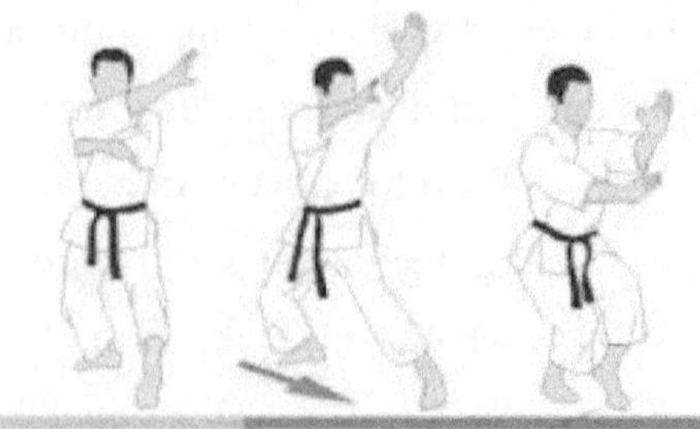

moves of Bassai Sho (抜塞小) as shown in the illustration to the left. The large hand movement, despite being done in slow motion, is an eye-swiping action before a *tsukami* and *hikiyose* technique. (The other hand is also doing a *tsukami* and *hikiyose* technique.) What happens in the actual *bunkai* (分解) is that when the attacker comes in with a *chudan oi zuki* (下段追い突き), the defender initially executes *metsubushi* and then grabs the attacking arm with both hands (*tsukami uke* [掴み受け, 'grabbing block']). As the defender pulls the opponent's arm (*hikiyose*), he sweeps at the same time. When carried out faster than what is shown in the *kata*, these actions cause the attacker to fall. The defender then executes the finishing move (a punch or a kick) either while the attacker is falling or after he has fallen. This final action is omitted or hidden in the *kata*.

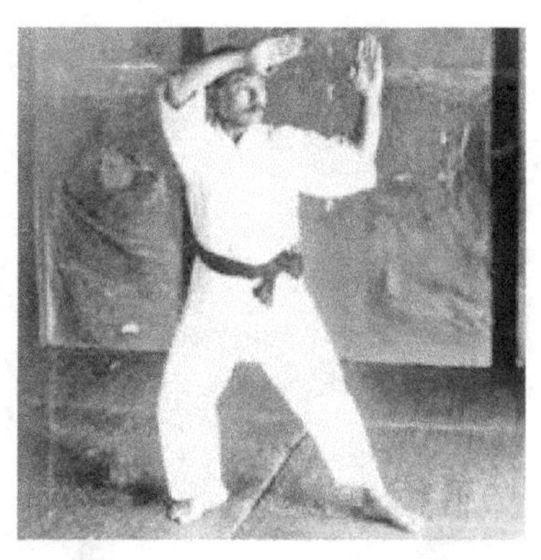

Why is this done slowly? I write about this interesting subject in Chapter 3: "Heian Bunkai Mysteries" of my book *Shotokan Mysteries*. Let me restate the reasons briefly here. One is to create a challenging technique (e.g., the first two moves of Heian Yondan). Another is to illustrate the pressing or resisting action, such as the one used in *tsukami waza* or *kakiwake* (掻き分け) *waza*. I believe the last two steps of Bassai Sho belong to the first reason, but, at the same time, I think there is a third reason.

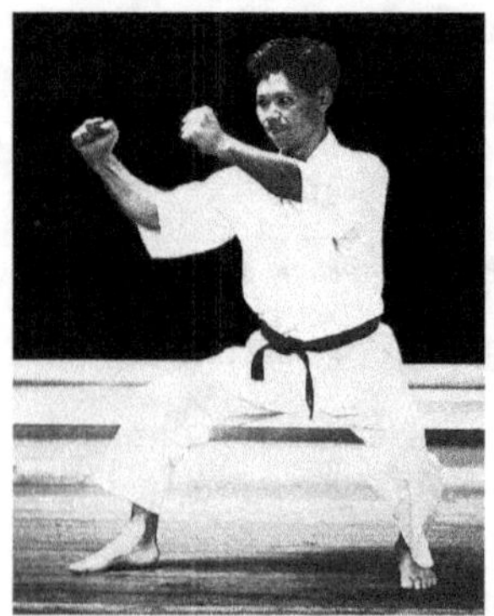

A certain move may be done slowly to show there are some options that are not included in the *kata*. I am pretty certain of this as an *uke* is not a final move. In other words, there must be a counterattack after an *uke*. I cannot believe the creator of a *kata* would design a form where the defender (*kata* performer) only sweeps the attacker and then moves on to the next *waza* combination, especially in an advanced *kata* such as Bassai Sho.

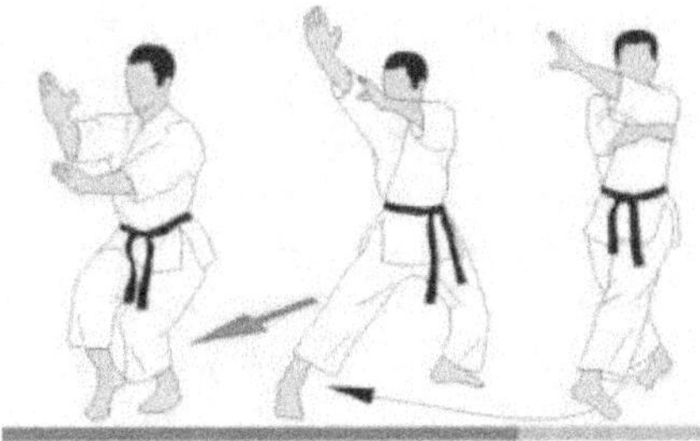

Without debating the point made in the previous paragraph, that overt upper hand movement (swinging the lead hand in a large circular movement) in the last two steps is an eye swipe. This action causes the attacker to lose momentum and have to stop in the middle of his action. This makes it much easier for the defender to sweep as he pulls the opponent downward, which makes the attacker very vulnerable to the counterattack.

Jintai Kyusho – The Vital Areas of the Human Anatomy

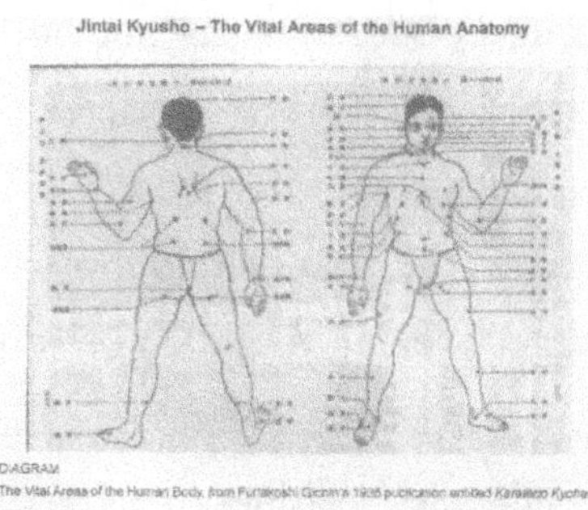

DIAGRAM
The Vital Areas of the Human Body, from Funakoshi Gichin's 1935 publication entitled *Karatedo Kyohan*

Metsubushi is only one way to achieve *suemono* in the opponent. Another popular way is to initially hit certain *tsubo* (ツボ, 'vital points'), such as the Adam's apple, solar plexus, groin, etc. The initial attack does not need to be too strong to achieve such an effect. (Of course, it could cause an instant knockout, too.) The timing and accuracy are more important than the power or strength of the blow (whether it is a strike or a kick). Right after the effect of *suemono* is achieved, you need to deliver the *kime waza* (極め技, 'decisive technique') to finish the fight.

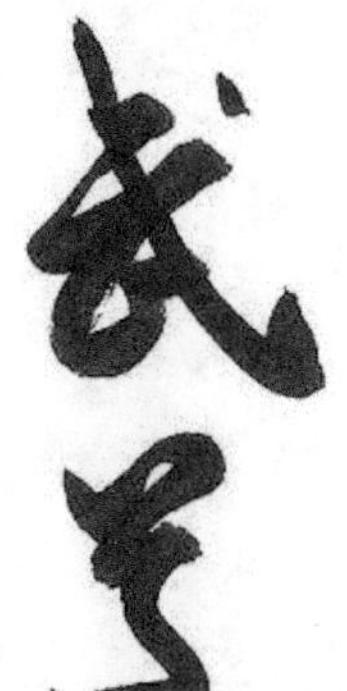

This timing is critical as you can easily fail if you allow too much time after the initial impact since the opponent is then able to see what is happening. This situation is quite different from the case of *metsubushi*, where you have much more time between the initial attack and the *kime waza* as the opponent is blinded by the initial attack for a second or two, or even longer, depending on the severity of the eye attack.

If you understand this concept and like it, you may want to evaluate different techniques that could cause a *suemono* effect.

Unfortunately, it is not too easy to deliver this in regular *kumite* training. This is what separates real fighting situations from dojo training. How to train in this kind of *budo* technique is another interesting subject that I hope to cover in a future work.

Conclusion

The true ultimate aim in karate is to keep peace and not to fight. However, once you choose to fight, you want and need to knock down the opponent with one devastating technique (*ikken hissatsu*). The ultimate aim in sport karate is totally different. There, it does not matter if your technique is of the one-punch-one-kill kind. This statement is not meant to degrade or totally reject sport karate. It has its place, and I respect it as an exciting sport. At the same time, I practice *budo* karate, which is purely based on the *budo* concept of real life-or-death fighting. From this perspective, I am afraid this valuable concept of making the opponent into a fixed target is being forgotten or is becoming a lost technique. I hope that this chapter will bring some attention to this subject and that more people will find and appreciate the old teachings.

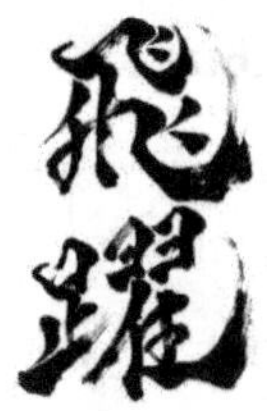

Chapter Two
第二章

Kumite Tempo
組手テンポとは？

組手 TEMPO

In *ippon kumite* (一本組手, 'single-attack sparring'), which I consider to be one of the most important items on the *kumite* training menu, there are many different tempos. You need to understand these tempos and be able to use them properly in order for you to improve your *kumite*.

2.0 Tempo

The most popular tempo in standard Shotokan (松濤館) karate is to block with one arm and counter with the other arm, the most typical technique being *gyaku zuki* (逆突き). This combination is a two-count tempo. Though it is the most popular, unfortunately, it is the least desirable. It is OK to teach this to beginners, but advanced students (brown belts and above) should stay away from it.

Why is this the least desirable tempo? It is obviously because it is the slowest one. You may say, "Well, we practice this combination thousands of times and can deliver the technique very quickly." You may be correct, but what I am referring to is not mechanical speed but rather tempo. I hope you understand the difference between these two terms and their meanings. In other words, a two-count tempo is structurally slower than a one- or one-and-a-half-count tempo.

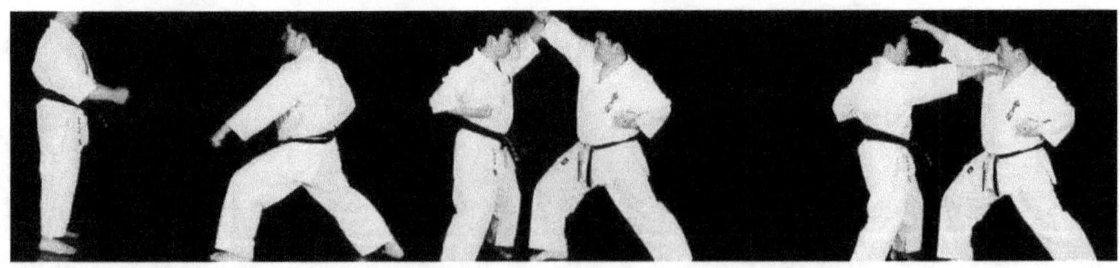

1.5 Tempo

There are faster and more advanced tempos, such as 1.5, 1.0, 0.5, 0.0, etc. I recommend that senior *karateka* master these as they advance their *ippon kumite* skills. Mastering these tempos will eventually help with *jiyu ippon kumite* (自由一本組手, 'semifree sparring') and *jiyu kumite* (自由組手, 'free sparring') as these *kumite* exercises allow much less time to counterattack, and greater skill is needed since the opponent is continuously moving in these advanced *kumite* situations.

A typical example of a one-and-a-half-count tempo is to use the same arm for both the block and the counterattack. Such a combination is structurally faster than a two-count tempo such as *jodan age uke* (上段挙げ受け) followed by *chudan gyaku zuki* (中段逆突き). Once again, I am not referring to speed but rather tempo.

Here is a video from one of the seminars I gave in 2016, in which I show a technique using a one-and-a-half-count tempo: www.youtube.com/watch?v=nPEsesOhma0. In this example, the technique is a combination of *chudan soto uke* (中段外受け) and *jodan ura zuki* using the same arm.

The key is to not execute the two techniques, i.e., *uke waza* (受け技, 'blocking technique') and *kaeshi waza* (返し技, 'countering technique'), as two separate motions. Doing this combination as two distinct moves defeats the whole purpose of the one-and-a-half-count tempo as it ends up becoming a two-count tempo. You need to make these two techniques (block and counter) into one smooth motion. In other words, you do not stop after the *uke*. You move your arm continuously after the *uke* and on into the *jodan ura zuki*.

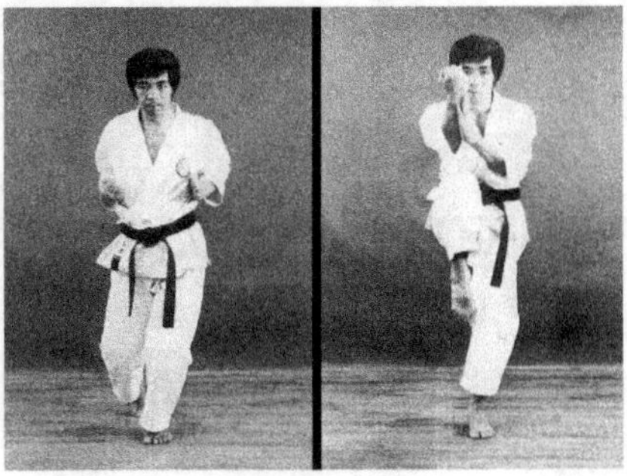

During the demonstration shown in the video, I mention that this *jodan ura zuki* technique (photo right) can be found in Kanku Dai (観空大). Another example can be found in Tekki *kata*, which happens to be an extremely important *kata* in Shotokan but is

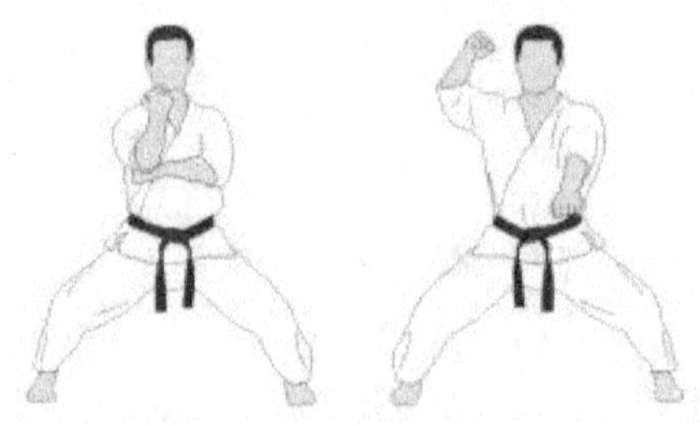

often ignored or undermined. The specific combination found in the *kata* is *jodan uchi uke* (上段内受け) and *jodan ura zuki* (illustration left). Try this combination in your next *kumite* training session. The challenging part is executing an effective counterattack with a short *jodan ura zuki*, which can be done if you are able to put your hips behind the technique.

1.0 Tempo

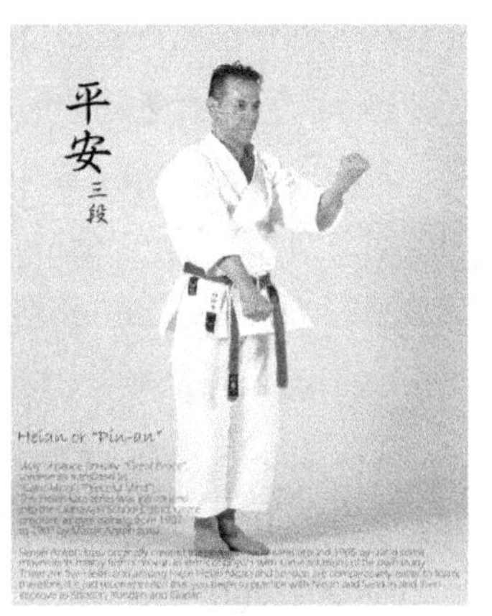

Now let me explain what a one-count tempo is. A one-count tempo means that when the opponent comes in with his attack, the defender blocks and simultaneously counterattacks. In other words, these two techniques (block and counter) are executed at the same time, and this execution is completed at the same time as the opponent's attack. I believe we have such techniques in all of the Heian (平安) *kata*. Can you identify them? Some are hidden and may be difficult to find, but they are there.

The combination used in this tempo is called *morote waza* (諸手技, 'two-handed technique'), which is more difficult to execute than a single-handed technique. You can easily see that using two different arms to do two different things at the same time is much more challenging than using just one arm at a time. Executing *age uke* with *gyaku zuki*, *chudan uchi uke* with *chudan gyaku zuki*, or other combinations is challenging, but these specific techniques

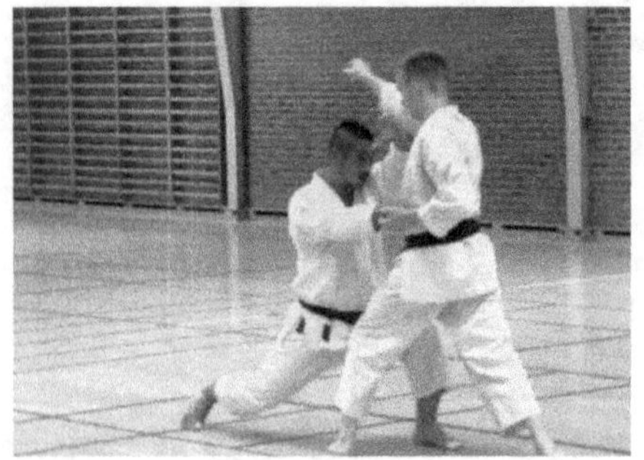

are not readily found in the Heian *kata*.

In Asai Ryu karate, we have some *kihon kata* (基本形, 'basic forms'), such as Junro Nidan (順路二段), to train in these techniques, which we did at a seminar in Goiânia, Goiás, Brazil, in May 2016. Here is one of the videos from that seminar showing a one-count combination of *age uke* and *chudan gyaku zuki*: www.youtube.com/watch?v=gmIan8cMCZk. If you are a brown belt or above, you should use this combination in *ippon kumite*. You will easily see that the opponent does not have a chance to deliver a second attack or to escape (in *jiyu ippon kumite*).

Up to now, I have explained what two-, one-and-a-half-, and one-count tempos are. I am sure the reader understands that a two-count tempo is twice as long as a one-count tempo and that a one-and-a-half-count tempo is fifty percent longer than a one-count tempo in the *kumite* concept.

Once again, I must emphasize that these numbers are used simply to describe the speed of the tempos. So, a one-and-a-half-count tempo is faster than a two-count tempo in terms of its biomechanical structure, even though an actual one-and-a-half-count combination could be slower if it is purposely executed very slowly. So, I want to make sure the reader clearly understands that the speed I am referring to is different from mechanical speed.

In fact, you can train in a two-count combination such as *age uke* with *gyaku zuki* to the point that you may be able to execute it as fast as a one-and-a-half-count combination (i.e., a block and a counter with the same arm or leg). Honestly, this practice of training repeatedly in only the two-count tempo is what I witness in most Shotokan dojo training sessions. I am writing this chapter to bring your attention to the fact that there are other, maybe better, options. It is up to you, but why not expand your repertoire of *kumite* techniques?

0.5 Tempo

Next I will briefly explain what a half-count tempo is. As you can see, it is faster than a one-count tempo, which is when the counterattack is delivered at the same time as the completion of the opponent's attack. Thus, in a half-count tempo, your counterattack is delivered before the opponent completes his attack, or in the middle of his attack. There are many situations in which a half-count tempo is used. I will mention only a few examples to give you an idea. As you are, I assume, an experienced *karateka*, I am sure you can think of many others.

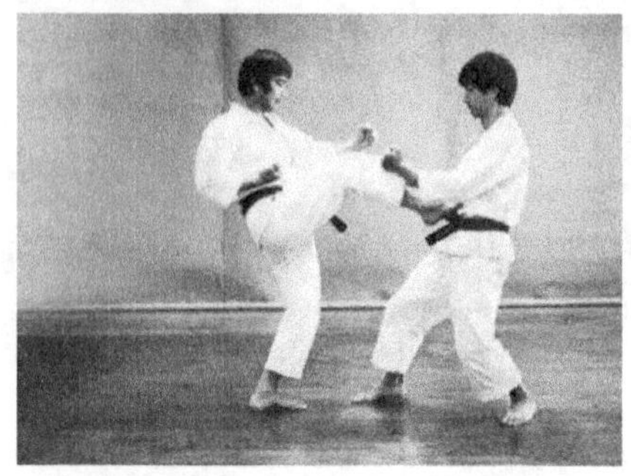

One example is to throw *mae geri* as the opponent lunges forward with *oi zuki*. The photo to the left shows a classic *kumite* demonstration by Hirokazu Kanazawa (金澤弘和, 1931–), former *kancho* (館長, 'chairman') of the Shotokan Karate-do International Federation (國際松濤館空手道連盟 [SKIF]) attacking a young Hitoshi Kasuya (粕谷均, 1948–), now chief instructor of the World Shotokan Karate-Do Federation (世界松濤舘空手道連盟 [WSKF]), with *mae geri* as the latter lunges forward with *oi zuki*. You can execute another half-count tempo using *oi zuki* instead of *mae geri*. This technique is referred to as *deai* (出合い, 'meeting head-on').

Another example would be *jowan osae uke* (上腕抑え受け, 'forearm-pressing block'), in which you step forward to block the opponent's elbow area and then press farther to execute either *enpi uchi* (猿臂打ち, 'elbow strike') or *yoko kentsui uchi* (横拳槌打ち, 'side hammer-fist strike') almost simultaneously (illustration right). This technique is another *deai*.

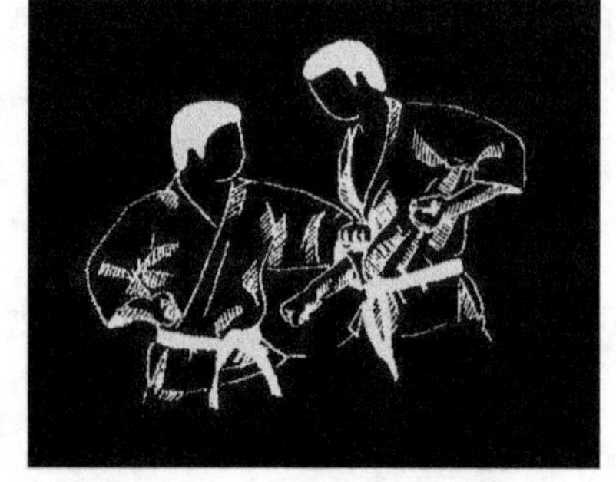

Lastly, many may not know one of the more realistic *bunkai* for the first move of Bassai Dai (抜塞大), demonstrated by Funakoshi in the photo at the top of the following page, which comes from his book *Karate Do Kyohan* (空手道教範 [Kobunsha, 1935]). Many people have been mistakenly taught that this is *chudan uchi uke* (中段内受け, 'inside middle block').

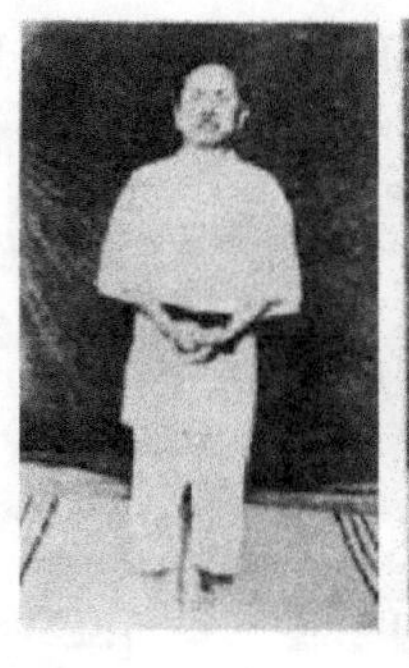
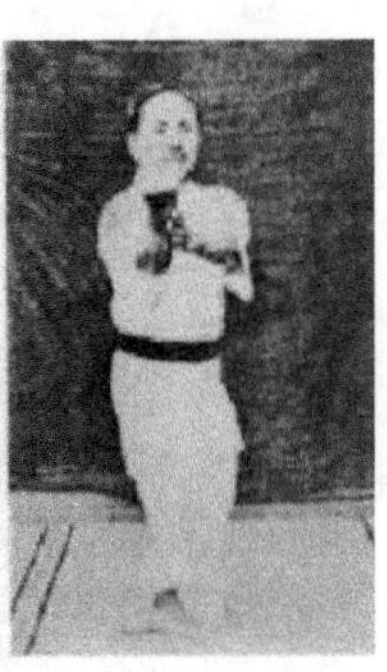

Of course, it can be done that way if you wish to do a less effective *bunkai*. A better *bunkai* is either *chudan* or, more effectively, *jodan uraken uchi*. The photo below shows *neko ashi dachi*, whereas it is *kosa dachi* (交差立ち) in Bassai Dai. The use of *kosa dachi* typically means that the technique executed will be followed by a throw, which is the case with the *bunkai* for the first move of Bassai Dai. You take a large step and almost jump in with this first move. This means it is a *deai* technique.

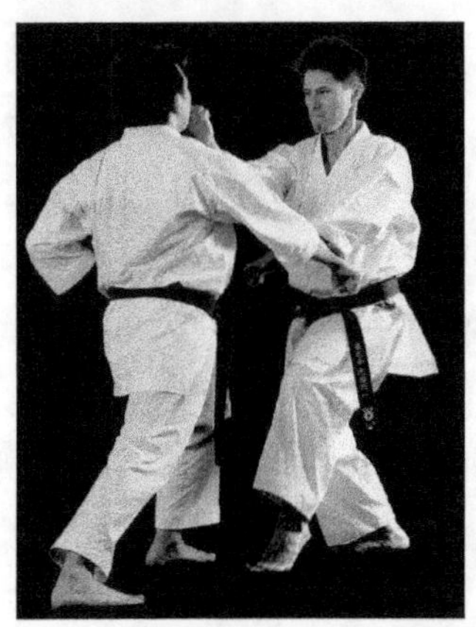

Interestingly, in the Shorin Ryu (小林流) *kata* Matsumura Passai (松村パッサイ), which can be found here: www.youtube.com/watch?v=oo9-d2dfkyU, you take two steps forward rather than using the big jump that is found in Shotokan's Bassai Dai. I prefer the Shorin Ryu approach as I consider it to be more realistic in a real fighting situation to quickly step in instead of jumping in. Regardless, both moves show that this is a strong *deai* technique.

This is typically called a *sen no sen* (先の先) technique, but, depending on the situation, it can be a *go no sen* (後の先) technique. It would take too much space to explain this here, so I will write more about *sen no sen* and *go no sen* in the future.

0.0 Tempo

Finally, I will cover a tempo that is even faster than countering with a *deai* technique. I will attempt to explain what a zero-count tempo is. This concept, I expect, will be understood by many readers. However, it is extremely difficult to have the ability to execute this technique. Of course, you need to train hard to attain this ability.

A zero-count tempo means that you execute the counterattack *as soon as* the opponent starts his attack. I must emphasize that the timing is not after he starts to move, and this is why I stressed the words *as soon as* in the previous sentence. If your countering action comes after the start of his attack, even slightly, it is considered to be a half-count tempo.

The timing here is rather critical and almost invisible. It is at the very moment when he initiates an aggressive move. The indication of such a move would include a flinch in the arm or shoulder, a shift in the center of gravity, etc. So, your "counterattack" may look as though you are hitting the opponent before he attacks you. In other words, your opponent's aggressive move will most likely not be noticed or detected by a third person who happens to be watching the match or incident.

Even if you understand this timing, if you are a tournament *kumite* fighter, I suspect you will not care about it. Your concern is scoring points against your opponent in a *kumite* match; thus, the timing does not matter to you very much. Even if the opponent is not moving or initiating an attack, you can jump in and punch or kick him. So, this tempo is not critically important in tournament *kumite*.

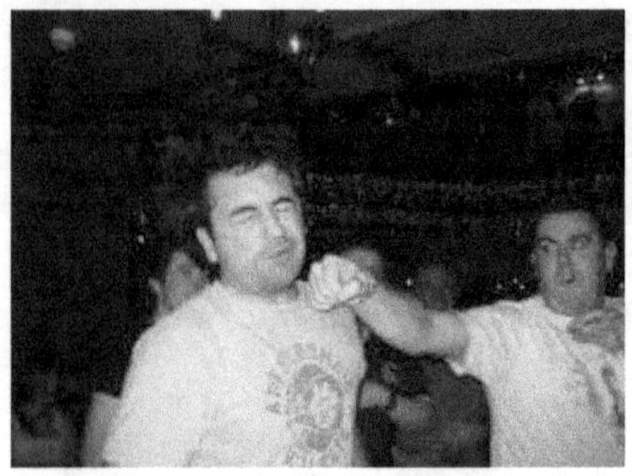

On the other hand, this becomes extremely important in a street fight. However, I must caution you to be very careful about when you use this tempo. Imagine what would happen if you hit the attacker as he just stood there as if he were an innocent bystander. You would be sued by him for "attacking him first" (even if he had the ill intention of hitting you at that moment).

In this case, you would most likely lose in a court of law. I am sure the court proceedings would include circumstantial evidence, such as a description of the scene, the preceding actions, the verbal exchanges, etc. I am not a lawyer, so I cannot say for sure, but I think you would lose your case no matter how hard you tried to explain to the judge that you detected the attacker's initial move when you saw him flinch.

So, in a fist fight, you may have to use a half-count tempo to protect yourself. But, in other, more life-threatening situations, knowing zero-count tempo may save your life. How about if the attacker has a gun or a knife and intends to harm or kill you? You will want to use this tempo in a situation where a guy is drawing a gun or pulling a knife out of his pocket. In this case, even if the guy is not pointing the gun or knife at you, you may want to attack him immediately.

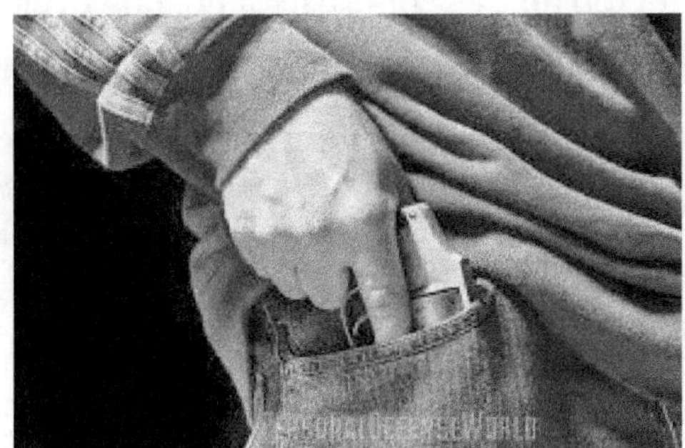

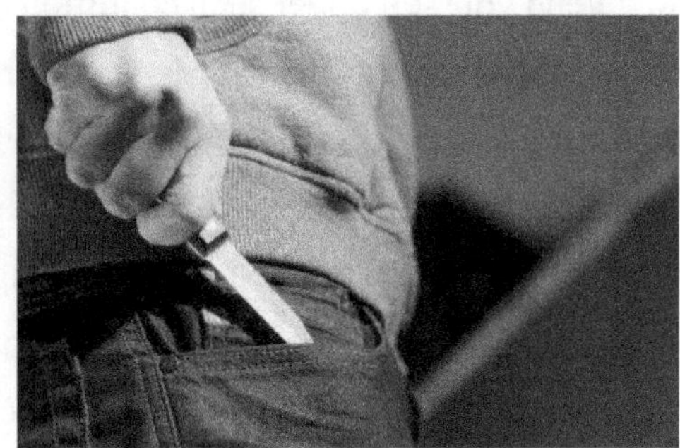

I consider the very act of pulling a gun or knife to be an action that threatens my life. This is where a judgment factor comes into play. He may be doing this only to steal your wallet without particularly wanting to harm you. In this case, it may be a wiser decision to give him your wallet rather than taking the chance of becoming a dead hero. On the other hand, if you know for sure that this guy is trying to harm or kill you—you will need evidence later—then you need to move as soon as the gun or knife is pulled. Your chances of survival decrease dramatically after the attacker aims the gun directly at you or has the knife only a few inches away from your body.

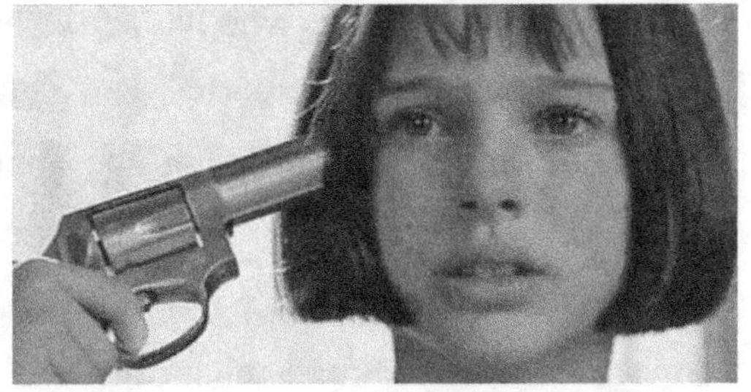

It could be a case where the guy is grabbing your clothes at the neck and cocking his arm over his head. In this case, he is visibly threatening you. If he is only threatening, then you have the option of not hitting first. But, if you see or feel that

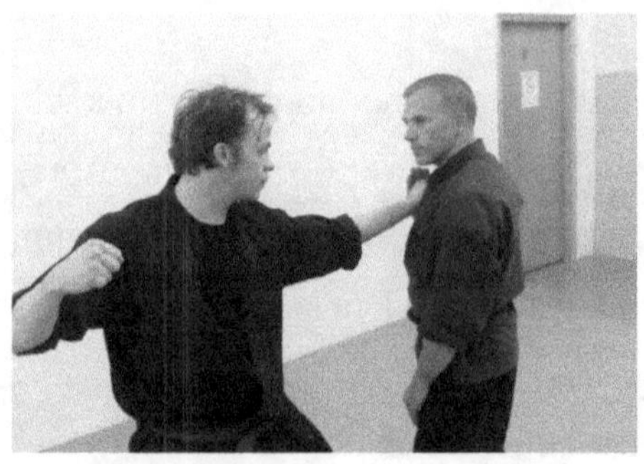

his intention is to punch you, then you can deliver a zero-count technique at that moment. The distance is very short, so if you wait until he starts to throw the punch or kick, that may be taking too great a chance unless you are in total control of the situation and have full confidence in your ability to defend yourself under such conditions. Not too many people can or do, however.

Whether or not this case is considered to be a zero-count tempo is debatable. Some readers may say, "Wait! Isn't it a half-count tempo if you wait until the attacker grabs your lapel with his fist in the air?" These readers are technically correct. Once the attacker engages in an aggressive act, your reaction will not be a zero-count tempo. This is why I say that these readers are technically correct. At the same time, I do not consider it wise to take action prior to a visible show of aggression only because of legal and ethical reasons.

From a legal point of view, without knowing the true intentions of the attacker, if you punch this guy based on just a flinching shoulder (before he grabs you or raises his fist), you will lose in court. Since I am not a lawyer, I am only guessing that this is the case, at least in Japan and possibly in the U.S., but I am interested in hearing from any readers who happen to have a legal background.

From an ethical perspective, can you justify punching this guy based on a flinching shoulder without being one hundred percent sure of his intentions? Of course, you can only if you know that he intends to harm you or if he seriously threatens you by saying, "I will kill you." Then, it may be a different situation. In that case, you may take the chance to act as soon as he flinches his arm or shoulder. However, if the guy is that serious about harming you, he will not be standing still, and deciding when is the right time to act or react will be challenging and difficult.

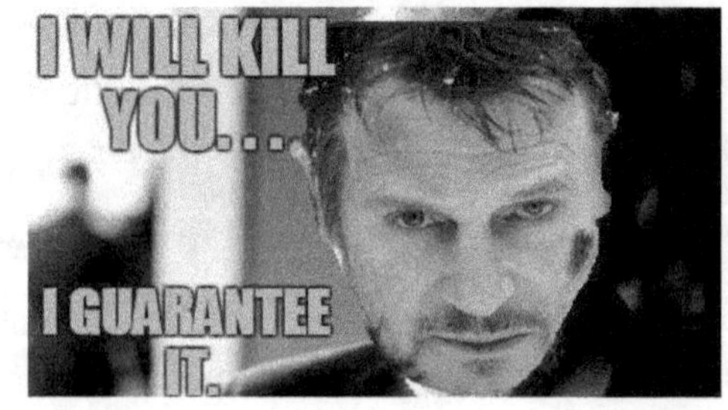

In other words, in the case of an attacker without a weapon, it is difficult to determine precisely what physical action can be considered an overt attack. Is it when he grabs your lapel or shoulder? Do you have to wait until he raises his fist? Is it when he says, “I will kill you”? Isn’t it extremely difficult to define an aggressive act, even though you may “feel” his ill intention?

In summation, a zero-count tempo means that there is no wait between the initiation of the attacker’s aggressive act and your action (attack or restraining technique). This tempo may not be considered to be important in tournament *kumite*, but in a real street fight or a life-threatening situation, it can save your life.

-0.5 Tempo

There is another tempo, which is a negative-half-count tempo, but I will not go into this here. It involves detecting the opponent’s ki and nerve impulses, and I am afraid too many Western readers would have an issue with this concept, so I will not venture into it in this chapter. However, sometime in the future, I will attempt to write about this very interesting subject, particularly when I touch on *sen no sen* and *sensen no sen* (先先の先).

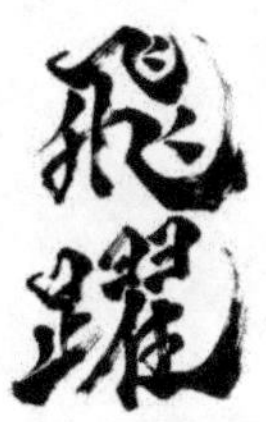

CHAPTER THREE
第三章

WHAT IS MEOTODE?
夫婦手とは何ぞや？

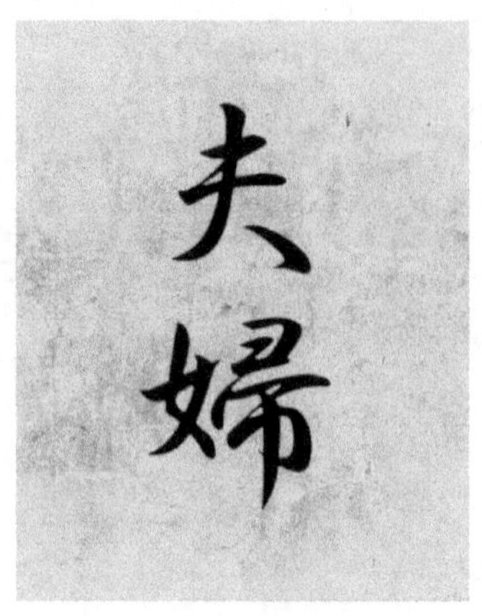

Let's look at the literal meaning of the word *meotode*. In fact, this word consists of two separate sections: 夫婦 and 手. The first section is pronounced *meoto* or *fufu* and means 'married couple'. I figure most practitioners are familiar with the last character, 手. Yes, this is *te* ('hand'). Because of *rendaku* (連濁, 'sequential voicing'), the pronunciation changes to *de*, but the meaning remains the same. When put together, *meotode* means 'hands of a married couple'. OK, you understand this, but does it make sense to you? Maybe some readers can figure it out. You will understand better if I explain the concept of *meoto* as we understand it in Japan.

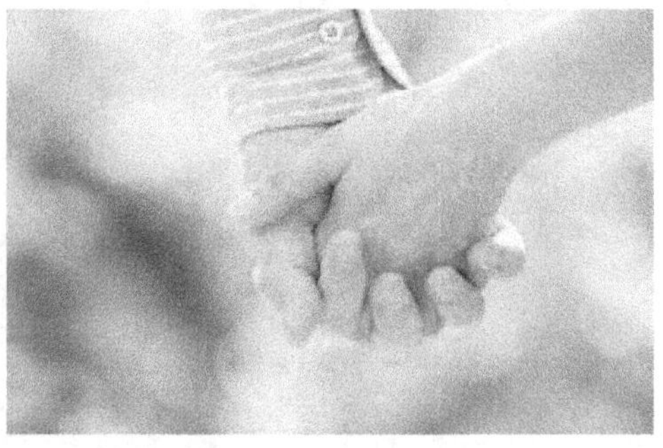

In Japan, we consider a married couple to be a team. They are equal but have different functions or roles. In Japan, a wife is expected to support her husband as he is considered to be the head of the family. Since this is not a sociology term paper, we will not discuss whether the Japanese concept I present here is right or wrong, appropriate or inappropriate. I ask the reader not to pass judgment on the cultural concept regarding married couples in Japan. Instead, I ask that you understand this concept, whether you agree or disagree, so that you can understand the karate concept of *meotode*.

So, this does not refer to the literal hands of a husband and wife. We all have two hands (or arms) and consider the front hand to be the stronger or more aggressive one. This is the husband hand. On the other hand (no pun intended), the function of the rear hand (i.e., the wife hand) is mainly to support the front hand. In other words, both hands have to work as a team. That is, we are to use them in concert instead of using them separately. Now, this is the most important part. You may say, "Oh, I know this. Isn't it the same as *morote waza*?" My answer is yes and no. Let me explain.

Morote (諸手) means 'both hands', and *waza* (技) means 'technique'; therefore, *morote waza* (諸手技) refers to a technique in which you use both of your hands. However, it does not define the function or role of the front and rear hands. Of course, if you stand facing the opponent in *kiba dachi* (騎馬立ち), *heiko dachi* (平行立ち), etc., there is no front or rear. In that case, the technique can be called *morote waza*. Though it is possible, the opponent and you are not likely to continuously stand still during a fight. Therefore, one side of your body will most likely be closer to the opponent, and the hand on that side is considered to be the front hand if it is used. In short, *morote waza* is a technique using both hands in general, and *meotode* is a specific kind of *morote waza* where one hand (most likely the front) is used to attack or counterattack, and the other hand (normally the rear) is used for support or to execute an *uke* (受け). Sometimes the roles of the hands can be switched, but this is normally the case.

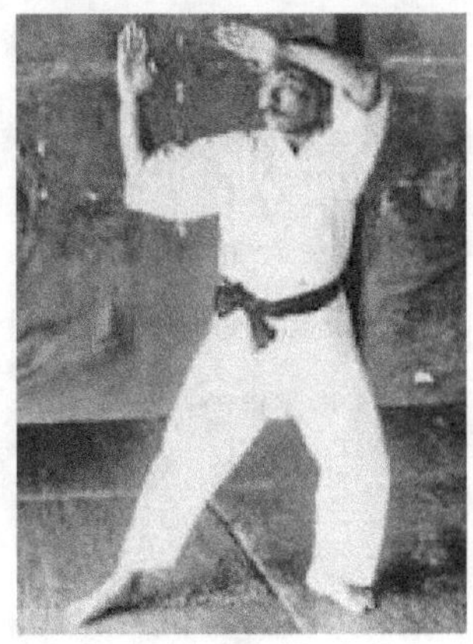

Given this explanation, I expect many people would object to my statement. You might say, "In *kata*, we find that many techniques are executed with a single hand and mostly with the front hand." Others might point out that in most of the *kihon kumite* (基本組手, 'basic sparring'), we learn to use the front hand to block (*uke*) and the rear hand to execute a counterattack, such as *gyaku zuki*. I am well aware of this, and this is exactly why I have brought up this karate concept and am spending time explaining it. Below are two key points that have been de-emphasized lately.

1. Simultaneous Use of Both Hands

It is recommended to use both hands at the same time. In other words, *morote waza* should be preferred to the individual use of each hand. Why? I write about this in Chapter 3: "What Does 'There Is No Gyaku Zuki in Karate' Mean?" of my book *Karatedo Paradigm Shift*. There I talk about tempo in *kumite* and explain that the individual use of the hands—such as executing *age uke* (挙げ受け) with the front hand first and then *gyaku zuki* with the rear hand—is the slowest tempo (not speed). There are other techniques that are much faster, and the use of *morote waza* enables this faster tempo. It is definitely faster if you counterpunch at the same time you block.

Believe it or not, there are many *morote waza* in our *kata*, including all of the Heian *kata*. Unfortunately, the correct *bunkai* for those *morote waza* is not being taught in many dojo. Thus, many people do not know, for instance, that the *shuto uke* (手刀受け) in Heian Shodan (平安初段) is a *morote waza* and also a *meotode*. There are many other misunderstandings, such as with the first moves in Heian Nidan (平安二段) and Heian Yondan (平安四段). The *kosa uke* (交叉受け, 'cross block') in Heian Sandan (平安三段) is visibly a *morote waza*. There are also a few *morote waza* in Heian Godan (平安五段), and they should be used as *meotode*. A good example is the seventh move, which is a *chudan uchi uke* with the rear hand held at the forearm of the front hand. I will explain these *morote waza* further in the next section.

2. Attacking Role of the Front Hand

Another forgotten concept is that the front hand should be used to attack or counterattack. Most readers may say, "I do not agree that this concept is being forgotten. We use the front hand in many of our attacks, such as *oi zuki* (追い突き)." You are absolutely correct, but I would like you to think about counterattacks.

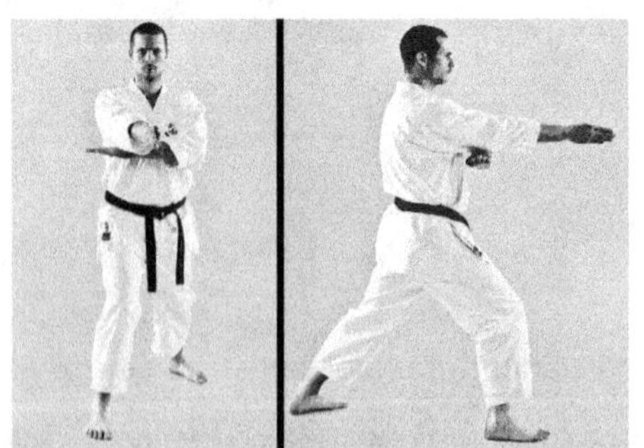

Then, you may say, "OK, counterattacks with the front hand are different. First of all, how can you throw a *gyaku*

zuki with the front hand?" This is a good question, but I am not suggesting that you throw a *gyaku zuki* with the front hand. We can find a typical *meotode* in Heian Nidan. It is a right *shuto nukite* (手刀貫手) with a left *osae uke* (抑え受け), which is shown in the photo on the previous page. This is an excellent example, and everyone will agree that this shows the *meotode* concept.

At the same time, there are many other *morote waza* that should be understood as *meotode* but are not. This is why I claim that this concept seems to be ignored or even forgotten. Here I will address several other *morote waza* and explain the *bunkai* based on the *meotode* concept.

Let's start with Heian Shodan. There is a sequence of four *shuto uke* at the end of this *kata* (illustration right). This technique is very popular in Shotokan *kata*, and you can find it in Heian Nidan, Heian Yondan, Kanku Dai, etc.

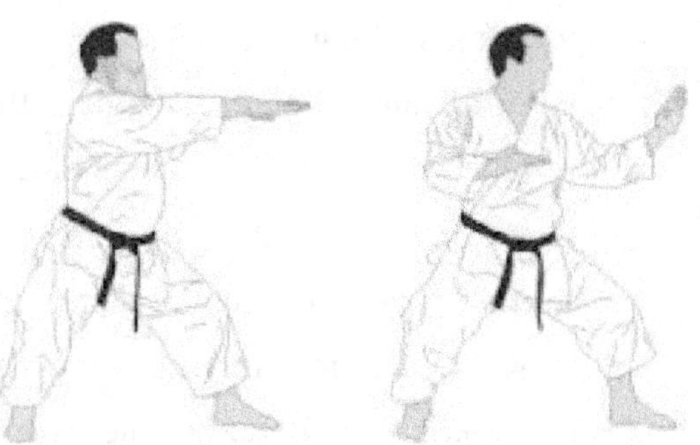

In most cases, this technique is executed in sequences of two or four, which are mirror images of the left and right sides. In a sequence of two *shuto uke*, the first and second ones have different functions (and this is the same with the third and fourth ones). The first one is a simple *shuto uke* against the opponent's *chudan zuki* (中段突き). The second one is not an *uke* but rather a strike. In the first *shuto uke*, you blocked with your left hand. As you step in a diagonal direction, you grab the opponent's arm or *karategi* with your left hand and then deliver a counter *shuto uchi* (手刀打ち) to the opponent's neck with your right hand.

There are many *bunkai*, and most of them are correct. The only incorrect *bunkai* is the one that does not work. An advanced *bunkai* technique can be found even in the first *shuto uke*, as well, but it is too difficult not only for white belts but also for colored-belt practitioners.

Maybe a brown belt could start practicing the following technique. I am sure you have learned that you need to cross your arms before executing *shuto uke*.

In other words, your striking or *uke* hand is placed in the rear. You were taught to bring the striking hand back because you need to allow a greater distance for the hand to travel so that you will have a strong strike or *uke* when it is executed. That point is OK, but have you asked about the other hand, that is, the hand that is extended forward in the arm cross before the execution of *shuto uke*? If you have, your sensei most likely told you that it provides protection for your midsection or that it is just a simple *kamae* (構え) and has no meaning. This is OK for white belts; however, for advanced students, that sensei must have another explanation. The rear hand that is extended forward is a *tsukami uke*. Yes, it is difficult to catch the opponent's striking arm. It is impossible for white belts; however, it is very possible for advanced students. Again, this is OK as we need to have different *bunkai* for the same technique, depending on the student's ability.

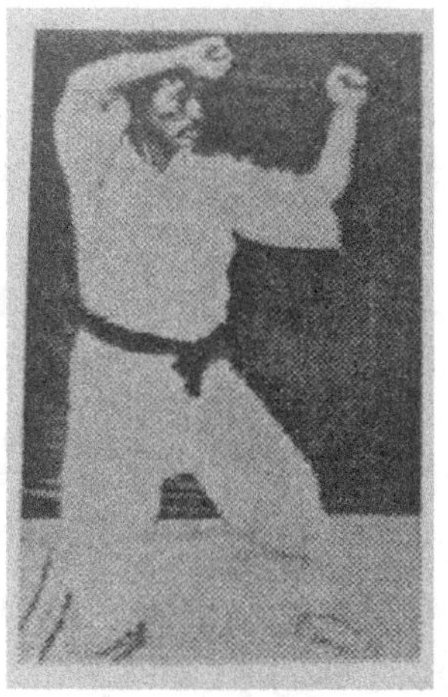

Let me address another *meotode* technique. You know the first move of Heian Nidan is a *morote waza* (photo right). But, most readers were not taught that this is a *meotode* technique. In other words, the typical *bunkai* I see in most of the Shotokan dojo I visit is that the front hand is a *jodan uchi uke*. Then, what is the purpose of the rear hand? I suspect you were taught that the placement of the rear hand at the forehead is only a *kamae* or is used for protection of the forehead. I am not going to say this is an incorrect *bunkai*. This idea is possible, of course, and maybe it is OK to teach this to beginners. However, advanced practitioners should know the *meotode bunkai*, which I believe is the original *bunkai* that was taught on Okinawa.

So, how does this *morote waza* work as *meotode*? The front hand is, in fact, an attack, such as *jodan ura zuki* or *jodan uraken uchi* (上段裏拳打ち). You may say that this cannot be because the front hand movement for *jodan ura zuki* or *jodan uraken uchi* is quite different from that of *jodan uchi uke*. It is true that you move your front arm in a semicircular motion to execute *jodan uchi uke*, whereas you need to move your front arm almost completely vertically to execute *jodan ura zuki*. For *jodan uraken uchi*, though, the forearm moves in a semicircle but also in a more vertical (rather than horizontal) motion. You are correct that the movements are all different, but the fundamental upward arm movement is the same, and once you reach the black-belt level, the adjustment of the arm movement is not too difficult.

In addition, did you know that the fist direction of the front hand was changed by Master Funakoshi? In our *kata*, the little-finger side of the front fist faces the opponent. Take a look at how this technique is executed in Wado Ryu (和道流), the style that spun off of Shotokan before Funakoshi made these changes. You will find that the direction of the front fist is different. In other words, the back of the fist faces the opponent (photo above). This fist position proves that the movement can be used as a *jodan ura zuki* to the opponent's chin.

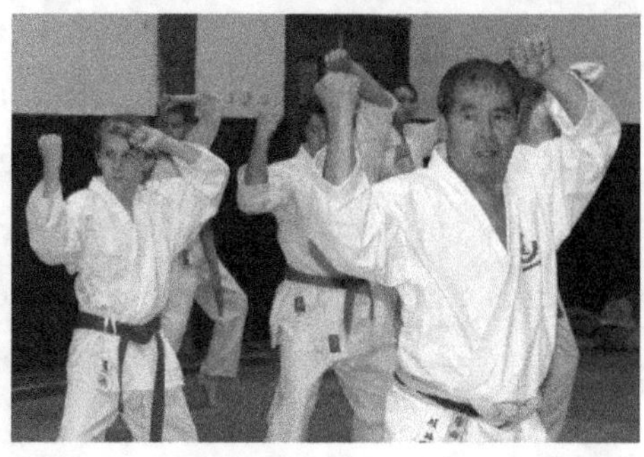

You may accept my explanation for the front hand, but you will probably ask about the rear hand. Do you really believe it is only a *kamae*? Does it really make sense to hold up an arm in front of your forehead? If it is only a *kamae*, then why not hold it at the chest as we do in *shuto uke*? Of course, anything is possible, but I really think this explanation of its being just a *kamae* is inappropriate and unrealistic.

I hope you agree that it makes sense that the rear arm movement has a meaningful *waza* rather than just being a *kamae*. If so, then what is the technique? The answer is easy. If you look at the position of the rear arm carefully, you will know the answer. What does it look like? Yes, that is the *jodan age uke* position. You guessed correctly that the rear arm is used for *jodan age uke*. The first technique is a *jodan age uke* with the rear arm, and you simultaneously perform a *jodan ura zuki* or *jodan uraken uchi* with the front fist.

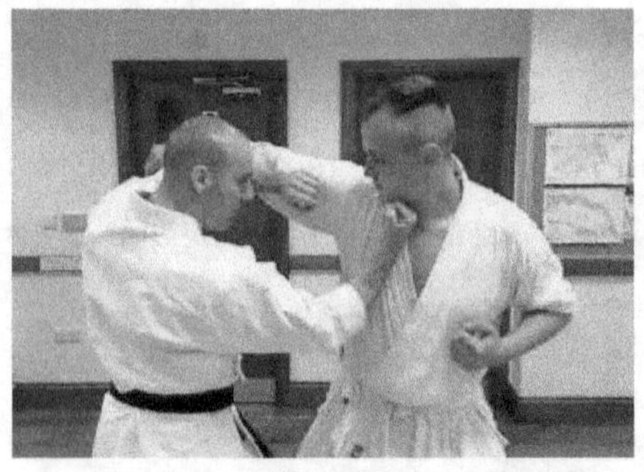

Now, we wonder why this *bunkai* (photo left) is not more popular or more commonly taught. That is a good question, but the answer is also simple. This *bunkai* is much more difficult to do. Just try it, and you will see it right away. First of all, you need to step forward with your left foot instead of backward with your right foot—interestingly, this is exactly what you do in this *kata.* Naturally, you will discover by stepping forward that the distance from the opponent is much shorter. Therefore, you can immediately understand that this *bunkai* is not fit for beginners. This is exactly why another *bunkai* has been taught by most Shotokan instructors. That *bunkai* is much easier but, unfortunately, much less realistic and effective.

You will probably agree that the commonly taught *bunkai* is easier, but you may not agree that it is less realistic and effective. Why do I make such a negative statement? Let me explain. There are typically two common ideas for the arm cross in the second move (illustration below).

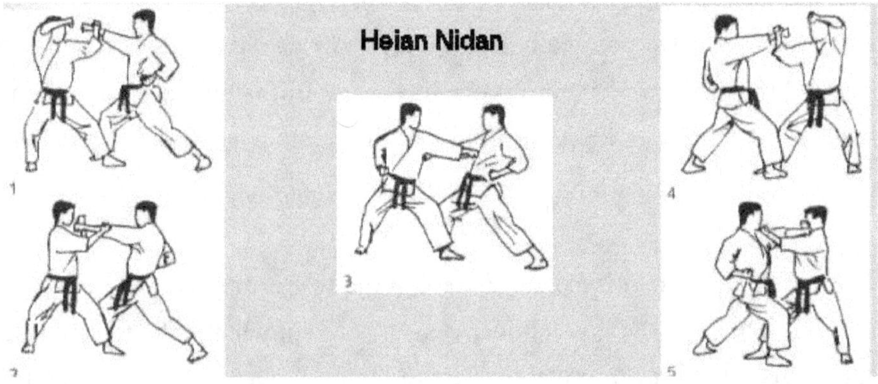

One idea is to catch the opponent's second punch by crossing the arms. First of all, I would like to ask if you have tried to do this at a normal speed. If so, were you successful? I would also like to ask if this *bunkai* technique is really appropriate for seventh-*kyu* students, but, regardless, that is not the point. Let me continue.

The second idea is to execute *jodan ura zuki*. I do not believe seventh-*kyu* students will have learned how to execute *ura zuki*, but let us assume they can. This is not the reason this is unrealistic or less realistic, either.

By the way, I must point out that the *bunkai* on the right side of the illustration shown on the previous page, which uses an *uke*, is very challenging, too. Since it is an illustration, not too many people will notice, but you will see this if you try it with a partner. He executes *jodan uchi uke* with his right wrist (so far so good). Then, he must execute *jodan soto uke* (上段外受け) against the attacker's *gyaku zuki* with the same arm. Just as with the first idea, the attacker has to be awfully slow with his second attack for this to work. In addition, the defender has to bring the arm around to catch the second punch. But, this is OK, too. We can assume the attacker is extremely slow and these two ideas would work. However, I am talking about a situation where the practitioners are at the same or a similar level instead of assuming one side is very slow. I say a counterattack with the rear arm after the block does not work effectively.

The reason for my statement has nothing to do with what kind of counterattack you may execute with the rear arm as the attacker's second punch is too fast if the skill level of both the attacker and the defender is the same or similar. The defender's second attack can only be fast enough if he is significantly more advanced, such as a situation in which a black belt defends himself against a seventh-*kyu* attacker. If you do not believe my statement, I suggest you try this at your dojo.

Now do you agree that countering with the front hand while blocking with the rear arm at the same time is more realistic? I know some of the more diligent Shotokan practitioners will object to this. They will probably say, "Yes, I agree it is faster to hit the opponent on the first move, but this technique does not square with the fundamental Shotokan philosophy that *kata* begins and ends with a block. What do you say to this?"

I may cause some uproar, but I have to say that you have been misinformed. This is a sensitive subject, and I am afraid it has been sort of hidden or avoided; thus, not too many people know this. If I were to explain in full what is involved in this statement, I would have to write a much longer chapter, so I will share only a summary of the historical background.

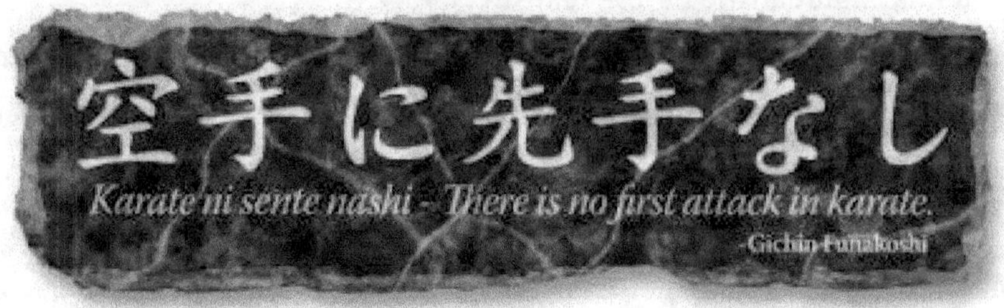

As many of you know, Japan lost the last World War, which ended in 1945. The occupation army prohibited all martial arts across Japan for fear that they would foster a militaristic mind-set among the Japanese people (even though this was propaganda that was completely incorrect). Regardless, karate was considered to be one of these dangerous arts, and karate practitioners were prohibited from practicing or giving instruction in karate. An interesting side story is that U.S. soldiers who were stationed on Okinawa during that period would beg the Okinawan masters to teach them karate and would supposedly receive some secret instruction.

Anyway, on mainland Japan, it was a serious situation for professional karate instructors whose livelihood depended on teaching karate. To make a long story short, the senior instructors, including Master Funakoshi, had to approach General Headquarters (GHQ) for permission to teach karate. At that time, they had to say that karate was not a barbaric fighting art but a peaceful art of self-defense and that all *kata* began and ended with a block, not with an aggressive first strike. I am not sure how Master Funakoshi felt about having to say this to the GHQ officers, but one thing we know is that these instructors received permission to resume their karate activities (both practice and instruction) within a few years, whereas kendo (剣道) had to wait five years. In fact, karate was the first *budo* to receive this permission.

OK, let's get back to *meotode*. The photo of Hirokazu Kanazawa (金澤弘和,

1931–) to the right shows another *morote waza* whose applications are commonly misunderstood. This technique is typically used at *chudan* (中段, 'middle level') as seen in the Shotokan version of Heian Godan. Since this technique is referred to as an *uke*, we all assume it is a *chudan uchi uke* as shown in the photo. The *uke* itself is not the problem. What we need to pay attention to, again, is the rear hand. A popular explanation is that the rear hand is supporting the *uke*. In other words, the rear hand is making the block stronger. I am sure many practitioners have believed this explanation. But does it really do that? Just try it and see if it does. I am not going to waste your time here. I am afraid it is like the rear arm in the first move of Heian Nidan. In other words, I may sound radical, but this is just a fabrication. The rear arm movement must have a more significant role.

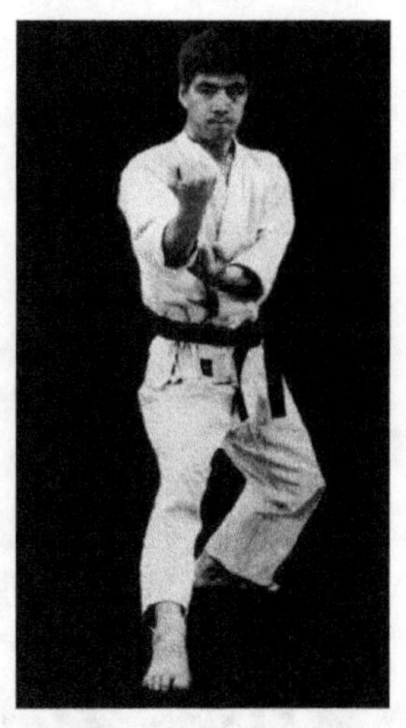

So, what is the rear arm for? Once again, it is same as in Heian Nidan. One of the better interpretations is that the rear arm is used for the *uke*, while the front arm is used for the attack. The *meotode bunkai* for this technique is to execute *uraken uchi* to the opponent's solar plexus (*chudan*) or chin (*jodan*) with the front fist while simultaneously executing *osae uke* against the opponent's *chudan zuki* (photo left). In the case of using the front arm as the block, the rear fist is used not as a support for the block but rather as a short-distance *ura zuki* to *chudan*.

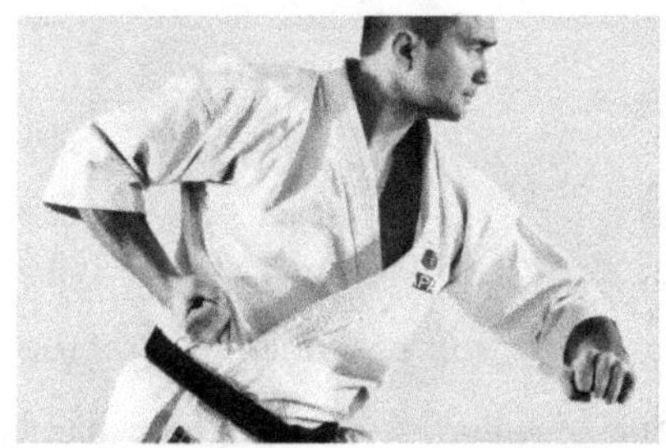

The important thing is the timing. You need to move in toward the opponent and deliver *osae uke* while his arm is still bent. Press down on the inside of the opponent's elbow for an effective *osae uke*. Once the opponent's arm is fully extended, it is too late to execute *osae uke*. When you think of how the block is executed (at a very short distance), then you can easily see that the front fist is used for *uraken uchi*, which is also an effective short-distance attack. If the attacker comes in with a right *oi zuki*, the defender can execute *osae uke* with the left (rear) arm. In this application, the right (front) arm is not used as a block but rather as a simultaneous counterattack to *jodan* in the form of *uraken uchi*.

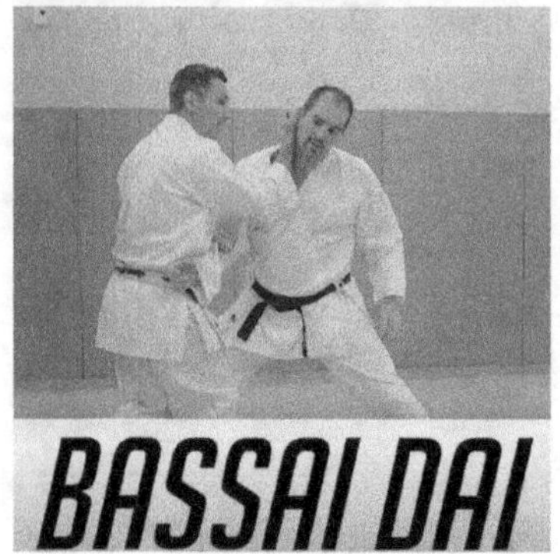

I would like to add a short explanation of the first move of Bassai Dai. In that move, your rear hand is open instead of closed in a fist; however, the meaning is still the same. You execute *osae uke* with the left (rear) palm or forearm while simultaneously executing *uraken uchi* with the right (front) fist (photo left). I suspect this may not be not the *bunkai* most readers have learned. Which *bunkai* makes more sense, the more aggressive one shown here or the one where the rear hand is used only to assist the front arm as it executes the block?

I could come up with many other *morote waza*, but I will leave that work to you so that you can try to find new *bunkai* based on the *meotode* concept in your own training. Good luck and enjoy.

Conclusion

Many different *morote waza* are found in our *kata*, and we are familiar with the techniques. On the other hand, the concept of *meotode* has not been taught among most Shotokan practitioners. The basic idea of *meotode* is to use the front arm mainly for the purpose of attacking and counterattacking while using the rear arm to support the front arm with a block. As we are not taught *meotode*, we commonly see many *bunkai* in which the front hand is used as the *uke*, and many of these *bunkai* do not make sense. Now we know why. By understanding the basic concept of *meotode*, we can learn a new way of thinking about *bunkai*.

One other benefit to taking *meotode* into account is that it solves the disparity between *kata* and *kumite* with regard to distance and techniques. In *kata*, we find that almost all of the steps move forward. On the other hand, we learn to step back

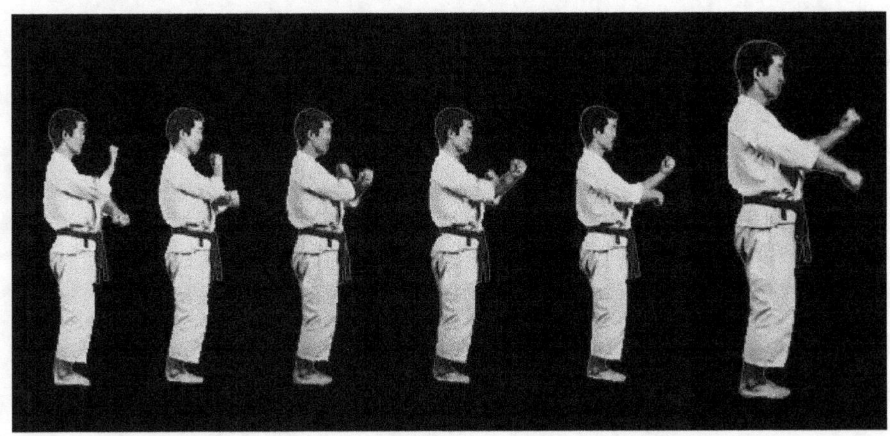

when we learn *gohon kumite* (五本組手, 'five-attack sparring'), *sanbon kumite* (三本組手, 'three-attack sparring'), and even *kihon ippon kumite* (基本一本組手, 'basic single-attack sparring'). The ancient masters left us their techniques in *kata*, and they are definitely telling us to step in when we fight. If you step in, the distance from your opponent becomes very short, which requires a short-distance fighting method. This is where the *meotode* concept becomes very useful. Let us not forget this important concept of *meotode* that was left to us by the ancient masters.

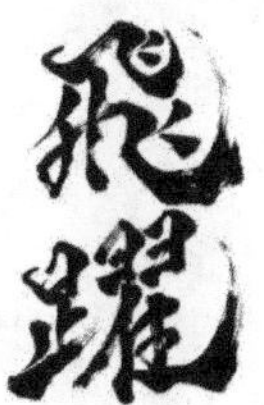

Chapter Four
第四章

What Is the True Objective of Team Kata?
団体形：真の目的は？

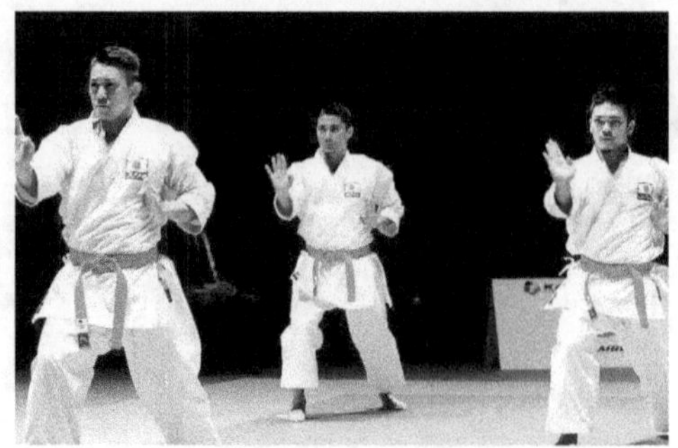

Even though I have very little interest in karate tournaments, I have heard and read comments and questions about team *kata* by so many people that I have decided to write about this subject.

Those who have been involved with or have participated in a major tournament know what team *kata* is. It is a *kata* performance given normally by a team of three people but occasionally by a team of five. As you know, the objective of the team is for each member to perform the same *kata* synchronized as perfectly as possible. The team that can perform a *kata* as if it were being run by a single person gets the highest score and wins. It is as simple as that.

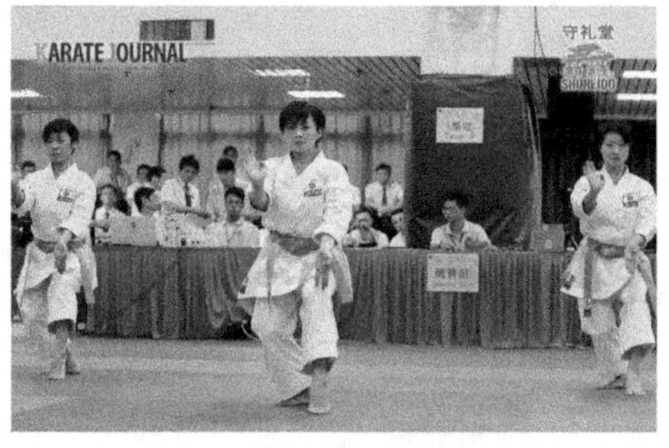

Many karate practitioners, including those who are in favor of karate tournaments, question the purpose or the benefit of team *kata*. Some people may point out that a team environment encourages the team members to be motivated to practice. This is true. If one member feels lazy or not motivated to practice, the other members may be able to entice that person to practice with them. Another benefit may be had if the leader is an excellent *kata* performer as the other team members can learn from that person and thus improve their *kata* faster and more easily by imitating the leader.

Having said that, synchronization seems to be more important than accuracy of technique, correct timing, etc. If this is the case, most of the emphasis and effort of the training will be spent on synchronizing the moves instead of performing the *kata* according to the individual's feeling or understanding of the moves. So, many people—maybe even you—wonder how this training will benefit the practitioners or karate itself. Don't you think this is a very natural and reasonable question?

Dr. Rupert Sheldrake (1942–) is a biologist and author who is best known for his hypothesis of morphic fields and morphic resonance. Dr. Sheldrake's website (www.sheldrake.org) has the following to say:

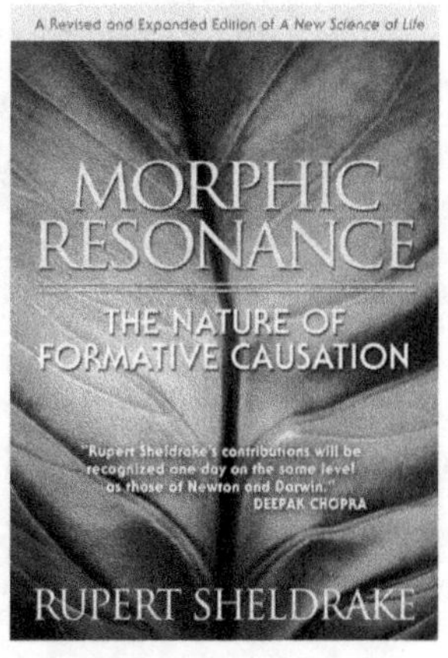

> Morphic resonance is a process whereby self-organising systems inherit a memory from previous similar systems. In its most general formulation, morphic resonance means that the so-called laws of nature are more like habits. The hypothesis of morphic resonance also leads to a radically new interpretation of memory storage in the brain and of biological inheritance. Memory need not be stored in material traces inside brains, which are more like TV receivers than video recorders, tuning into influences from the past. And biological inheritance need not all be coded in the genes, or in epigenetic modifications of the genes; much of it depends on morphic resonance from previous members of the species. Thus each individual inherits a collective memory from past members of the species, and also contributes to the collective memory, affecting other members of the species in the future.

He brings up several very interesting and amazing points about animals, including human beings. I want to share three of his concepts that I believe give us some hints as to what we are capable of. The first is telepathy, the second is premonition, and the third is collective behavior. Let me go a little more deeply into each point.

The first two are classified as the sixth sense. *Sixth sense* is another term for extrasensory perception (ESP), including clairvoyance, premonition, intuition, etc. We perceive the visible world through the five physical senses (smell, taste, sight, touch, and hearing) plus our mind (feelings) and intellect (decision-making capacity). The sixth sense (the capacity for subtle perception) is our ability to perceive the unseen world. Let's start with telepathy first.

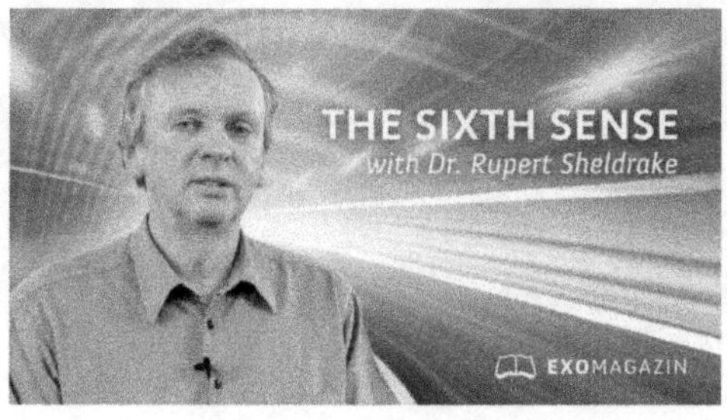

1. Telepathy

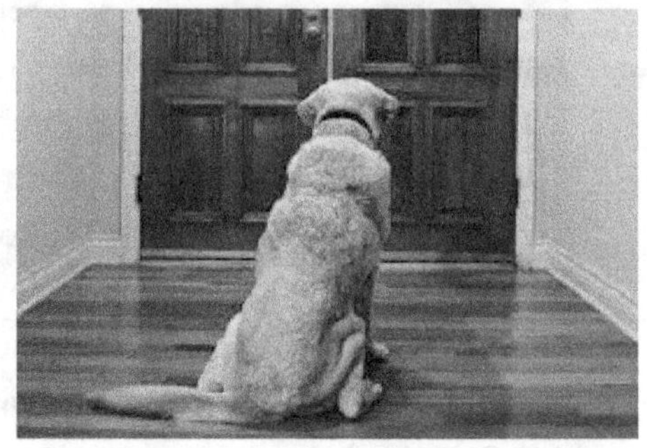

Whether you believe this or not, it is a fact that dogs, cats, and other animals have shown the ability to sense their master's return. They wait at the front door of the house or at a window looking down at the door. This happens even if their master's return may be unscheduled or unexpected. They seem to "know" way before he is near the house. If you have a pet, maybe you have experienced this.

How can they do this? Some people, including some serious scientists, believe there is some form of telepathy. A dog can know as early as the moment at which its owner decides to go home. It may sound too incredible to believe, but this has been proven to be true by many scientific experiments. In this case, the decision-making brain waves trigger the dog's brain, and it goes to the front door to wait. In many cases, the dog arrives at the door only to wait a few minutes before its master's return. In this case, maybe this is accomplished not by the act of making decisions but rather by being able to sense the brain waves of the master as he approaches the house.

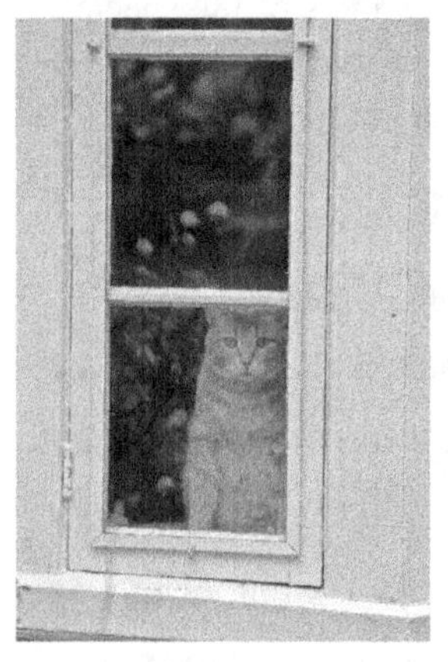

2. Premonition

Premonition is a strong feeling that something is about to happen, especially something unpleasant. When I think of this, I remember a particular scene from the classic samurai movie *Seven Samurai* (七人の侍 [Toho Studios, 1954]). It is a testing scene where a samurai is hiding behind a door, and the candidates,

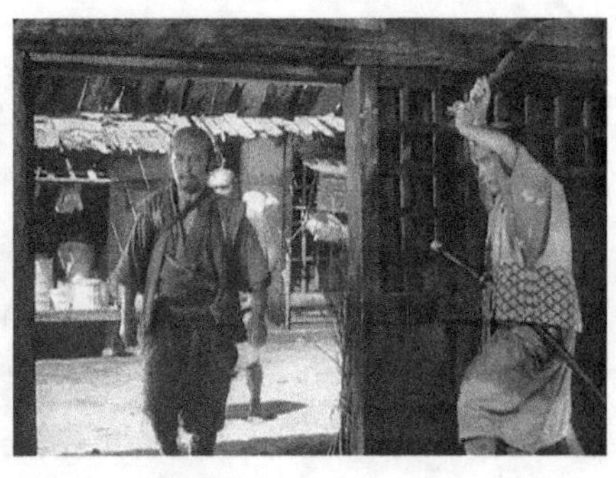

who are unaware of his presence, are asked to go through the door. If you have seen this movie, you remember that some candidates failed when they were hit with a wooden sword. However, one passed because he could tell someone was hiding behind the door (photo right).

You may say, "Hey, that kind of story may be interesting in a samurai movie, but that is only in the world of movies. The real world is different." Not so fast. I am well aware that many people can be skeptical about this subject, but it is also true that real samurai experiences of this nature have been documented. One famous one involved Munenori Yagyu (柳生宗矩, 1571–1646 [photo below left]). Let me share a detailed story about his experience.

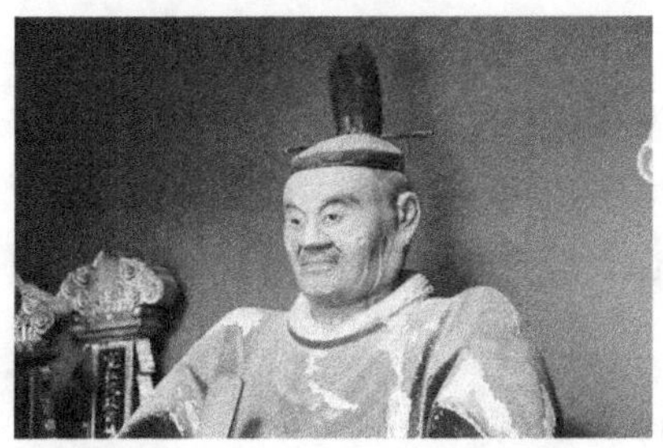

If you are a kenjutsu (剣術) practitioner, you may know that he was the founder of the Edo branch of Yagyu Shinkage Ryu (柳生新陰流) kenjutsu. This was one of two official kenjutsu styles authorized by the Tokugawa shogunate. The other was Itto Ryu (一刀流), founded by Ittosai Ito (伊東一刀斎, 1560–1653). Yagyu began his career in the Tokugawa administration as a direct retainer and eventually received the title of *Tajima no Kami* (但馬守).

His story goes like this. One morning, he was enjoying the view of the garden from his house. A young servant samurai was sitting behind him. The young samurai was also a kenjutsu student under Yagyu and knew how excellently skillful Yagyu was with his sword. Yagyu looked very defenseless as he had his back turned toward the student while he looked out at the garden. So, the young samurai thought to himself, *No matter how good Master Yagyu may be with his swordsmanship, I bet he could not defend himself if I attacked him right now*. At that very moment, Yagyu turned around, quickly walked into his room, and closed the door behind him.

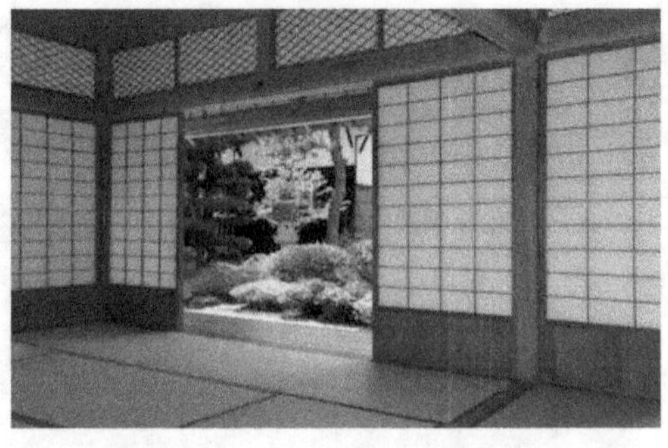

He stayed in his room alone all day, which was very unusual. So, in the evening, the young servant asked his master what was wrong with him. Yagyu answered, “When I was looking at the garden, all of a sudden, I felt someone was coming to attack me. However, you, whom I trust, were the only one who was around me. So, I thought maybe I was sick; thus, I decided to take it easy in my room all afternoon.” Upon hearing this, the young samurai felt very guilty, so he confessed his secret thought, expecting to be severely punished. However, Yagyu smiled and said, “Oh, I am glad that you told me this. Now I know why I felt that way. I am relieved now.” Yagyu did not punish the young servant but rather thanked him for having tested him.

Since this story was documented by his servant, it must have really happened. I will not bring up other instances, but there were many other reported cases similar to this one during the seventeenth and eighteenth centuries. One interesting point is that this did not happen only with the sword masters. Some samurai of average skill with the sword also demonstrated this ability.

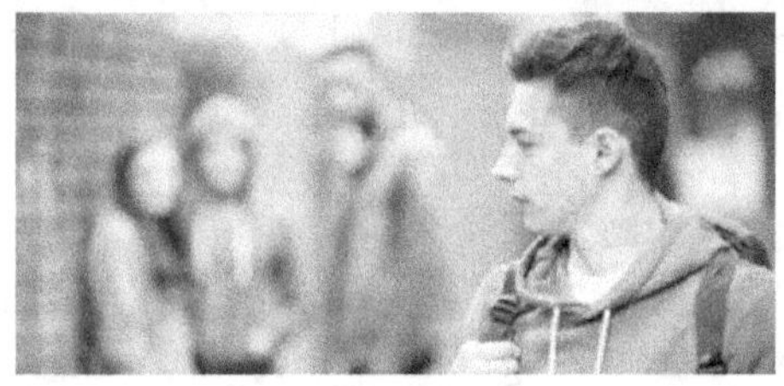

In fact, you do not need to be a samurai to experience this. Have you not had the experience of feeling that someone was watching you from behind and then turned around to find that someone was indeed staring at you? This is a very common occurrence, especially for women. This ability to detect another person’s stare feels like ESP, but, in fact, the perception originates from a system in the brain. Believe it or not, this system is devoted to detecting where others are looking. This “gaze detection” system is especially sensitive to determining if someone is looking directly at you.

I can give you another known example of this special sense or ability. It is

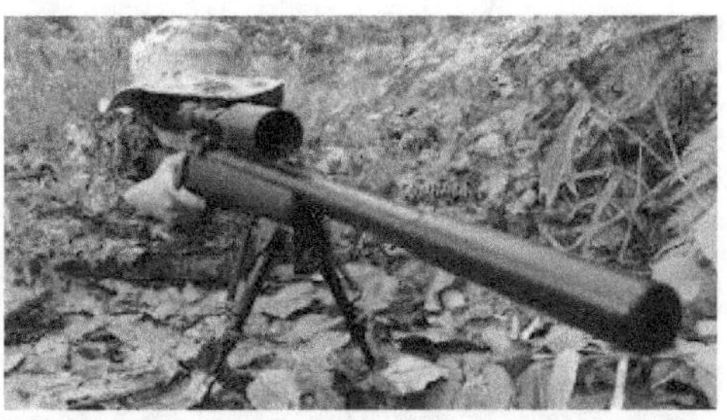

found in the case of professional hunters and photographers who deal with wild animals. Of course, they need a hideout or a camouflaged suit to make them less detectable. In addition, they claim that they must not stare at the prey when it appears. If they do, the prey seems to sense it. Well, they are wild animals, so they must have this kind of special sense. What is more interesting is that there have been many incidents in which hunters report that they felt they were being watched by their prey. As a result, they turned around and found that an animal was staring at them or sneaking up behind them. This special sense or ability saved their life.

3. Collective Behavior

Collective behavior occurs in large groups of similar animals and can be witnessed in flocks of birds or schools of fish as they swarm together. Birds flock together when they migrate, but I am particularly interested in another occasion. Birds and fish of many kinds behave according to collective decision-making. They not only flock together but also change the form and direction of their course to protect themselves from predators.

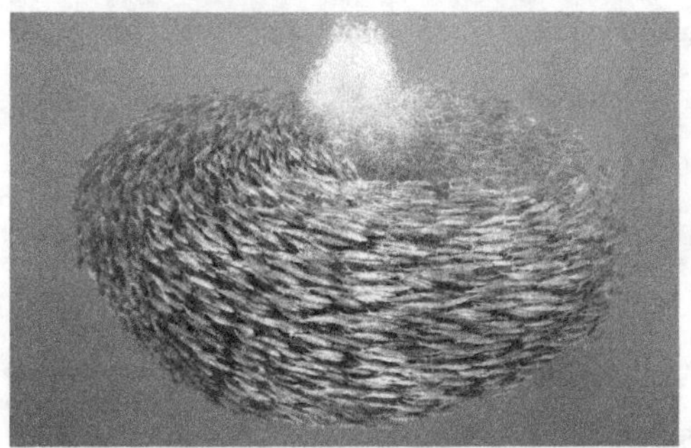

A school of fish, say, herrings, swims as one unit (photo left). Individually, each one is a small fish, but by keeping the size of the school large, they can intimidate their predators. What is amazing is that the school can change its direction almost instantaneously, which makes it look like one fish. Each fish cannot be making an individual decision to change its course as it would be too slow to react in time. Thus, the fish must be behaving according to a collective decision-making process.

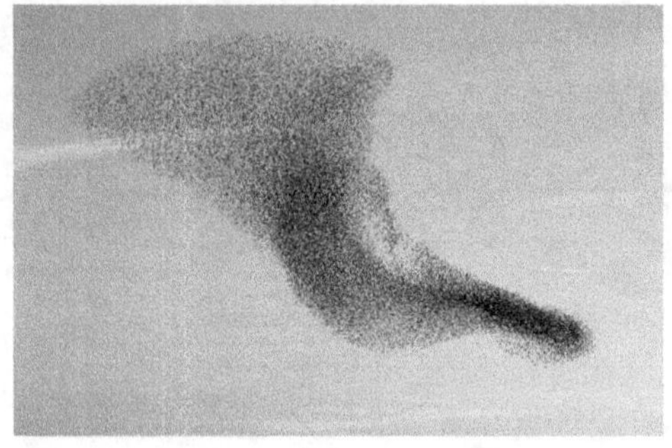

A flock of birds, say, a few hundred, flies as a group (photo left). They all change direction as one, and no individual bird ever crashes into the bird next to it. It seems as if their brains were almost tied together. Is this possible? It obviously must be because they successfully demonstrate such unified behavior.

Conclusion

I have brought up these abilities and explained them in depth because I believe most of us have forgotten that they exist in us. I also believe that we can regain them with some special training. One way to achieve this is to practice team *kata*.

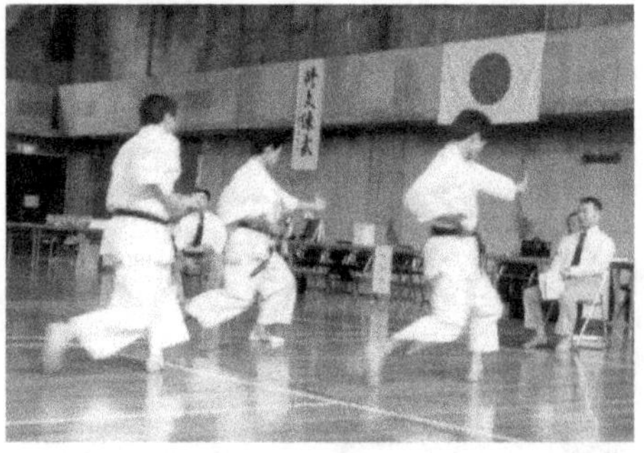

In my twenties, I used to compete in tournaments in Japan, and team *kata* was my favorite event, so I was certainly one of the team *kata* members (photo right). Our sensei, Sugano, told us not to depend on our eyes to synchronize our movements since we could not see both teammates at all times. He told us to "feel" them with our internal senses. We even practiced many times with our eyes closed. Eventually, I could almost "see" my teammates who were performing behind me. We won first place in the prefecture tournament.

So, the objective of team *kata*, we all know, is to synchronize the movements of the team members. I am certainly aware that there are some downsides to trying to synchronize your movements with those of your teammates when running *kata* instead of running it according to your own rhythm. However, I do not agree with a few who view team *kata* as nonsense or meaningless. By practicing team *kata* intensely, a *karateka* may be able to develop the hidden or forgotten ability of the sixth sense. If that is possible, then how can we say it is worthless or meaningless?

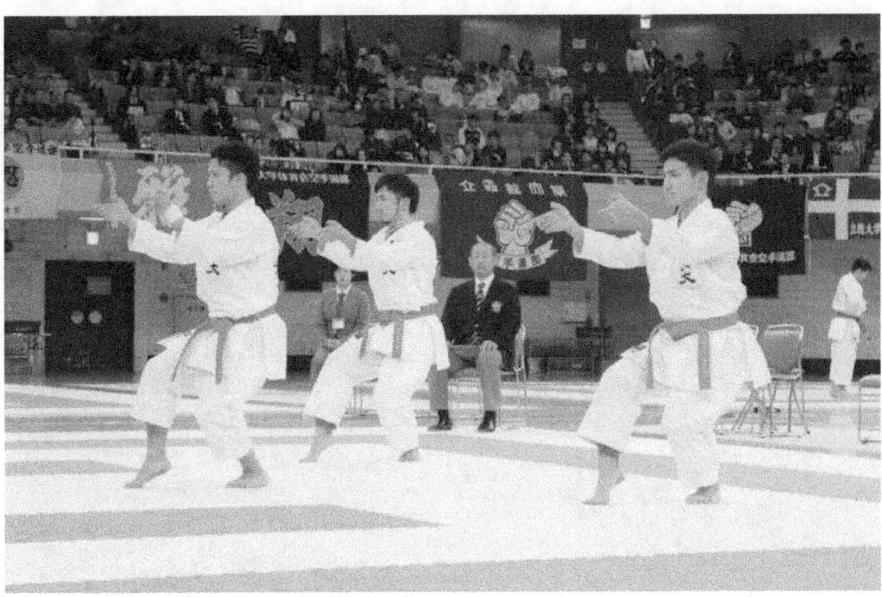

Rupert Sheldrake was a keynote speaker at the 2013 International Gathering of Eden Energy Medicine. Here is a video of his presentation for those who wish to learn more about morphic resonance: www.youtube.com/watch?v=MtgLklXZo3U. If you are interested in the detailed biography of Dr. Sheldrake, here is the URL for that page on his website: www.sheldrake.org/about-rupert-sheldrake.

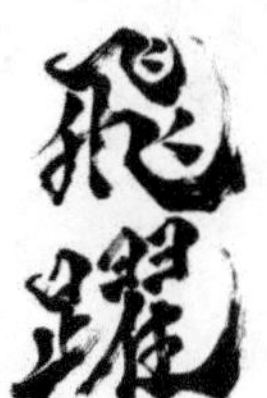

Chapter Five
第五章

Five Practical Training Ideas to Improve Kata and Kumite
形と組手を上達させる五つの案

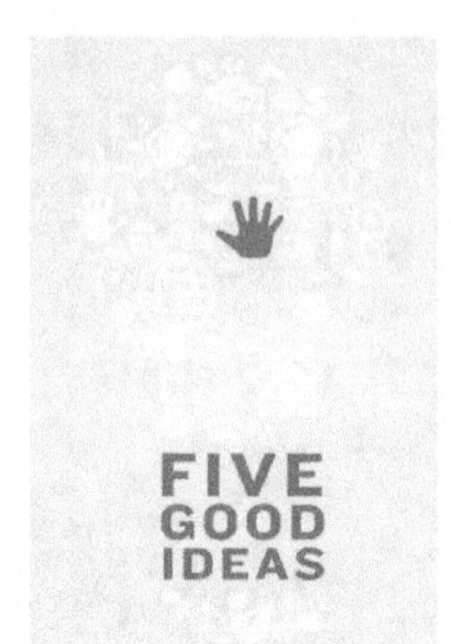

I travel around the world, visiting different dojo to teach Asai Ryu Budo karate (浅井流武道空手), which is based on Shotokan. In almost all dojo, I meet many dedicated practitioners. They are all interested in finding ways to improve their karate. I do my best to share my knowledge, hoping that what I pass on to them will benefit them.

Some of the young ones are quick to pick up the ideas and are flexible in adopting new concepts. They are young, so they are more relaxed about their improvement. On the other hand, I see a sense of urgency and near desperation among the senior practitioners who are over forty years old, and especially among those who are over fifty. Some of them have told me that they are practicing not to improve but rather to stop or at least delay deterioration. This is a shame, and I have been very disheartened upon hearing this.

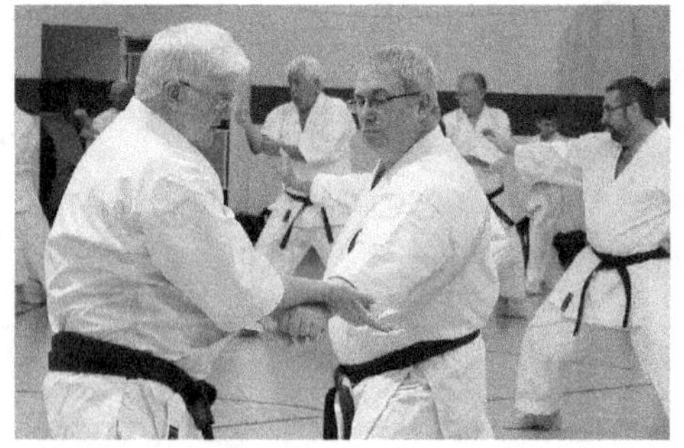

I sympathize with those who are frustrated, but I strongly believe that they should not give up. This is the very reason I have decided to write this chapter. I honestly believe in the amazing capability of human beings. However, we must know that as we get older, we may be able to access this capability only if we believe in it. I am confident that all of us can improve, no matter what age we may be or condition we may find ourselves in.

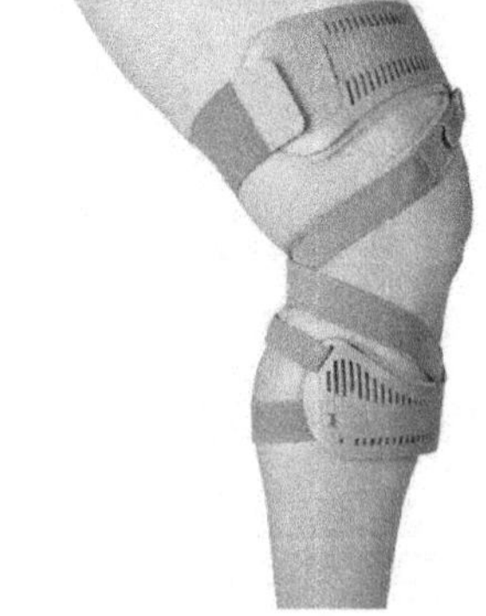

So, what we need to do first is to believe in ourselves. Then, we make a new commitment that we will train a little differently for a period of at least three to six months.

I am aware that different practitioners' situations and circumstances vary greatly. Some may have developed some physical limitations, such as bad knees or hips. I also realize that each person needs a different solution that addresses his specific needs. There may not be one silver bullet, but I think I can come up with some useful ideas that can benefit all practitioners. However, I cannot guarantee that my ideas will work for you. I can only suggest that you read on and see if they sound like a solution for you. The only thing you have to lose is about ten to fifteen minutes of your time to read the rest of this chapter, so why not?

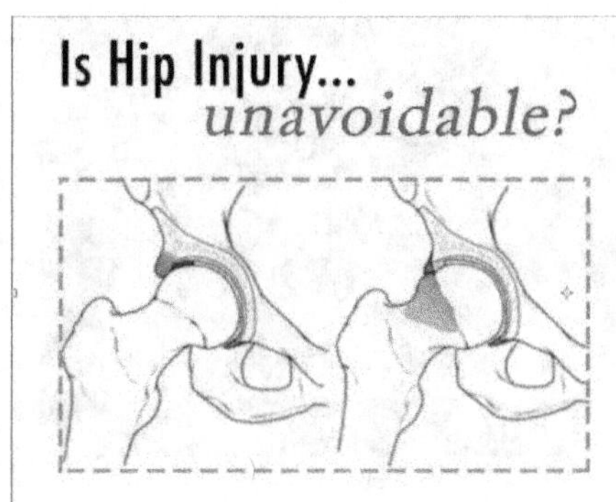

I will discuss the *kata* and *kumite* segments separately. In each segment, I will explain what the most common errors are and what challenges are faced by senior practitioners. Then, I will provide the reasons they are encountering these challenges and hindrances. At the very end, I will provide my ideas as to how they can train to improve their *kata* and *kumite*.

Before we discuss the specifics of these ideas for improvement, I must bring up one very important subject. It is a mind-set or a belief that practitioners have that I think is the biggest barrier to improvement. In fact, two ideas must be recognized in this mind-set.

First, you need to admit that whatever you have done or tried so far did not work well or was not able to improve your performance to your satisfaction. This does not mean what you have done was wrong. It simply means you were not able to find a solution to meet your expectations.

Second, you need to acknowledge that in order to achieve your goal, you must find a different solution. This is very important, and you must realize that you are your own worst enemy. In other words, you naturally desire to stick with what feels natural and comfortable to you. All of us prefer to move our body in a comfortable way. For instance, we are well aware that we are supposed to keep our upper body upright when we throw a side kick. However, we tend to lean down.

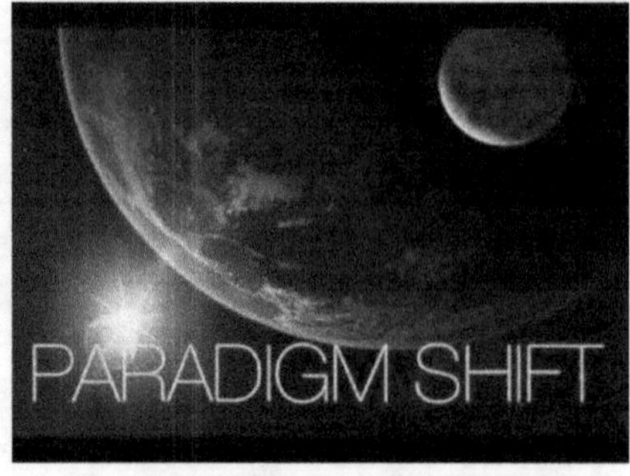

Why? It is simply because we want to kick higher, even if we destroy our basic, correct form. You may have developed other bad habits without knowing it.

So, what I am asking is that you execute your karate techniques and training in exactly the way I will share in this chapter. You need to promise that you will not execute them according to your natural, normal, or usual way. Doing it your own way may be the most comfortable, but being stuck in your old ways will not change anything, which means there will be no improvement.

OK, we can move on if you are willing to accept these prerequisites. Now I will present some specific training ideas that may help you improve your *kata* and *kumite*. We will start with *kata*.

Kata

Idea 1: Elimination of Personalized *Kata*

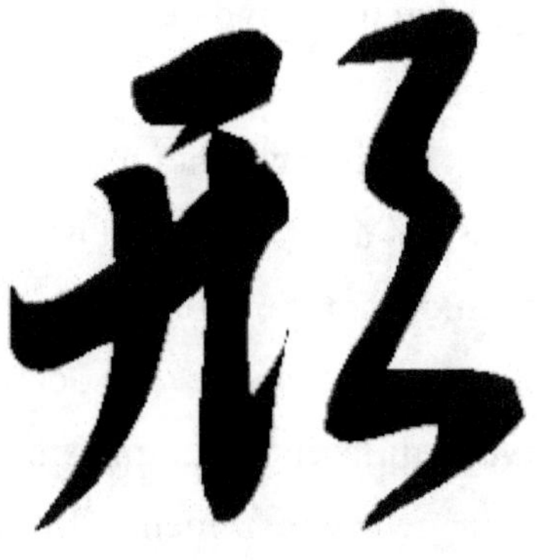

Many believe that once a practitioner reaches a high rank, such as *sandan* or *yondan*, he can modify *kata* to his liking. It is also considered not only acceptable but almost desirable for one to have his own style of running *kata*. If you are successful in achieving the ultimate level, this concept may apply. However, for most of us, we must not encourage changing any part of *kata*.

Thus, if you are running your *kata* your own way, I have to ask you to stop. I know this may be a big challenge and may seem impossible, but no matter how challenging it may seem, this, unfortunately, is a mandatory requirement if you wish to improve.

This is another mind-set requirement. It may be a paradigm shift for your mind about how you run your *kata*. If you accept this, then it is worth reading the rest of this chapter. If you do not, then you can skip Idea 2 and jump to Idea 3 if you wish, or you can stop reading altogether.

Idea 2: Return to Textbook *Kata*

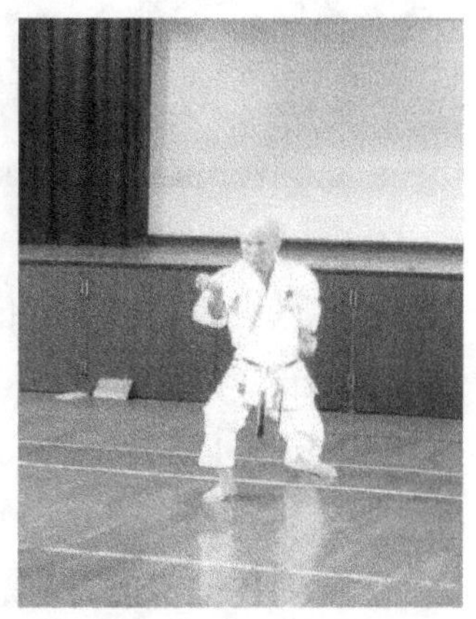

Now you have promised to go back to how the *kata* is run in the textbook. Whether your style is Shito Ryu (糸東流), Goju Ryu (剛柔流), or Shotokan, each style has published a textbook version of the *kata* in book and/or video format. These are available either by purchasing the textbook or video or by simply accessing reputable resources on *YouTube*.

I caution you not to pick a video of a *kata* champion unless it is published as an official *kata* of that style. I say this because the champion will most likely run the *kata* in his own style and not necessarily according to the textbook method. If you try to imitate him, then you are trying to run his *kata*. Since you cannot imitate him one hundred percent, your *kata* will deviate not only from his version but also (and most likely even more so) from the textbook version.

You might have felt that the first two ideas were not specific or concrete regarding how you can improve your techniques and *kata*. The first one addressed your mental attitude. The second one was to set a standard that you will follow with your *kata*. Though you may not believe these two ideas are that important, I cannot overemphasize that they are required if you wish to improve your *kata* performance. I need to ask you to promise now that you will accept them and strictly follow them. You need to think about this before you proceed to the rest.

The last three subjects are the ones that touch on the fundamentals or the essence of *kata* performance. They are not secrets or unknown teachings. You may remember that you learned these key points when you started karate but may have forgotten them a long time ago.

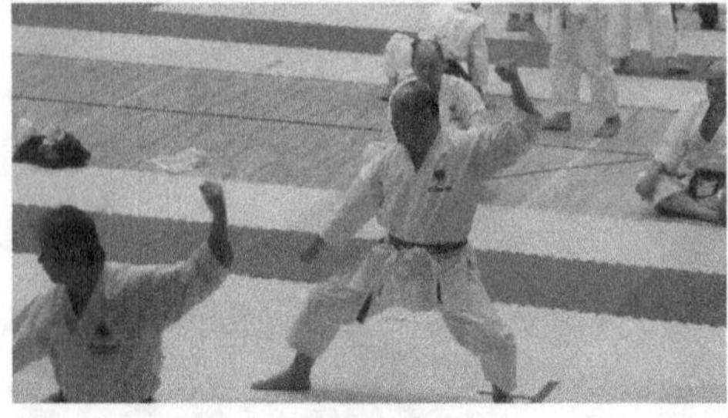

The three key points of *kata* are *chikara no kyojaku*, *waza no kankyu*, and *karada no shinshuku* (including *iki no chosei*). These are the main three essential points of *kata* taught by Master Gichin Funakoshi. I see great value in them, and we should check your *kata* performance and see if it satisfies these key points.

Let's review each of these key points in depth, and I will present the common mistakes that are found among senior practitioners. You can check and see if any of those mistakes fit your case.

Idea 3: *Chikara no Kyojaku* (力の強弱)

This term literally means 'strength and weakness of power'. This teaching is fairly straightforward and easy to understand. We understand that we need to put power into some parts or techniques within *kata*, while other techniques must be done softly. Right?

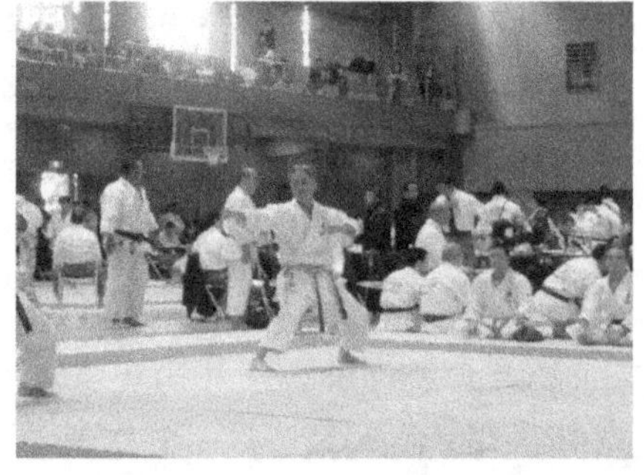

You may say, "Yes, I know this very well. I am pretty sure I am doing it exactly the way it is supposed to be done." But, you could be way off if you happen to believe that power should be placed where the *kiai* (気合) are and that soft techniques should be placed where you typically go slowly.

Surprised? The points I made above are not incorrect. What I am saying here is that you may be missing something that is much more important. We must never forget that strong and weak points exist not only in certain places within *kata* but also in certain places within each and every technique.

For instance, let's take a simple technique like *shuto uke*. You have to bring your *uke* hand back to your neck (on the opposite side of the body) before you strike forward. In the process of bringing your hand back, you need to be relaxed to have a fast and smooth movement going forward. However, many practitioners apply too much power and tension when bringing the hand back. They wish to move the hand quickly, but, sadly, their tension slows them down. This action is counterproductive because tension works like a brake. It not only slows you down but also reduces the amount of power or *kime* at the completion of the technique.

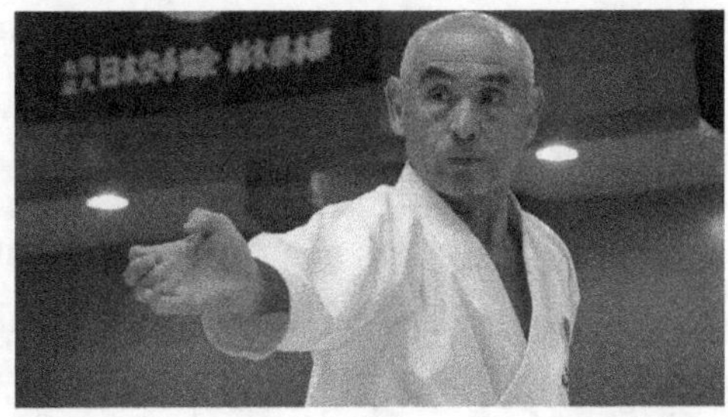

Many people say that the movements of Shotokan karate are not fluid. People from other styles accuse Shotokan practitioners of being too tense, and the latter argue that they are generating *kime*. In general, there are two kinds of *kime*. One is short *kime*, which is sharp; the other is long *kime*, which uses a pushing motion and takes more time.

You can find long *kime* in Jion (慈恩). It is on the second-to-last movement, the left *chudan nobashi zuki* (中段伸ばし突き), which is a *choku zuki* (直突き) delivered to the left side of the body. You can also find this type of *kime* in almost all other *kata*, starting from the Heian *kata* (such as on the *kakiwake uke* [掻き分け受け] in Heian Yondan and the *morote tsukami hikiyose* [諸手掴み引き寄せ] after the *jodan juji uke* [上段十字受け] in Heian Godan) all the way up to and including the *morote kaishu kakiwake uke* [諸手開手掻き分け受け] in Unsu (雲手), the left *nobashi zuki* after the right *mae geri* in Sochin (壯鎮), and the very first movement in both Gojushiho (五十四歩) forms.

Most of the time, this long *kime* is not a problem. The more challenging one is the short *kime*. It is challenging because many practitioners cannot make it sharp.

Why? It is simply because the amount of time they use to generate this *kime* is too long. In other words, they apply the brakes too soon, and it ends up being long *kime*.

What you have to do is go full speed until the very end of the technique. Just imagine it is like driving a car at 60 mph (roughly 96 km/h) and needing to instantly come to a full stop without applying any braking action. I know your car cannot do it. The only way to have this happen is for you to collide with a stone wall. Then, you can achieve a dead stop (and probably be dead yourself, too).

Your body is like your car, and a dead stop of your fist or foot is hard to achieve. But, your arm length is limited, so you can achieve full extension, which will make your fist come to a dead stop. So, all you have to do is go at full speed until your car hits the wall (i.e., your arm reaches full extension). Well, this is easy to say, but the problem is that you tend to apply some braking action before the arm reaches full extension.

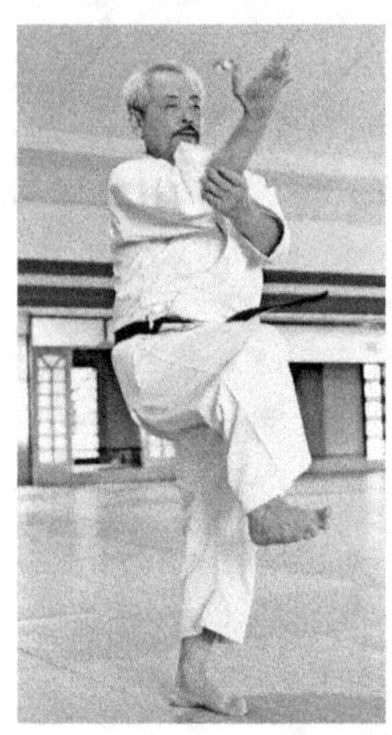

You may point out that it is dangerous to let your arm fully extend at high speed. This action (*choku zuki*) could cause physical damage to the elbow, something similar to tennis elbow. I understand this concern or fear. In fact, many practitioners have suffered from this as they have tried to achieve last-moment *kime*. But, I must point out that this physical harm was caused not by full extension of the arm but rather by incorrect bone alignment in the arm. I talk about this important point in Chapter 11: "The Relationship between Choku Zuki and the Elbow Position" of my book *Karatedo Paradigm Shift*. In that chapter, I explain in detail how you should align your elbow when you deliver *choku zuki* at full speed. By doing this correctly, you can avoid the elbow problem, even if you fully extend your arm at high speed.

If the *kime* is to be performed at the very end of the technique, what you need to do is work on relaxation during movement. This makes up more than ninety-nine percent of each technique. Now you are aware of this, but you will point out that to move your arm, you have to tense the muscles in the arm, shoulder, etc. This is true, and what makes it more difficult is the need to tense only the necessary muscles. This means you want to perform the minimum amount of work to move your arm and hand. This concept goes for all techniques.

An excellent model of this concept is the cracking of a whip. Since a muscle cannot extend itself, in order for your arm to extend, one muscle (or group of muscles) must tense while the other muscle (or group of muscles) must relax and allow itself to be stretched. If the relaxed muscle tenses, it will work as a brake, and the action will be slowed down. If the power of both muscles is equal, then the arm will stop and not go anywhere. A good example of this is when you flex your arm to show off your biceps as a popular symbol of strength.

So, I recommend that you do a lot of relaxation exercises before you perform your *kata*. Shake your arms, legs, neck, and body. Make your body soft and limber like a whip. The arms and legs are almost always relaxed. Whether it is an arm technique (a punch or a block) or a leg technique (a kick or a block), you control your technique from your lower *tanden* (丹田), which is the handle of the whip. As you are a seasoned *karateka*, I do not need to explain further on how to generate power using the *tanden*.

Idea 4: *Waza no Kanky*u (技の緩急)

As you know, *waza* (技) means 'techniques'. What is *kankyu*? *Kan* (緩) means 'mild' or 'slow'. *Kyu* (急) means 'fast' or 'quick'. Together, these two characters make up the word for 'tempo'. So, the whole phrase refers to the slow and fast techniques, or the tempo, of *kata*. In the previous point, I discussed how to execute each technique. Here, I am talking about the rhythm or flow of the entire *kata*.

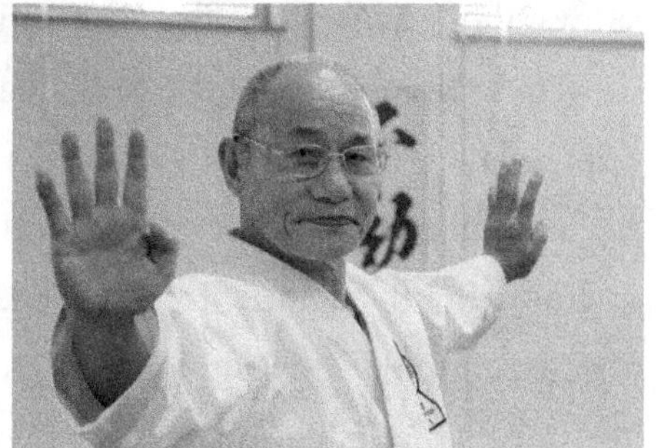

With the popularity of competitions,

many practitioners falsely believe they need to make all techniques fast. The speed of all techniques is not uniform. Some techniques may be extremely fast, but others may be neither fast nor slow. Depending on the technique, the speed will be different. This is the same not only for punches and blocks but also for kicks and body shifting, including turns.

To show the contrast between fast and slow techniques, in some places of tournament *kata*, the performer will come to a complete stop and intentionally hold this dead-stop position. This concept may work in competition *kata*, but in *budo*, this is a strong no. The *budo karateka* considers *kata* to be like a living thing. A full stop means virtual death. *Kata* must flow like a river and must never stop. If the river stops at any one point for too long, the water goes bad. There may be a few places where *kata* movement seems to stop, but the practitioner must maintain the continuous but invisible movement that connects one technique to the next. If you are familiar with Japanese brushed calligraphy, you will have seen the small drips between the kanji. This shows that the brush was lifted after completing one kanji as it traveled to the next. Even though there is no visible line connecting one kanji to the other, those few small drips signify the connection.

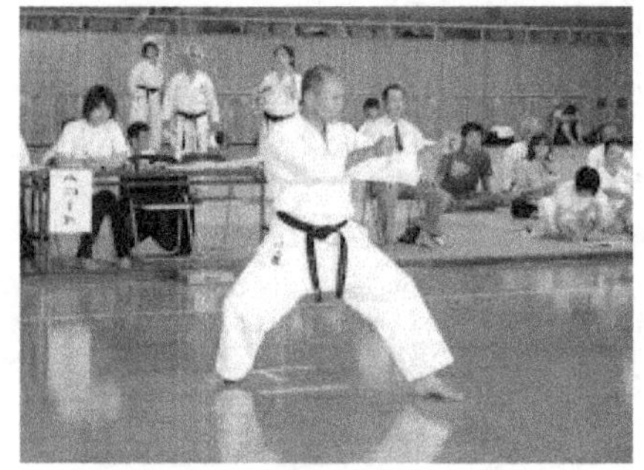

Since this continuous movement is invisible, we cannot show it with our body movement, so how do we show it? One way is through breath control. The other comes from the tension and relaxation of specific muscles of the body, which shows, though invisibly, the preparation of those muscles for the next move.

These hints may be too technical and the techniques too difficult to acquire right away. I suggest that you watch videos of demonstration *kata* performed by Japanese masters. I do not particularly suggest videos from tournaments. No matter how calm the competitors may be, their performance is affected by the pressure of competition. I suggest videos that were created for instructional purposes so that you have a model performance. I know Shotokan and Shito Ryu have these kinds of videos. I am sure other major styles also have similar instructional *kata* videos that can be easily accessed.

If you are lucky enough to study under or have access to a high-ranking Japanese sensei, you can watch his *kata* performance and imitate the correct *kata* rhythm. Then, you can ask him to watch your *kata* and give you advice on the *kata* rhythm.

Idea 5: *Karada no Shinshuku* (体の伸縮) and *Iki no Chosei* (息の調整)

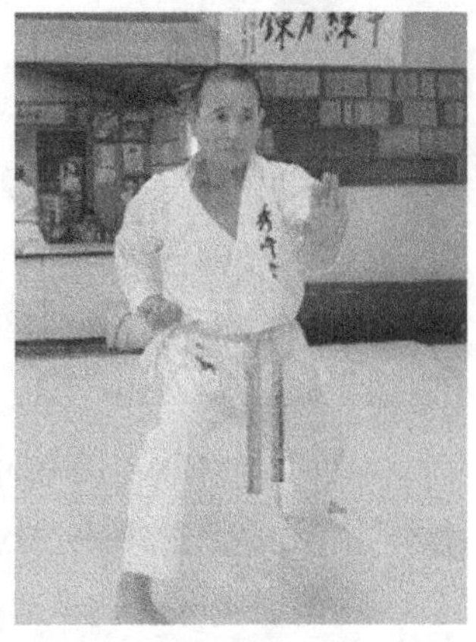

This is the last important element of *kata*. In fact, this applies to all karate techniques. There are two parts involved in this element. One is body control, and the other is breath control. Let's look at these two parts.

The first one is *karada no shinshuku*. *Karada* (体) means 'body'. *Shin* (伸) means 'expansion' or 'stretching'. *Shuku* (縮) means 'contraction' or 'shrinking'. So, the whole term means 'expansion and contraction of the body'. The important thing is that this applies not only to the expansion and contraction of the muscles but also to the movement of the body itself.

Let me give you an example. When you cross your arms as when you are preparing to execute *chudan shuto uke*, you sort of collapse the front part of the rib cage and open up the back side. Therefore, in this movement, you tense the front part of the chest but expand the area near the shoulder blades. At the same time, the arms must be relaxed and must not be tense. When you complete the *shuto uke* technique, you expand the chest area but tense the underarm and back muscles. Full expansion of the *uke* arm is more important, and remember that the full contraction of those muscles must not happen until the last moment. Failing to do this will cause your technique to be small and jerky. Your *kata* will not have enough power and will not look dynamic.

Another contraction may be found in *neko ashi dachi*. The supporting leg and lower *tanden* are tense in this stance. At the same time, the front leg must be relaxed and ready for kicking. Though your *tanden* may be tense, your upper body must be relaxed.

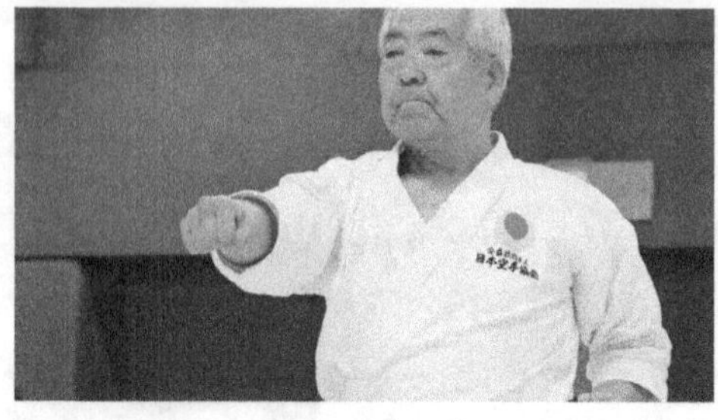

So, the key point is that when we talk about tension and relaxation, we are not only thinking of a sequence that moves from one to the other as separate actions. They most likely happen at the same time but in different parts of the body. In fact, this makes it very challenging as we tend to focus on one area at a time and forget the other parts of the body.

How can we pay attention to all parts of the body and be able to apply the correct amount of tension and relaxation? It is not easy, so you are virtually an expert if you can do it easily. My idea is to learn how to relax more. Most practitioners are typically too tense. I suggest that serious practitioners spend more time relaxing their muscles. In other words, do more stretches and relaxing body movements.

Another idea is to increase the flexibility of the major joints at the hips and shoulders. Having more flexibility will allow you to stretch more and thus relax more in your body movements.

The second part of the last element of *kata* is *iki no chosei*. The meaning of this term is 'breath control' or 'breath management'. This idea or technique is, in fact, coordinated with and, therefore, included in *karada no shinshuku*. In other words, as you expand and contract your body, you must coordinate the body movements with natural and correct breathing.

Being able to do correct breathing is very difficult, in fact. As you may have seen in your dojo, most beginners (and even some senior practitioners) hold their breath too long and too often during techniques. Typically, you expand your body as you inhale and contract your body as you exhale. This means that you normally relax as you inhale and then tense as you exhale.

In general, what I have described regarding the timing and objective of inhalation and exhalation is correct. However, the subject of breathing is much deeper and more complex than this. The ancient martial artists realized that tensing too much or too often was not desirable. This moment of tension is called *itsuki* (居着き) and is considered one of the worst errors in martial arts training. The martial arts experts wanted to stay relaxed and mobile at all times, even when they exhaled. Thus, they came up with many different breathing methods.

One of these is a reverse breathing method, in which you contract as you inhale and expand as you exhale. Typically, expansion of the body, especially with long, deep inhalation, is translated as relaxation. The reverse breathing technique of tensing as you inhale is not found in sport karate. It may sound contradictory and unachievable; however, it isn't that difficult once you have learned how.

An easy example for understanding this mechanism is a rubber band. If you expand it, you will feel the tension. By doing this breathing, you can keep your *seika tanden* (臍下丹田, 'lower abdominal *tanden*') tense while keeping your upper body relaxed. The best *kata* for training in this breathing method is Hangetsu (半月). I write in depth on this subject in Chapter 11: "Hangetsu" of my book *Shotokan Myths* (available in both paperback and electronic format through *Amazon*).

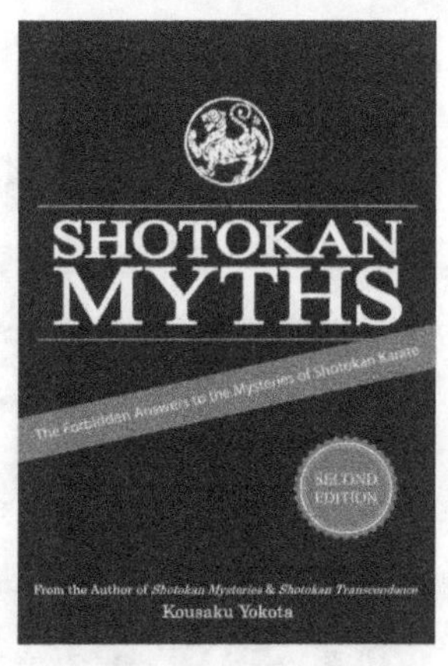

Finally, I suggest that *kata* practitioners run the *kata* much more slowly so that they can pay more attention to the details of the body movements. You can always speed up once you can perform your *kata* correctly at lower speeds with the right rhythm and tempo. Running a fast *kata* with poor techniques simply results in a fast, sloppy *kata*. Do not fall into mindless repetition of your *kata* practice. In other words, it is much easier to just run with a *kata*, which means you run your *kata* without thinking. Though it is tiring and demanding, you must think and pay full attention to each move you make. This is why I suggest that you run your *kata* much more slowly, maybe at half or even a quarter of the normal speed. If you are not paying much attention when running slow *kata*, it will just be a slow, sloppy *kata*. You need to keep all the other elements I have discussed above in mind, such as the power and rhythm of the *kata*. Let us move on to *kumite*.

Kumite

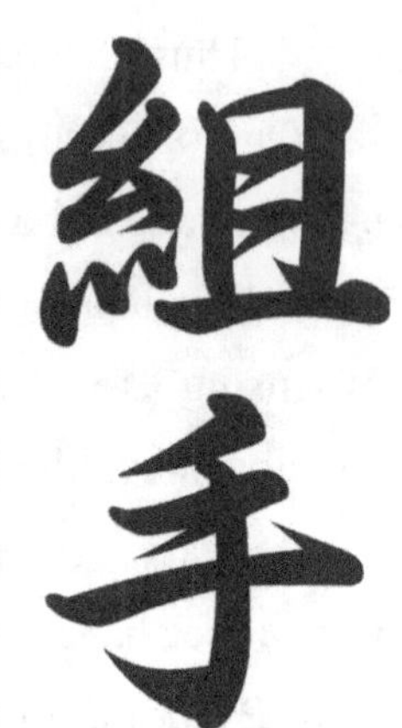

Here are five training ideas to improve your *kumite*. When I say, "*kumite*," here, I am talking about *jiyu kumite*. I want to call your attention to the fact that I am not thinking about tournament *kumite*. Therefore, I must ask you to remember that my ideas and suggestions may not make you a better tournament fighter. If you are only interested in tournament *kumite*, and your objective is to score points or win tournament matches, this chapter may not be of interest to you, and you may be disappointed. The techniques and ideas I will be discussing are related to *budo*, and though they are not directly designed for street fighting, the basic concept can be applied in those situations.

I will provide five training ideas that senior practitioners can try so that they can improve their *kumite* skill. Before I start with the specifics of the ideas, I have to ask you to drop *gohon kumite* and *sanbon kumite* from your *kumite* drills (in case you are still doing them). Instead, I recommend that you spend all your *kumite* training time on *kihon ippon kumite* and *jiyu ippon kumite*. If you are practicing only *jiyu kumite*, then drop that, too. Go back to *kihon ippon kumite* and *jiyu ippon kumite* drills, which are the main themes of the following training ideas.

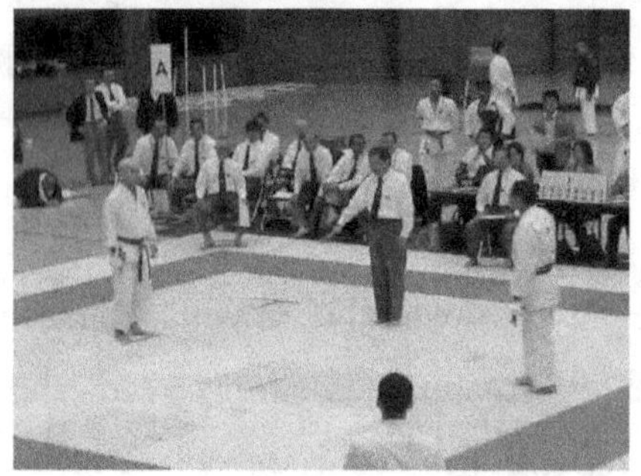

I am sure you have practiced *kihon ippon kumite* many times in your karate life. Maybe you feel that you do not need to practice this to improve your *jiyu*

kumite. I disagree. I have found that many senior practitioners can benefit from reconstructing their *kumite* skill by practicing *kihon ippon kumite* in a different way. Here I break down the idea into two parts: (Idea 1) as a defender and (Idea 2) as an attacker.

Idea 1: *Kihon Ippon Kumite* Defense

There are three key elements to remember when you practice for the defending side: not stepping straight back, using a fast tempo, and waiting until the last moment.

The first element is to not step back when you are the defender. Practice stepping forward at an angle. In other words, step toward the one- or two-o'clock position when you move to your right side and toward the ten- or eleven-o'clock position when you move to your left side. Stepping toward either the three- or nine-o'clock position is acceptable, but try to learn *irimi* techniques, which are much better.

Irimi (入り身) is a very popular term in aikido and jujutsu (柔術), but it is not so well known in most karate dojo. Let me give you a brief explanation of what it is. This Japanese word consists of two parts: *iri* (入り), which means 'enter' or 'step in', and *mi* (身), which means 'body'. Thus, *irimi* refers to techniques where one enters or steps in to an attack instead of standing still or stepping backward to block or dodge it.

After practicing *gohon* and *sanbon kumite* for so many years, we are conditioned to step back when we are attacked. This is the worst choice for positioning. What you need to do is position yourself to a side (right or left) of the opponent in every situation. The most important thing that this body movement will give you is this: you will not be on the opponent's attack line, while your attack line will face straight at the opponent. This is what you need to develop in *kihon ippon kumite* and also eventually in *jiyu ippon kumite*. Of course, the final objective is to realize this skill in *jiyu kumite*.

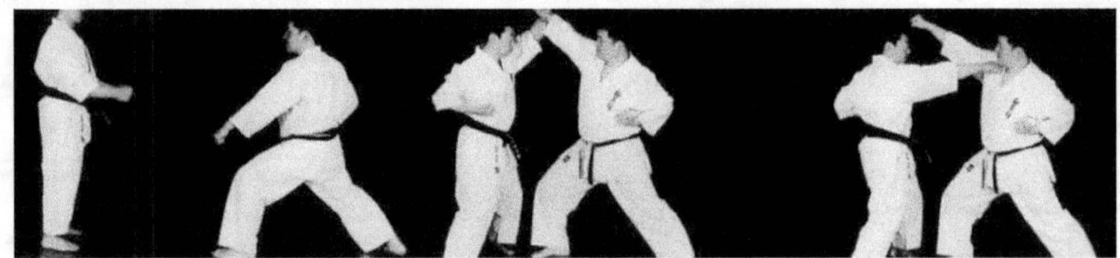

The second element is to not execute the *uke* with one arm and then follow up with a counterattack using the other arm (e.g., *age uke* with the left arm followed by *gyaku zuki* with the right arm as shown in the photo above). This combination is called *two-count tempo*. It is very popular among Shotokan practitioners, including the senior ones. Unfortunately, this tempo is too slow and not very usable in *jiyu kumite*. You must practice only the one- or one-and-a-half-count combinations.

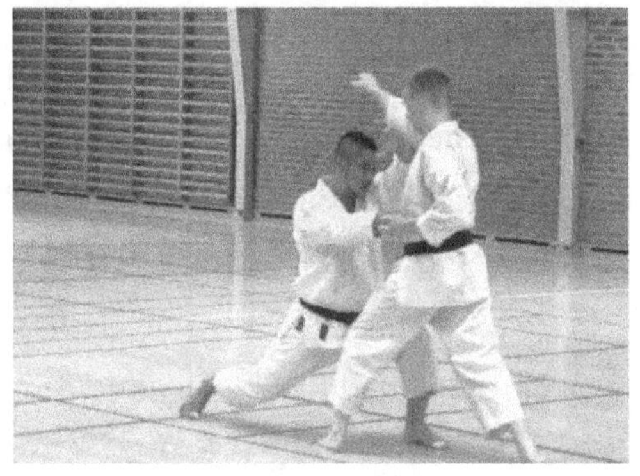

A one-count tempo is when you execute the *uke* and the counterattack at the same time, which is called *doji waza* (同時技, 'simultaneous technique' [photo right]). A one-and-a-half-count tempo is when you execute the *uke* and counterattack with the same arm. Of course, when you are familiar with these two tempos, you can advance to the even faster tempo of *deai* (0.5 tempo), which is *sen no sen*. In a *deai* technique, you execute the counter, with or without the *uke*, before the opponent completes his attacking technique.

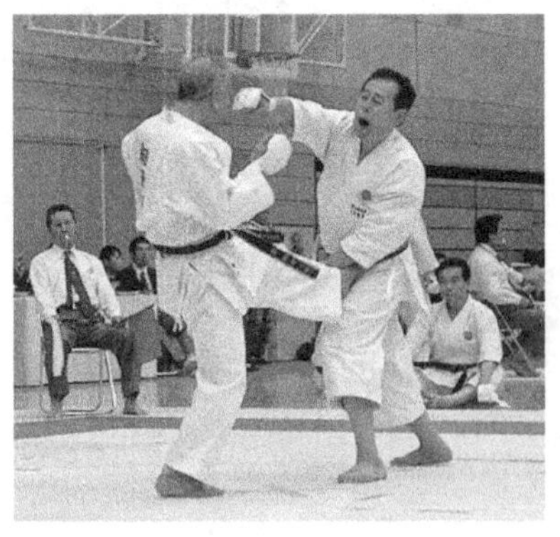

The third element is the most challenging. You need to delay your reaction until the very last moment. In other words, you need to let the opponent commit to his attacking movement. We tend to react as soon as the attacker makes a move. If this is a fake, then the reaction to it will put you in an unfavorable position. So, what you must do is remain in the *shizentai* (自然体) position until the attacker's fist or foot almost touches you. At the very last moment, you take your *irimi* step to dodge the punch or kick by a space no greater than the thickness of a sheet of paper. Too often the defender wants to dodge the attacking technique by more than several inches. This is OK for a white belt, but if you are a senior practitioner, this is wasted time and distance.

Waiting until the last moment is indeed risky, and, for many, it is a scary practice. To practice this as a gradual process, you can ask your partner to slow down initially until you get used to the speed. Then, you can ask your partner to speed up a little and eventually get up to full speed.

Idea 2: *Kihon Ippon Kumite* Attack

There are three key elements for the attacking side, as well: minimizing body movement, bending the front knee, and increasing distance. Even though you are attacking, believe it or not, you are in an unfavorable position. This is because the defender knows your attacking techniques and is waiting for your move. Even though he does not know exactly when you will deliver the attacking technique, he is definitely in an advantageous position. So, you need to train to turn this disadvantage around and put yourself in a more advantageous position.

The first element is to minimize body movement. The defender knows your attacking technique, say, *jodan oi zuki*. As soon as you move the upper body or head, the defender gets a warning and becomes ready to block your punching arm. So, what you have to do is minimize your body movement before you attack. In other words, you must hide your movement and make your attack as stealthy as possible. You need to minimize the up-and-down as well as the left-and-right body movement. You need to move straight toward the opponent by

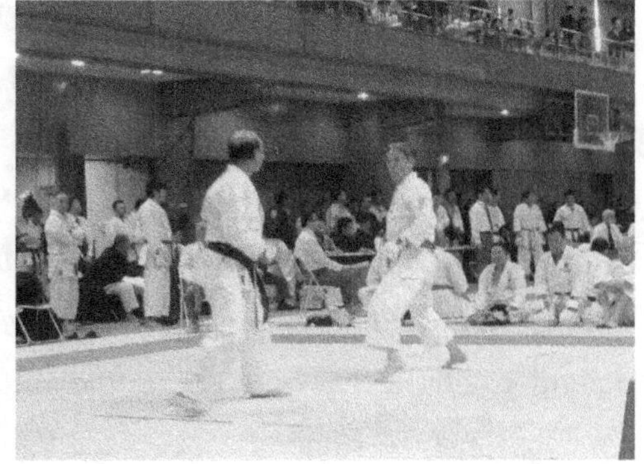

bending your front knee and keeping your upper body at the same height. Making yourself stealthy when attacking with a punch is rather easy. It is much more challenging when attacking with a kick.

How do you train for this? I can suggest two ways. One is to use a full-length mirror you may find in your dojo. Stand in front of it just as you are going to attack. You can see yourself and make the necessary adjustments. The other way is to ask your partner to tell you after each attack if he could detect the attack.

The second element is to bend your front knee so that it is farther forward than your big toe without lifting your heel. In other words, you bend your front knee so far forward that you almost fall toward the front. I think of this position as being like when a trigger is pulled or a bow is fully drawn. If your front knee is not fully bent, it will need to be before you can take a step forward. This means a delay in time, if only for a split second, but it could make a big difference.

In addition to the two points above, the third element you can try is to put more distance between you and your opponent. At first, this will put you in a more unfavorable position. You will need to cover more distance by taking a larger step. Attacking from a greater distance without being detected is much more challenging to do. You need to practice stretching your step (without telegraphs and/or up-and-down body movement, of course). If you can do this successfully in *kihon ippon kumite*, it will certainly improve your *jiyu ippon kumite*.

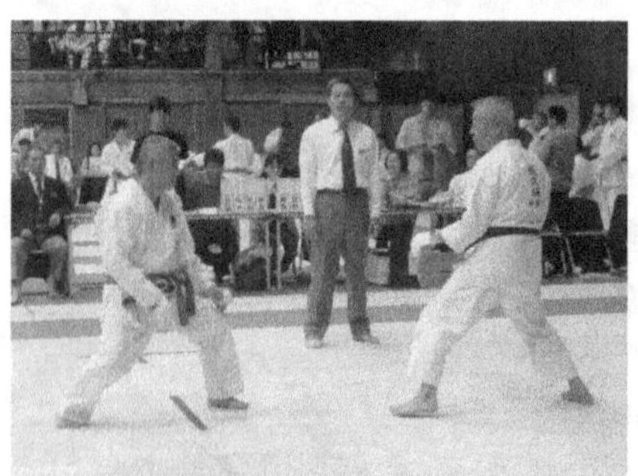

Once you improve your *kihon ippon kumite*, you will advance your *kumite* training to *jiyu ippon kumite*. This is the most important step, which requires much more intense and precise practice. The biggest difference between *kihon ippon kumite* and *jiyu ippon kumite* is that in the former, the distance is fixed as the defender stands in *shizentai*, whereas in the latter, the attacker and defender both move about before they attack and defend.

Obviously, distance is one of the key elements that you practice in *jiyu ippon kumite*. You must remember that the *maai* (間合い, 'distance') when you are an attacker is different from when you are a defender. Therefore, you focus on finding these two different distances by using the techniques in the *kihon ippon kumite* training. Here again, we will have separate sections for the defender (Idea 3) and the attacker (Idea 4).

Idea 3: *Jiyu Ippon Kumite* Defense

First, let's look at the defender's key points. We need to apply all the key points that we worked on in *kihon ippon kumite*. Let me point out several key points for *jiyu ippon kumite*.

A. First of all, I find that often the defender tends to step back when the attacker steps in. Just as in *kihon ippon kumite*, stepping back is a bad move that must be avoided. If you feel you must move, then step to either the left or the right side. In other words, you need to execute *taisabaki* (体捌き, 'body shifting') away from the attacker. If possible, move toward the attacker (which is much more challenging and requires you to be ready to be attacked). If you move in to either side of the attacker, it will be very difficult for him to deliver the second attack.
B. You must be sure to make the counterattack decisive enough that the attacker cannot carry out a second attack (though he would not actually do this in *ippon kumite*). In other words, if you think the first counterattack is weak or not decisive enough, you must execute a second counterattack right away. 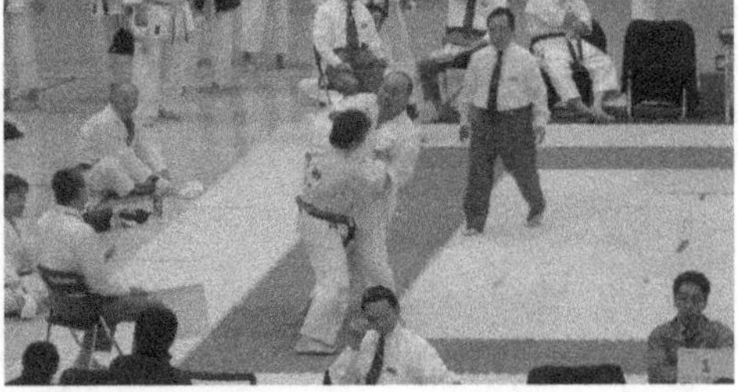
C. You must practice facing straight at the attacker, always keeping him in front of you, even after your counterattack. This is a very important habit you must

develop to get ready for *jiyu kumite*. I am sure you know that not facing straight at the opponent creates an opportunity for the opponent to attack you.

D. After the counterattack, you must leave enough distance to make it impossible for the attacker to carry out a second attack (though he would not actually do this in *ippon kumite*). In *jiyu ippon kumite*, there is no second attack; thus, the defender tends to drop his guard in both feeling and action. I often see the defender staying very close after the counterattack. Of course, if the counterattack is decisive enough, then there will not be a second attack. However, we must always think about this situation. If the counterattack is indecisive, then the attacker can carry out a second attack, especially if you are within attacking distance. This is why you must develop the habit of keeping a sufficient distance from the opponent. This is called *zanshin movement*.
E. Finally, you must keep your arms up in *kamae* after your counterattack. Again, I often witness the defender drop his arms right after the counterattack. This is a bad habit, which must be corrected. You must always keep the *zanshin* feeling with your *kamae* until your sensei tells you to stop or until the opponent recovers from his attacking posture to show the end of the attack.

As a defender, your objective after training in all these points is to reach a stage where you can block and decisively counterattack any and all attacks you receive, regardless of the distance and timing of the attacker.

Idea 4: *Jiyu Ippon Kumite* Attack

Now, let's look at the key points for the attacker. Through repetitive practice, you need to find the proper distance from the opponent which will be most effective when you attack. As in *kihon ippon kumite*, the attacker in *jiyu ippon kumite* is also in an unfavorable position. Since the defender knows your technique, he can block and counterattack most of the time. Here are the key points:

A. One advantage you have is that the defender does not know exactly when you will attack. You must exploit this advantage. Most often, the attacker does not really choose the time, in other words, the right time. He just steps in after starting the *kumite*. What you need to do before you attack is position yourself patiently at the most advantageous distance and then attack at the right time, such as when the defender crosses his legs or drops his arms. You cannot move around for more than a minute without attacking, but you have plenty of time to position yourself if you spend, say, thirty or even fifteen seconds.

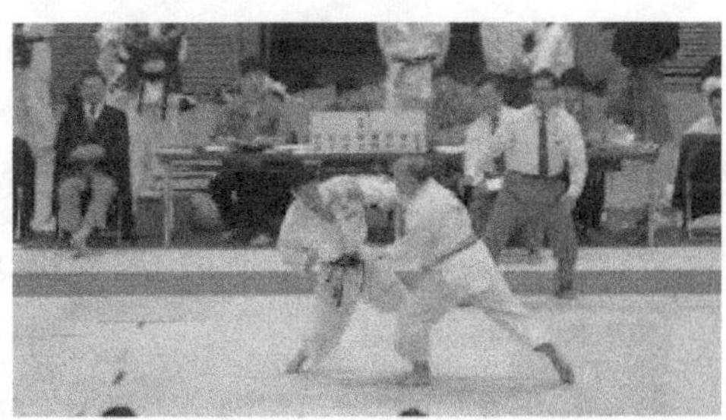

B. You must try to attack from both short and long distances. In other words, I am sure you have a very comfortable distance from which you like to attack, and you will most likely be successful if you attack from there. What you want to develop is the ability to attack from both a very short distance (almost *gyaku zuki* distance) and a very long distance (one-and-a-half-step distance).

C. When you finish the first attack, you must be sure to face the opponent squarely in front and not at an angle. In addition, you must be at the right distance in case you carry out a second attack. What you are practicing here is being ready for a second attack (even though you are supposed to use only one attacking technique in *ippon kumite*). Here, you are preparing for *jiyu kumite*, and you need to develop a readiness for a second attack.

Idea 5: *Yakusoku Jiyu Kumite*

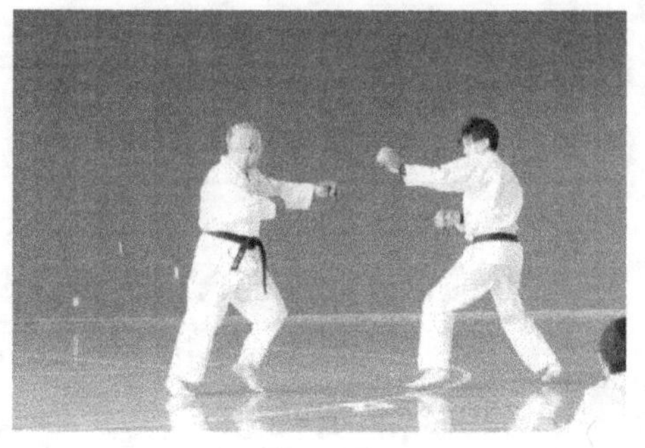

The final exercise to prepare you for your improved *jiyu kumite* is *yakusoku jiyu kumite* (約束自由組手). This exercise is typically designed for the attacking side, even though you can improve your *kumite* by practicing it from the defending side, especially if you wish to work on *go no sen* tactics.

Yakusoku (約束) means 'agreed', so there is one agreed-upon rule to control *jiyu kumite*. The rule is that only one side initiates all of the attacks. The other side is the defending side, which means that this side only executes blocks and counterattacks and cannot initiate attacks. You and your partner switch roles so that you can train in both attacking- and defending-side techniques.

The attacking side takes the initiative and continues to attack the opponent, who only reacts by blocking, shifting, and countering. In this training exercise, the attacking side needs to learn how to initiate and continue the attack with many different combinations. In *jiyu ippon kumite*, you can attack only once, so, even though your aim is to be successful with one definitive technique, often your opponent blocks your attack. In *yakusoku jiyu kumite*, however, you can use combination attacks.

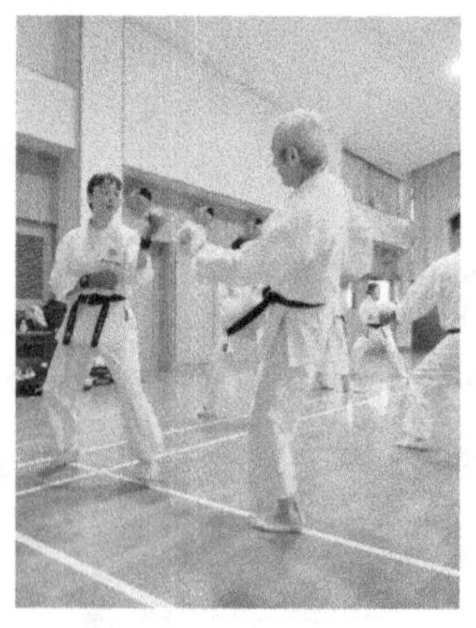

One big caution is that you must not skip *jiyu ippon kumite* training or take it lightly. You must spend a lot of time and gain confidence in your single-attack ability (as well as your ability to defend) before shifting your training to *yakusoku jiyu kumite*. This is because you need to develop a decisive single-attack ability. If you depend upon your techniques from combinations only, then your first attack tends to lack commitment or be indecisive. In other styles, combinations and successive light techniques are encouraged. Though we respect this fighting concept, in Shotokan, we believe in the concept of *ikken hissatsu.*

The key point for the defending side in *yakusoku jiyu kumite* is that you either get out of the way, block so as to get the opponent off-balance, and/or counter before the opponent executes any follow-up attacking techniques. When you get out of the way, you must never step straight back as this move will surely invite a second and third attacking technique from the opponent. You must apply the same stepping techniques as you practiced in *jiyu ippon kumite*, which are moving forward or getting to the side of the attacker so he cannot continue his attacking techniques.

These are the five ideas, which are designed for you to move up one by one like the rungs on a ladder. You must evaluate your performance at each step before moving on to the next step. In this process, you must be honest with yourself. If you have not achieved the goals of the key points, then you must stay in that stage until you become confident that you have.

I have one more request here at the end of my suggestions. I request that you not do any *jiyu kumite* training until you have completed all five steps. You can compare your *jiyu kumite* performance much more clearly after six months or even one year of specially programmed *kumite* training. I strongly recommend this not only for the above reason but also because, frankly, doing *jiyu kumite* during the program period will dilute the development of your techniques and thus your progress. You need to build the structure of the techniques as you would build a tall building, starting from the foundation and working toward the rooftop.

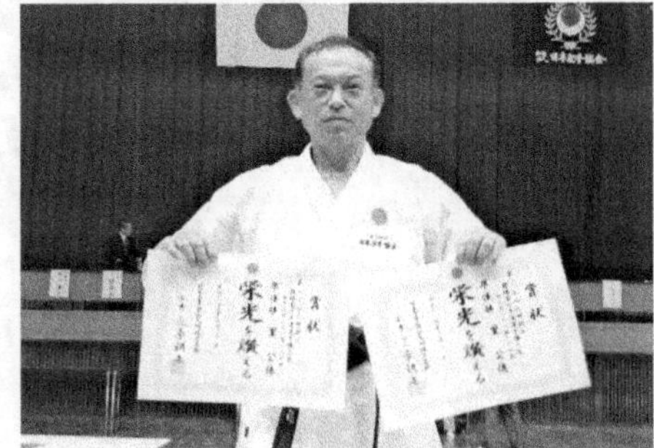

I have presented five practical training ideas for *kata* and *kumite*, specifically for senior *karateka* with the goal of achieving continued and ongoing improvement in karate. Even if you complete all these ideas, I cannot guarantee that you will be the national or even regional champion of *kata* or *kumite*. However, if you accept the training ideas presented here and stick to the program for at least six months (or longer where necessary), I am pretty certain that your *kata* and/or *jiyu kumite* will improve significantly. If you are not happy with your karate performance, why not try these ideas? You have nothing to lose. It is never too late.

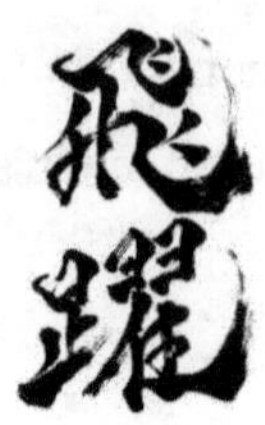

Chapter Six
第六章

The Truth about Foot Stomping
踏み込み足の真実

For senior karate practitioners, the *fumikomi* (踏み込み, 'foot-stomping') technique must be very familiar. The reader knows that this technique is found in many of the Shotokan *kata*, including Heian and Tekki. I could have chosen any of these *kata*, but, for this chapter, I have decided to pick Jion to discuss this subject and will explain why later.

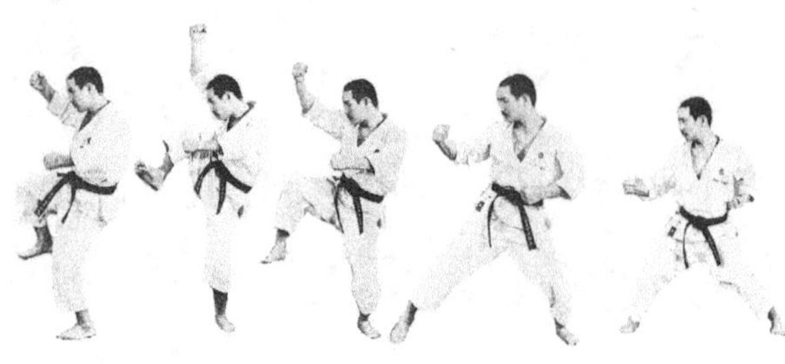

Kuro obi (黒帯, 'black belt') practitioners know that Jion *kata* has an interesting sequence of techniques, which consists of *fumikomi* and *chudan uchiotoshi uke* (中段打ち落し受け, 'middle downward-swinging block'), on the forty-third, forty-fourth, and forty-fifth steps (photo above). When I learned this *kata* more than forty years ago, I was taught to stomp down and hit the floor as hard as possible with my foot. The *bunkai* for this combination was an *otoshi uke* (落し受け, 'dropping block') against a *chudan oi zuki* attack with a simultaneous stomp to the opponent's front foot. Our sensei told us we should imagine that we were a big sumo wrestler when we did this technique. We were to deliver the stomp so that the impact would almost put our foot through the floor. I am pretty sure that this is similar to what the reader is familiar with.

You may be shocked, but I am writing this chapter because I need to inform you that this instruction is incorrect. Maybe *incorrect* is too strong a word, so I should use the word *insufficient*. In other words, the standard way in which the stomping technique has been taught all around the world is only for beginners. When I say, "beginners," I am not referring to *dan* rank or belt level but rather to degree of experience with this technique. What I am saying is that you need to learn this technique as a strong stomp down on the floor with a great impact. But, once again, this is only for learning the movement. Once the practitioner learns this, he must move on to the next level, which is a better way of delivering this technique.

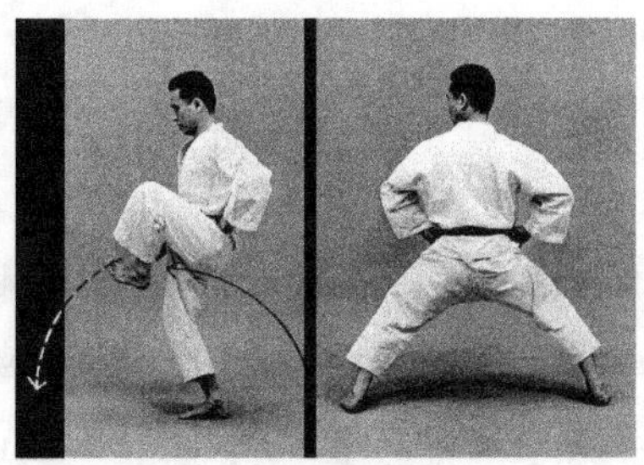

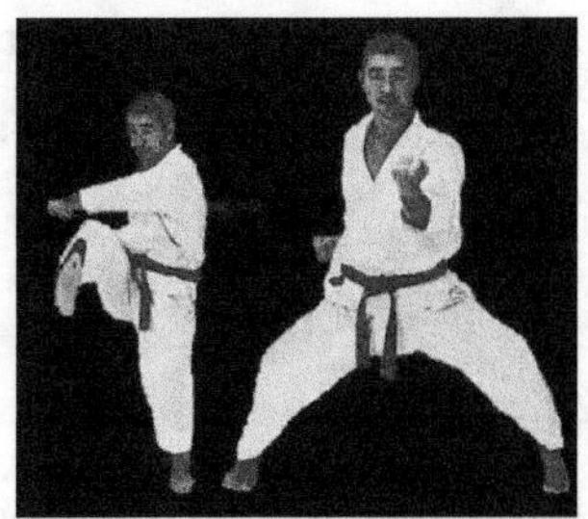

In fact, you can find *fumikomi* in Heian Sandan (photo above left), Heian Godan, Tekki (photo above right), Jutte (十手), Jion, etc. Understanding the true delivery of this technique is too advanced for students below black belt. If your instructor knew this technique, he might have shared this knowledge when he taught you Tekki Shodan. If he did not, he probably wanted to wait until you earned your black belt. Understanding how to deliver *fumikomi* correctly is indeed reserved for *dan* ranks.

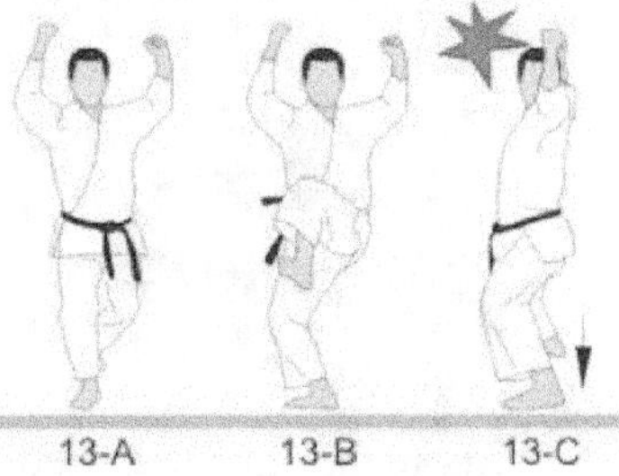

I could have picked Jutte for this chapter as we find a sequence of three *fumikomi* in that *kata* (illustration right). However, I find that Jion is a better *kata* for explaining the *fumikomi* technique. Why is this? It is because *fumikomi* is delivered with an *uchiotoshi waza* (打ち落し技, 'downward-swinging technique' [illustration below]) to emphasize the downward motion.

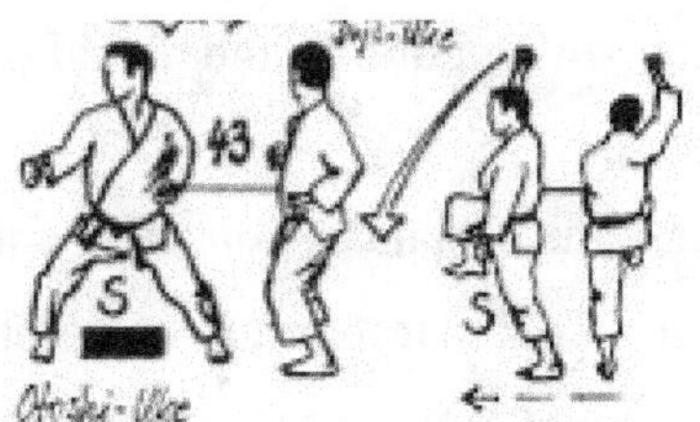

So, you must be asking, "How do we deliver this technique in the correct way?" Though it may sound contradictory, the short answer is that we need to learn how to not stomp the floor. My statement may sound puzzling to many readers. You may even think that this does not seem right. Yes, I am aware of this. It sounded strange to me, too, when I first learned about it. Believe it or not, it is not too difficult to mentally conceptualize how to deliver this technique. On the other hand, physically executing the technique correctly requires a lot more body management than you can imagine.

OK, let us go further to understand what this technique is all about. What we need to do here is study how this technique is practiced in kung fu, the forefather of karate. It is unfortunate that we have to do this since in-depth understanding of this technique has not been taught by most traditional karate styles, especially Shotokan. If you are a fan of Shaolin kung fu, you may have seen the dents in the stone-block training floor in the temple (photo below left). Yes, these dents came from repeated stomping by the Shaolin monks who have trained there for many years (photo below right).

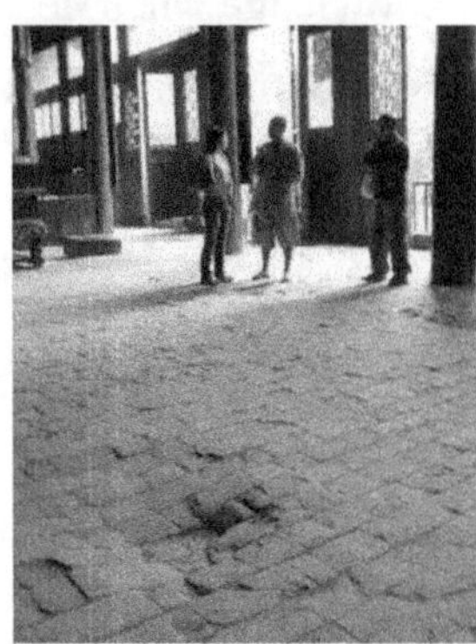

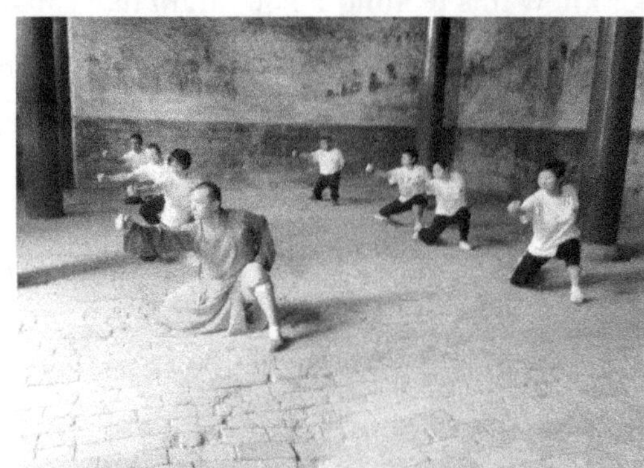

This technique is called *shinkyaku* (震脚), which literally means 'leg vibration'. Of course, this does not mean that the leg itself vibrates but rather that the stomping of the leg vibrates the floor or the earth like an earthquake. *Shinkyaku* is found not only in the Shaolin style but also in many other kung fu and tai chi styles, and there are several different ways to deliver it.

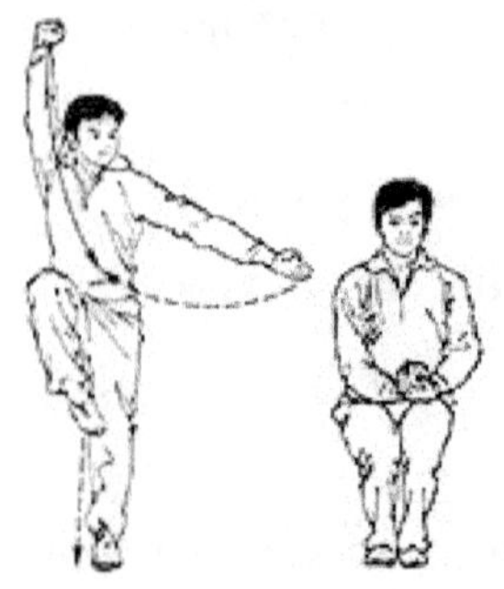

One way is from a natural stance. You raise one leg and then stomp it down. The illustration to the left shows a practitioner raising his right arm and right leg in a manner that is similar to that of the technique found in Jion. The difference is that here the practitioner stomps his right foot next to his left foot and simultaneously punches his left palm with his right hand in *uraken* position.

You are familiar with the fact that in Jion, we use *kiba dachi* and *uchiotoshi uke* (as shown in the photos below).

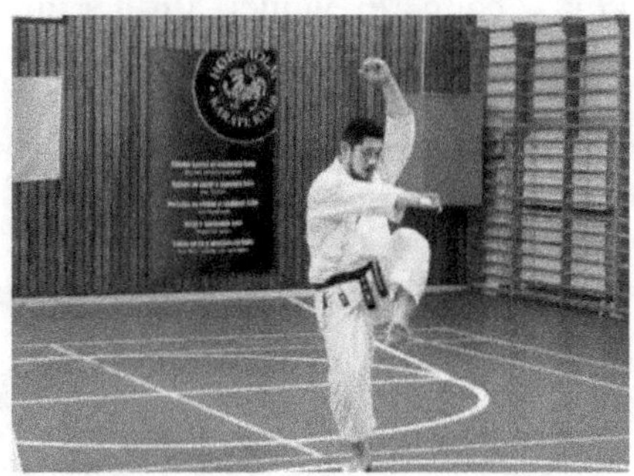

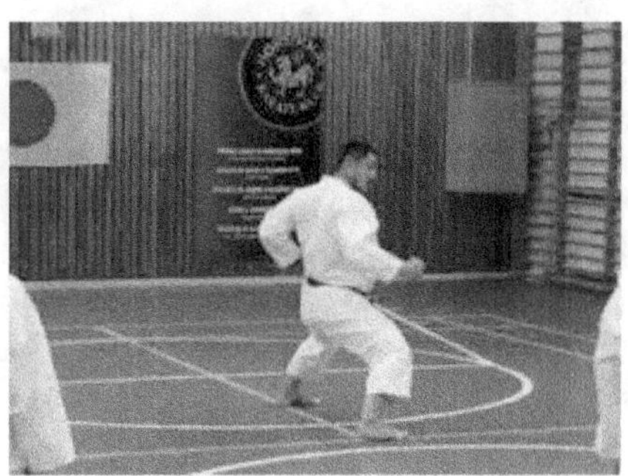

When we compare the techniques of these two different styles, it is very interesting to note that the preparation mode (i.e., raising one arm and one knee) is very similar. Also, notice how the knees are bent when the technique is completed in the kung fu method. The degree of the bend is identical to the one in our knees when we assume *kiba dachi*. If this kung fu practitioner spread his feet apart to about twice the width of his natural stance, then he would have a perfect *kiba dachi*.

Another way to deliver *shinkyaku* is to stomp with one leg from a longer stance, such as *zenkutsu dachi* (前屈立ち) or *kiba dachi*. An interesting method is to stomp with the rear leg (photo right), which is rather unique. In Shotokan, a rear-leg *fumikomi* from *zenkutsu dachi* is not taught. Even if the technique starts from *zenkutsu dachi*, *kiba dachi* is used at the time of the stomp (as in Heian Godan, Jutte, and Jion). This is an interesting subject, but I will not go into it in this chapter.

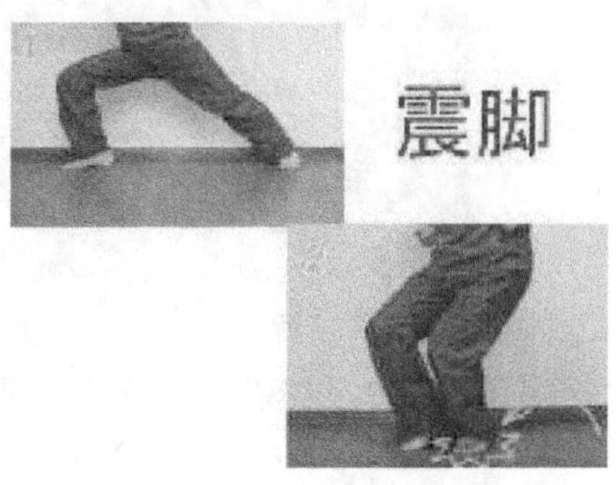

As you become familiar with the *shinkyaku* technique, you will be required to not make a stomping sound when you bring your foot down, whether it is delivered with the front or rear leg. In other words, the instructor will tell you not to direct the power downward but rather to bring it to an abrupt stop by squeezing the internal muscles in the lower *tanden* area.

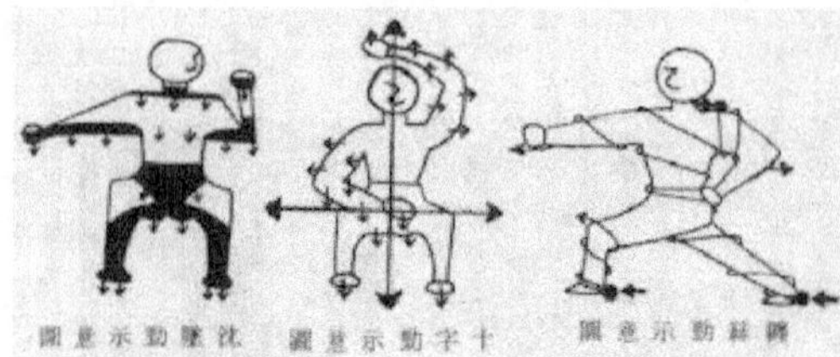

In one of the kung fu styles, Ba Gua Zhang (explained further in the following chapter), there is a technique called *chintsuikei* (沈墜勁 [read as *chénzhuìjìn* in Chinese]), which is shown in the illustration above. As I am not familiar with this style or its technique, I will not go into detail here. However, I do wish to share the basic and important concept of the technique that is taught in this style. In essence, you bring the body up first and then bring it down to generate power. The technique definitely uses this dropping power to deliver a strong punch (photo below left) or elbow strike (photo below right).

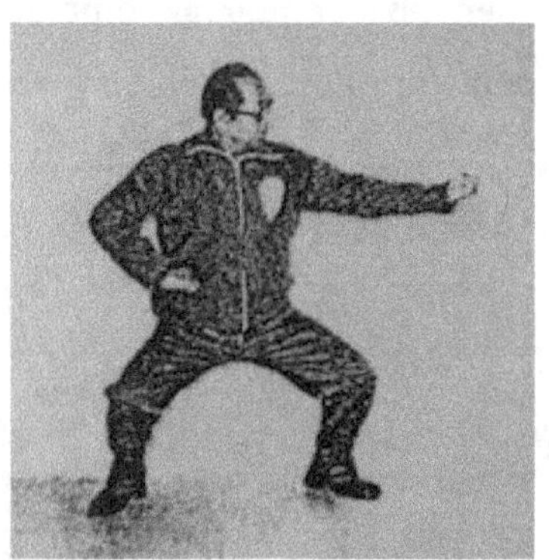

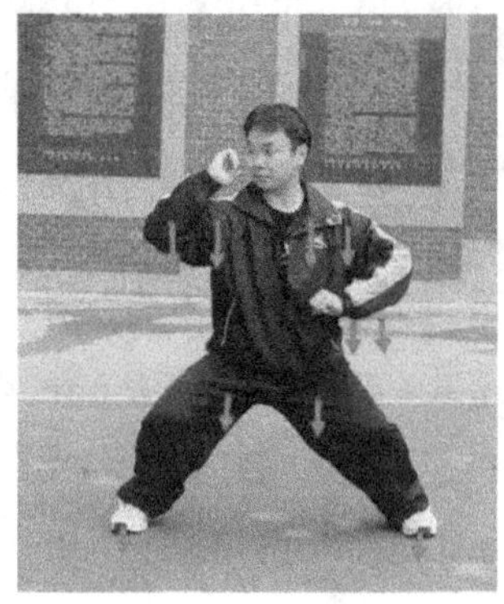

This is no surprise; however, it is not the main point. What the style teaches is that as you drop down, you are not to drop all of your weight. I know this statement is not clear and can be puzzling. Let me explain further. Toward the end of the stomp, right before your foot reaches the floor, you need to generate upward power by tightening the inner muscles of your lower torso so that the impact of your foot will be nullified. Does this make sense?

In other words, you freeze the downward power by tightening the core muscles within the lower part of your body. This power within your body works against the stomping leg. Maybe you can think of this as applying a braking action to the stomping leg at the very moment of impact. It is like a car. Imagine that you are driving a car. All of a sudden, something jumps out in front of you, so you have to apply a quick braking action to avoid a collision. Obviously, the challenge of this technique is that you need to put this "brake" on at the last moment and be able to avoid the collision.

If you are a senior practitioner, you may recognize that this sounds similar to how you generate *kime* when you punch. Believe it or not, this technique is managed using the same concept. The difference is that the leg technique is more versatile than the arm technique. You probably had the experience of holding *kime* too long with your punch when you were still at the junior level. If your arm and body were tense for too long, you would be stuck in a position for too long. In a *kime* situation, you were taught to relax right away so that you could continue to the next step or technique.

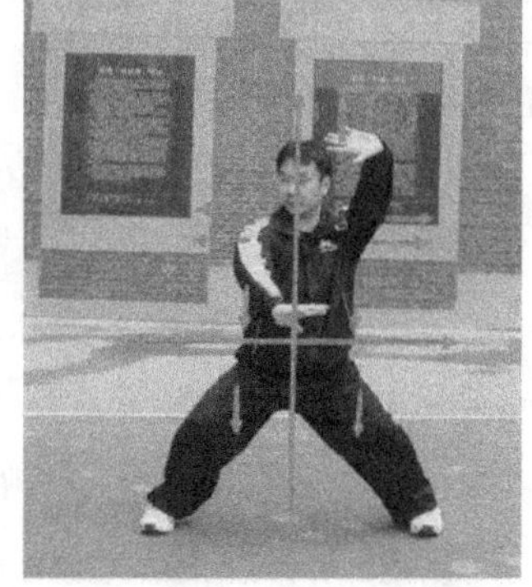

In the foot-stomping technique, when you drop your weight without a brake, two major disadvantages occur. One major problem is that you end up stuck in one spot, which is called *itsuki* in Japanese and is the most despised condition in Japanese *budo*. We consider *itsuki* to be the gateway to defeat or death. The other possible problem is the great impact of the ground reaction force on the foot at the time of stomping. This impact on the stomping foot may cause a serious joint (knee or ankle) problem.

By being able to do this leg-braking technique, you cause your body to "float" like a hovercraft or an ice skater. This means you are not stuck in one spot after the stomping technique. Rather, you are able to move around very easily in any direction. In other words, this technique allows you to remain mobile and able to shift. The analogy used to explain this state in this style of kung fu is that it is as if your head were being suspended and pulled up by a string. In other words, you become like a marionette, and your body floats like a suspended doll.

Let's go back to our *fumikomi* technique. I believe it has a similar concept.

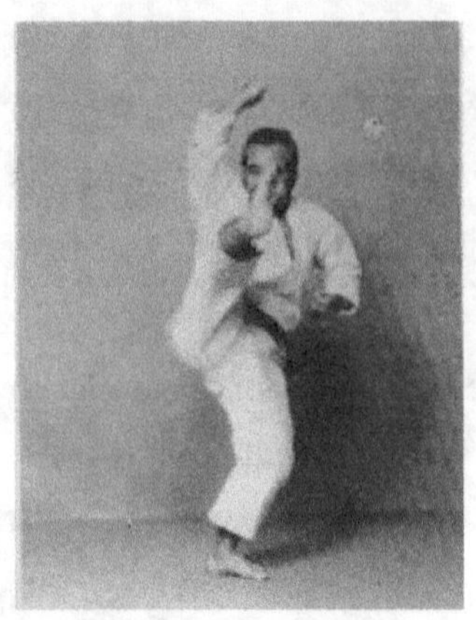

In other Japanese martial arts, this technique is called *fuminari* (踏鳴). It is usually used in *budo* with weapons, such as kenjutsu and jukendo (銃剣道, 'bayonet fighting'). It is also practiced in jujutsu and even in sumo (相撲); however, it is called *shiko fumi* (四股踏み) in the latter. Though this technique is not well known among karate practitioners, it remains one of the important high-level teachings in the Japanese martial arts. It is unfortunate for modern-day karate practitioners that this technique is now interpreted only as a stomping action of the leg and that the most important aspect, the nullifying action, has been forgotten.

Once you understand this concept and wish to experience its benefits, I suggest that you practice all the *kata* that have the *fumikomi* technique, such as Heian Sandan, Heian Godan, Tekki, Jutte, Jion, etc., in the new way. If you have developed strong inner muscles, this technique may not be too difficult to execute correctly. I hope you can feel the difference in your body when you execute the *fumikomi* technique with the last-minute braking action. I also hope you discover the forgotten benefits of executing *fumikomi* at a higher skill level.

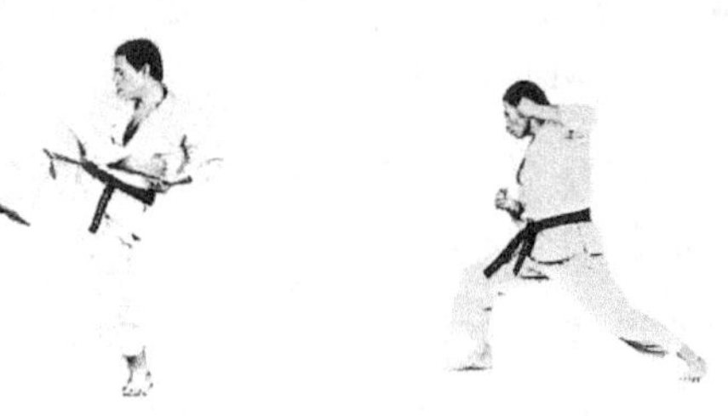

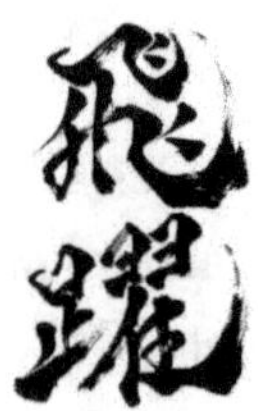

Chapter Seven
第七章

Internal Systems vs. External Systems
内家拳と外家拳とは？

I assume the reader already knows that there is some categorization within the martial arts that is used to show the characteristics that supposedly differentiate one style from another, but the fact is that all styles contain different amounts of the characteristics of opposing personalities. The categorization of a style itself does not result in any positive effect or merit. The benefit comes only when we better understand our style and are able to include some training that makes it more effective and meaningful.

So, let us start with a few popular categorizations. The most common one is probably the differentiation between *enkyori* (遠距離, 'long-distance') and *kinkyori* (近距離, 'short-distance') fighting styles. Shotokan is a good example of a long-distance style, while Goju Ryu, on the other hand, is a good example of a short-distance style. Asai Ryu is based on standard Shotokan but with the addition of techniques from a short-distance fighting style as White Crane kung fu, which is known as *hakutsuru ken* (白鶴拳 [read as *báihèchuán* in Chinese]), was incorporated into it by Master Tetsuhiko Asai (浅井哲彦, 1935–2006 [photo right]). This categorization is rather obvious and comparatively easy to grasp. I do not believe it needs further explanation.

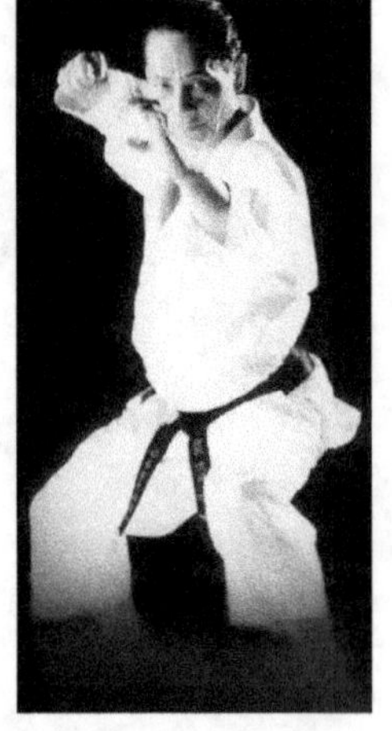

Another popular categorization is the differentiation between the Shorin (少林) and Shorei (昭霊) systems. Shorin is a system of fast, relaxed techniques and is exemplified by *kata* such as Enpi, Kanku, Gankaku (岩鶴), and Unsu. Shorei, on the other hand, is a system of powerful movements and slower techniques that is supposedly designed for larger-built *karateka*. Jion, Jutte, and Sochin are the typical *kata* of the Shorei system. This categorization has been explained by many other writers in the past. I have my doubts about its legitimacy but will not touch on that in this chapter.

One other popular categorization is the differentiation between Naha Te (那覇手) and Shuri Te (首里手) lineage. The words *Naha* and *Shuri* both indicate the particular regions of Okinawa where the different styles of karate were developed and practiced. Shotokan belongs to the Shuri Te line as it came from Shorin Ryu (少林流), the most popular Shuri Te style. The most popular Naha Te styles are Goju Ryu and Uechi Ryu (上地流).

The categorization I wish to focus on in this chapter is the differentiation between internal and external systems. As far as I know, this categorization has not been explained too well to Shotokan practitioners in the past. Among the Chinese martial arts, this categorization is as popular as the one that differentiates between northern and southern styles. The terms *internal system* and *external system* are written as *naikaken* (内家拳) and *gaikaken* (外家拳), which literally mean 'inside-house/family fist' and 'outside-house/family fist', respectively.

Most practitioners now explain the meaning of the phrase *inside house* as referring to the internal workings of the body, such as the mental and respiratory aspects of a martial art. However, it originally meant 'not staying with one's family' or 'not living in one's house', that is, living in a Buddhist temple instead. Therefore, the famous Shaolin kung fu (photo below) and its derivative styles—of which there are literally hundreds—are called *outside-house fist*.

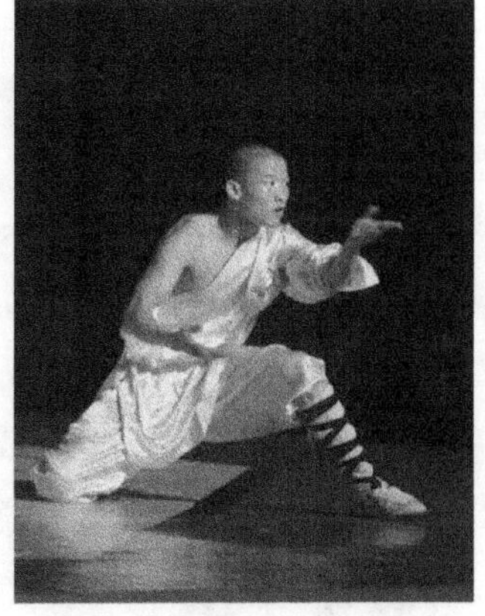

The term *Shaolin kung fu* (少林功夫) refers to a collection of Chinese martial arts that claim affiliation with the Shaolin Monastery, which is known as *Shorinji* (少林寺 [read as *Shàolínsì* in Chinese]). These styles generally emphasize long-range techniques, quick advances and retreats, wide stances, kicking and leaping techniques, whirling circular blocks, agile movements, and aggressive attacks. Due to numerous Hong Kong movies, Shaolin kung fu is well known in the Western world. However, there seem to be a lot of misconceptions and false beliefs about this fighting style. I suggest the reader learn more about it by reading the article "What's Shaolin Kung Fu?" by the Kunyu Mountain Shaolin Martial Arts Academy, which can be found here: www.chineseshaolins.com/what-is-shaolin-kung-fu.html.

The name of the other group, *inside-house fist*, means that the practitioner is not a professional monk. This is a group of fighting styles that are not linked to the Shaolin Monastery. The three most famous internal systems are Tai Ji Quan, Xing Yi Quan, and Ba Gua Zhang.

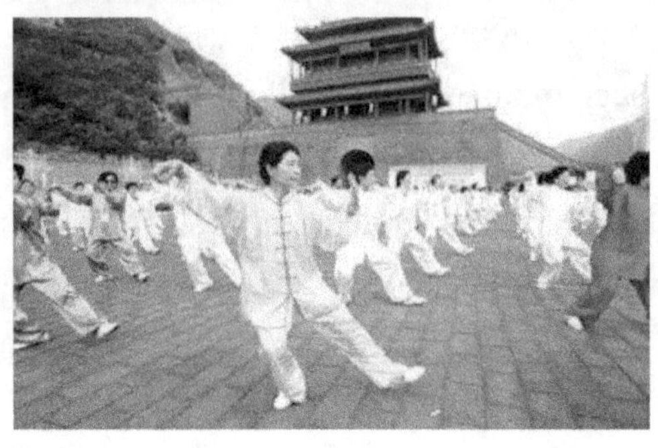

Tai Ji Quan (太極拳 [*tàijíquán*]), which is shown in the photo to the right, is a slow-motion meditative exercise for relaxation, health, and, to a lesser degree, self-defense. Tai chi, as it is more commonly known, has gained enormous popularity throughout the world for its health benefits. In Chinese philosophy, tai chi is the ultimate source and limit of reality, from which spring yin and yang and all of creation.

There are many different styles of tai chi, from a popular slow-motion style used mainly for relaxation and health purposes to a style that has some explosive moves and is a better fit for self-defense training. To learn more about tai chi, check out the article "What Is Tai Chi?" by Elizabeth Palemo on the *Live Science* website: www.livescience.com/38063-tai-chi.html.

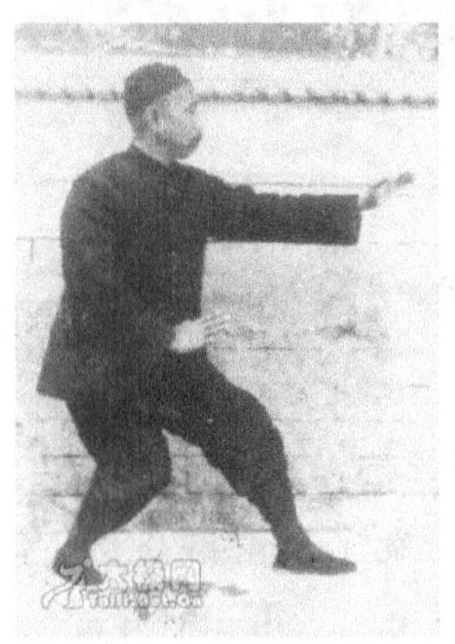

Xing Yi Quan (形意拳 [*xíngyìquán*]), which is shown in the photo to the left, may be a lesser-known internal system to the karate world, but it is one of the most well-known internal martial arts in general and is a very effective fighting style. The first two characters, 形意 (*xíngyì*), mean 'shape mind', and the last one, 拳 (*quán*), means 'fist'. The name derives from the style's imitation of the movements and inner characteristics of twelve animals: dragon, tiger, eagle, bear, chicken, hawk, horse, monkey, snake, phoenix, swallow, and alligator. The style was created by Marshal Fei Yue (岳飛 [read as *Yuè Fēi* in Chinese], 1103–1142), a famous general of the Chinese Song dynasty (宋朝).

One of the purposes of Xing Yi Quan training, like tai chi, is to improve ki (気 or 氣) circulation in the body and to maintain health. The training is supposed to build up a level of internal ki, which leads to the strengthening of both the physical body and its energy field. For more information on Xing Yi Quan, read the article "Xing Yi Quan" by Shen Wu Martial Arts, which can be found here: www.shenwu.com/hsingi.htm.

Ba Gua Zhang (八卦掌 [*bāguàzhǎng*]) is also one of the three orthodox internal systems. Its name literally translates to 'eight-trigram palm'. These trigrams are symbols that are used to represent all of the natural phenomena as described in the ancient Chinese text of divination *The Book of Changes* (易經 [*Yì Jīng*]). The character 掌 (*zhǎng*) means 'palm' as this system emphasizes the use of the open hand over the closed fist.

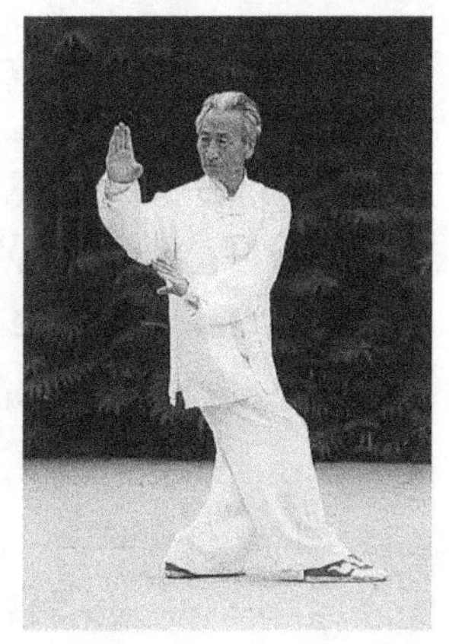

Ba Gua Zhang is based on the theory of continuously changing in response to the situation at hand in order to overcome the opponent with smooth, circular skill rather than brute force. Its *enbusen* (演武線) is very unique as it is built on complex circular lines, and the techniques are delivered not toward the direction of the moves but mainly toward the center of a circle or the side of the performer (photo right). I personally like this style as its footwork is based on normal walking steps, which I really think makes sense. The performer uses fast steps in circular lines and delivers the techniques while he is "walking." To learn more about Ba Gua Zhang, read the article "What Is Baguazhang?" by Beijin Baguazhang, which can be found here: http://bagua.freehostia.com/what.html.

There are also many good video clips of Ba Gua Zhang *kata* performances by some of the elder masters. Here is the URL for my favorite Ba Gua Zhang *kata*, Bāmǔ Zhǎng (八母掌, 'Eight-Mother Palm') as performed by Master Zhijun Sun (孫志君 [read as *Sūn Zhìjūn* in Chinese], 1933–): www.youtube.com/watch?v=n8agvbyMDkU.

OK, these are all Chinese-style martial arts, so you may ask, "How do these relate to our karate?" We need to look at another interpretation of internal and external systems. You will see the relationship as we go over the key points of internal and external systems according to this second interpretation.

I am aware that each martial art and karate style has some characteristics of all the categorizations, including internal and external systems, and that no categorization clearly divides the styles. The ultimate goal of this chapter is a better knowledge and understanding of our karate and possible improvement in training as this knowledge and understanding will, hopefully, be reflected in the training menu.

Let us start with internal systems. The focus of these systems is on such elements as the practice of awareness of spirit, mind, and ki (breath or energy flow) and the use of relaxed leverage rather than brute muscular tension. The principles that distinguish internal systems from external systems were described at least as early as the eighteenth century.

Components of internal training include stance training, muscle stretching and strengthening, and empty-hand and weapon forms. In addition to the solo practice of the forms, many internal systems have basic two-person training, such as pushing hands. A notable characteristic of internal systems is that the forms are generally performed at a slow or normal pace. This is thought to improve coordination and balance by using slow movements and low stances to increase the workload and require practitioners to pay close attention to their whole body and weight as they perform a technique.

In some styles, Chen Family Tai Ji Quan (Chén jiā tàijíquán [陳家太極拳]), for example, there are forms that include sudden outbursts of explosive movements. At an advanced level, the techniques are performed quickly. The ultimate goal is to learn to manage and control the entire body in every movement, to stay relaxed with deep, controlled breathing, and to coordinate the body movements

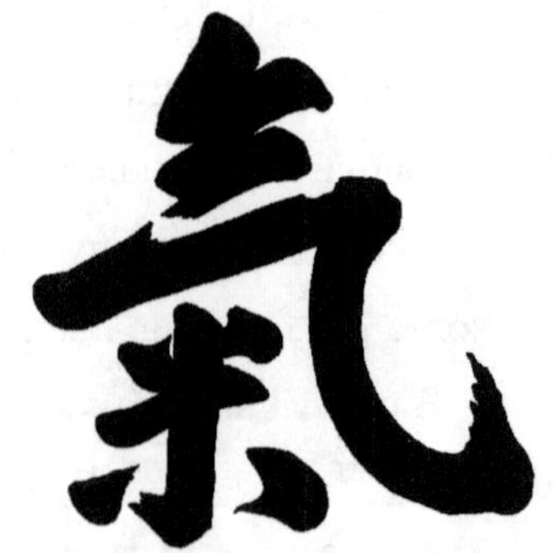

and breathing accurately while maintaining perfect balance.

Let's look at external systems next. External systems are characterized by fast, explosive movements. Their focus is on physical strength and agility.

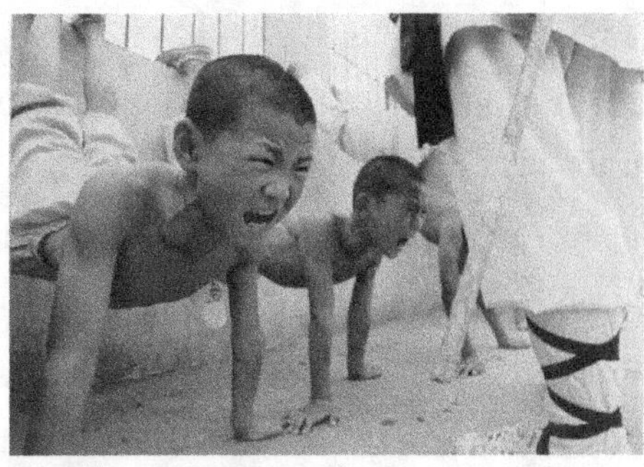

External systems include traditional styles, which focus on application and actual fighting, and modern styles, which are adapted for competition. Shaolin kung fu has many *wŭshù*, or *bujutsu* (武術, 'martial arts'), forms that include aerial techniques and explosive attacks (both with and without weapons). External systems begin with a focus on muscular power, speed, and application. They generally integrate *qìgōng*, or *kiko* (気功, 'ki training'), aspects into their advanced training after an excellent physical level has been reached.

Based on these definitions, to which group do you think traditional karate belongs? I guess the answer is easy. Traditional karate definitely has many characteristics of the external systems. By learning more about the characteristics of the other type of systems, we can identify the areas where our training may be lacking. I hope you can make your karate training more comprehensive by adding some exercises to supplement the missing areas.

So, what are the areas that are possibly lacking in our training? They may be ki training, breathing exercises, or softer movements. One of the main elements that I consider to be missing from the traditional karate syllabus is ki training. This is an important subject that should be seriously studied by all senior karate practitioners. It is also a deep subject that requires a lot of explanation and deep understanding, which I cover in Chapter 7: "What Is Ki?" and Chapter 8: "Ki Exchange with the Trees" of my book *Shotokan Transcendence*. If you are interested in this subject, I suggest you read those chapters.

One more thing I wish to call your attention to here is that deep breathing is closely linked to and critically necessary for ki training and exercise. Even if you do not understand anything about ki, when you do your deep breathing exercise, believe it or not, you are strengthening your ki at the same time. I have written an article on the subject of breathing exercises entitled "What Is the Belly Breathing Method?" This can be found on my blog at this URL: www.asaikarate.com/what-is-belly-breathing-method.

The missing elements may vary, depending on the particular karate style you train in. For example, Goju Ryu and Uechi Ryu practitioners may not see much need to increase their breathing exercises but may find value in training more in softer movements. For Shito Ryu practitioners, ki training and possibly more breathing exercises may be of interest. Coming from Shotokan myself, I believe all three of these elements (i.e., ki training, breathing exercises, and softer movements) can help Shotokan practitioners. I sincerely hope you can identify some of these that may be missing from your training syllabus.

Just as Asai Sensei introduced a short-distance fighting method into the standard Shotokan karate syllabus to make it more effective, you can add the exercises of the internal systems to your karate training syllabus if you feel that these important elements are missing. By doing so, you will expand your karate beyond the standard syllabus that you are familiar with into something more comprehensive that you can call an *internal and external system*. I hope this chapter has piqued enough of your interest to cause you to get outside the box and consider investing some time and energy into making your karate better.

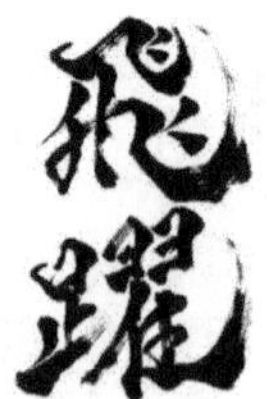

Chapter Eight
第八章

Eight Striking and Eight Nonstriking Points
八打八不打とは？

In Shaolin kung fu and Praying Mantis kung fu, there is a Chinese poem that describes the critical points, which is entitled "Hachi Da Hachi Fuda" (八打八不打 [read as *Bā Dǎ Bā Bùdǎ* in Chinese]). This literally means 'Eight Strikes and Eight Nonstrikes'. Most already know that *hachi* (八) means 'eight'. *Da* (打) means 'strike'. *Fu* (不) is a negative prefix (similar to *non-* or *un-* in English) and here combines with *da* to make *fuda* (不打), meaning 'nonstrike'. In some styles, they advocate for seven points instead of eight, but I will proceed with the eight-point concept here.

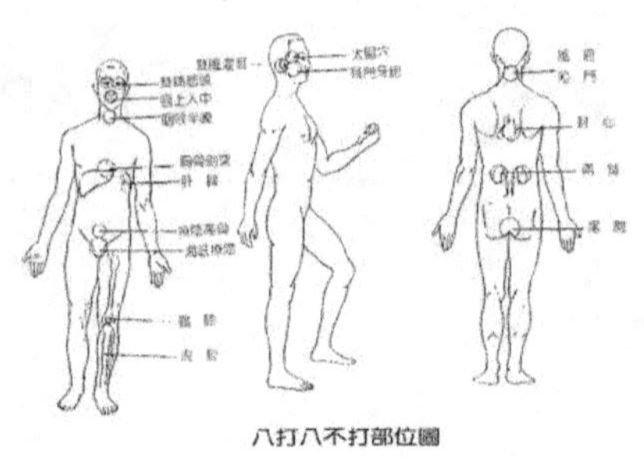
八打八不打部位圖

If you are a Shotokan practitioner, I suspect that you have never heard this saying, although some Okinawa styles, with their Chinese kenpo (拳法) lineage, may teach it. This concept of eight nonstriking points seems rather simple and straightforward. However, I believe there is a deeper meaning than what there superficially seems to be. We need to look more deeply to find more than just the literal translation of this saying.

What is meant by *hachi da*, or 'eight strikes', is the eight *kyusho* that, when hit, will limit or remove a person's ability to fight or cause him to lose his fighting spirit. What is meant by *hachi fuda*, or 'eight nonstrikes', is the eight *kyusho* that, when hit strongly, could possibly result in death; thus, the teaching is to avoid striking these points unless you really mean to kill the person.

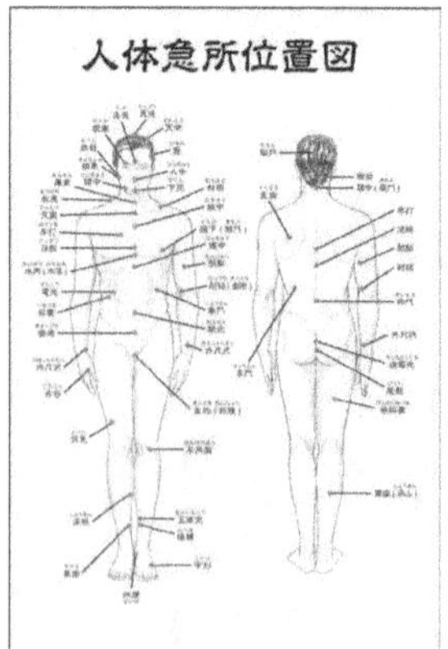
人体急所位置図

The locations of some of the *hachi da* and *hachi fuda* overlap somewhat, but others are slightly different. The positions of these points are now widely known and studied, but in the past, they were a big secret. However, even now, though you may know the locations, what benefit can you gain if you do not know how to strike or have the particular technique to strike with?

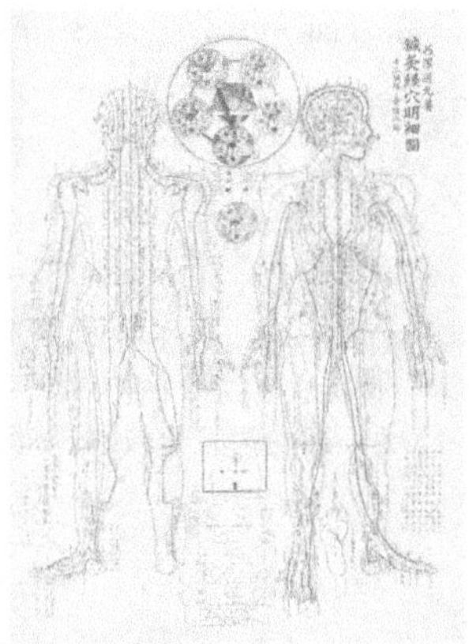

In our karate training, many senior practitioners have heard of *kyusho* (急所, 'critical points') or *tenketsu* (点穴, 'pressure points'). Though we may not have been taught specifically about *kyusho* and *tenketsu*, we almost instinctively know that some parts of the body are susceptible to a lot of damage, which can be dangerous. *Kyusho* are taught in many of the grappling martial arts, such as aikido and aikijutsu (合気術), as the techniques of these arts are closely connected to these points. In other words, practitioners of these arts grab or press specific points of the body instead of doing so randomly without paying attention to the exact locations of the points.

Some readers may say, "I have never heard of *hachi fuda*, but my teacher taught me some of the *kyusho*." This is great, and I am happy to hear this. At the same time, I wonder if your teacher also taught you about the other points, the *tenketsu*. These are the points that cause pain but not permanent damage. I have written about how Master Asai demonstrated his techniques on me, and you can find this story in Chapter 13: "Tenketsu Jutsu" of my book *Shotokan Mysteries*.

Interestingly, these points are also used in Asian therapeutic treatments such as acupuncture (*hari* [鍼]), moxibustion (*kyu* [灸]), and shiatsu (指圧). So, they can be used not only for harming or killing but also for healing the body. I write about these points in Chapter 7: "What Is Ki?" of my book *Shotokan Transcendence*.

Now, you may be wondering if these points are located at the same or different locations on the body. You may also be wondering if there are only eight or sixteen points. You must read on to find out more about these mysterious parts of our body.

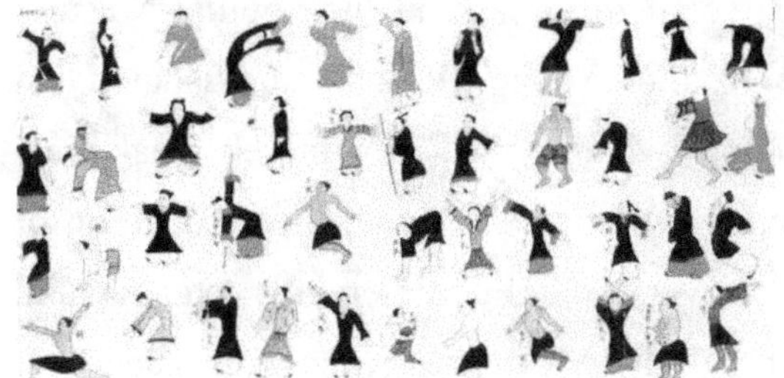

First, we need to look at what *kyusho* and *tenketsu* are. According to an article by James Highland published on www.livestrong.com on August 14, 2017, these critical points or pressure points are

> specific sensitive areas on the surface of the body. You can exploit a pressure point for many uses. Martial artists quickly disable attackers by using a simple but forced push on a pressure point. Stimulation of pressure points also helps to relieve pain and assists in massage therapy.

Tenketsu can alternatively be translated as 'chakra points'. According to an article by Sadhguru published on www.huffingtonpost.com on April 15, 2011,

> chakras are energy centers. Although most people have heard of seven chakras, there are actually 114 in the body. The human body is a complex energy form; in addition to the 114 chakras, it also has 72,000 *nadis*, or energy channels, along which vital energy, or *prana*, moves. When the *nadis* meet at different points in the body, they form a triangle. We call this triangle a *chakra*, which means 'wheel'. We call it a *wheel* because it symbolizes growth, dynamism and movement, so even though it is actually a triangle, we call it a *chakra*. Some of these centers are very powerful, while others are not as powerful. At different levels, these energy centers produce different qualities in a human being.

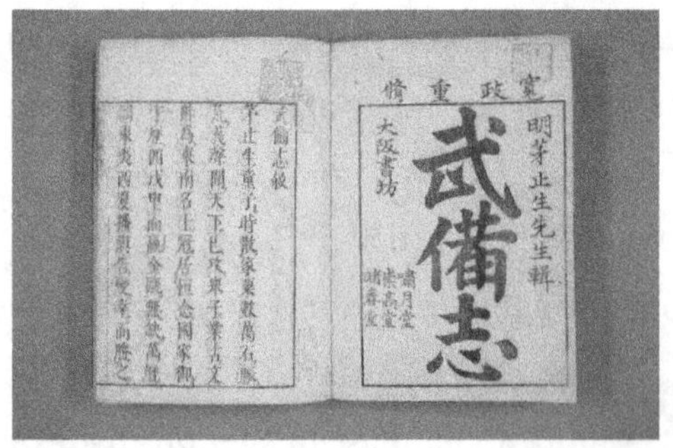

Exaggerated accounts of pressure-point fighting have appeared in Chinese kung fu fiction, both novels and movies. This eventually came to be known by the name of *dim mak* (點脈, 'pressure point') or *death touch*, in the popular Western culture of the 1960s. It is undisputed that there are sensitive points on the human body where even comparatively weak pressure may induce significant pain or injury. At the same time, the association of *kyusho* with the notion of death is controversial and commercially exaggerated. Regardless, if these places take a hit, there can be life-threatening consequences.

There are approximately forty locations inside and outside the body. In the martial arts, it should be noted that by attacking some of these critical spots, one can control or paralyze an opponent, though it may not endanger his life. Interestingly, the majority of these critical points are the same as the massage and acupuncture points; however, not all of them coincide. It is very important for a martial artist to know both maps of the two different methods. One map is for *kappo* (活法, 'life method'), which is a healing art for curing illnesses, and the other is for *sappo* (殺法, 'killing method'), which is a martial art for harming the enemy.

Now we have to study another Japanese term: *tsubo* (ツボ, 'vital points'). This is an acupuncture term that literally means 'jar' or 'vase' and refers to acupuncture points. This is, in short, a spot or point on the human body where an acupuncturist would stick a needle. For any therapist who performs treatment such as massage or acupuncture, having a thorough knowledge of these *tsubo* is mandatory.

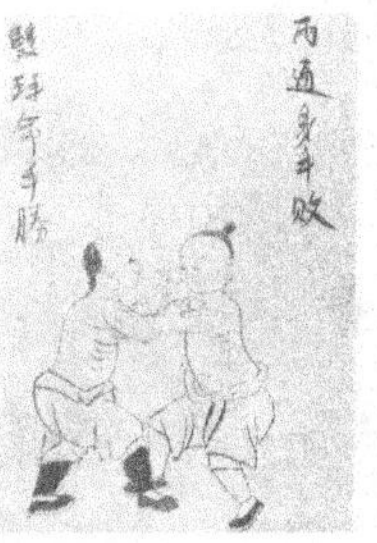

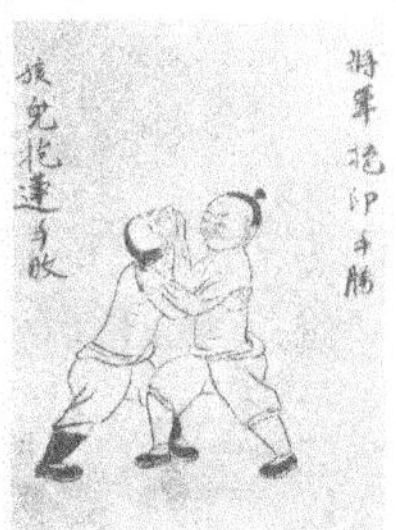

The number of vital points officially recognized by alternative medical professionals in Asia is 361. The lines that result from connecting them longitudinally are called *keiro* (経路, 'meridians'), and it is believed that there are fourteen of these *keiro* in our body. This is a very interesting subject, but it is not directly connected to the so-called death points, so I will not go any further into this subject here.

So, let us go a little more deeply into our investigation of the nonstriking points, or "death points," whether you believe there is such a thing or not. As it relates to karate, this term refers to the points that will cause serious damage, including death, if they sustain an excessive blow. In other words, these are the spots where *ikken hissatsu* becomes possible with the application of a strike or kick. It is interesting to note that in jujutsu, the number of *kyusho* is said to be 140, out of which about 50 are said to pose a high life-threatening risk. These critical points are categorized under four groups based on the results produced when they sustain an impact. All senior karate practitioners and instructors are advised to know them.

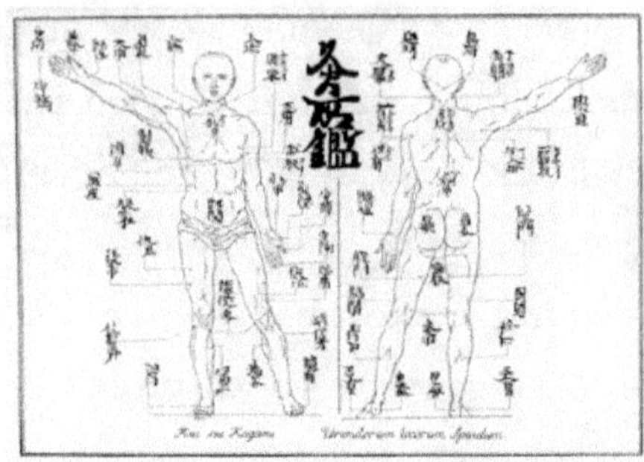

1. *Tsu kyusho* (痛急所, 'pain points') are points where one will experience intense pain. One example is the point between the thumb and index finger. Pinching this point causes great pain and can be used in submission techniques.
2. *Ma kyusho* (麻急所, 'hemp points') are points where one can be temporarily paralyzed. These are located in deeper parts of the body than pain points and are also used in submission techniques.
3. *Atekomi kyusho* (当込急所, 'thrusting points') are points where one can be killed or knocked unconscious. The first element of this term is related to *atemi* (当身, 'strikes'). These points are located in the chest and abdominal areas.
4. *Katsu kyusho* (活急所, 'activation points') are points that are used in first aid (*kappo*). They are found in the back, chest, and abdominal areas. These points are used for the exact opposite reason as *atekomi* points.

The size of one point is said to be about five-sixteenths of an inch (eight millimeters) in diameter. Thus, realistically speaking, it is quite difficult to know precisely where the spots are located. Consequently, it is also extremely difficult to attack any of these points accurately on an opponent. You not only need to be very familiar with the locations of the spots but also must acquire the specific techniques needed to deliver the proper attacks. What I recommend to instructors and senior practitioners is to memorize the approximate locations of these points.

As we approach the end of this chapter, I must touch upon one more subject. It looks as though Funakoshi Sensei studied the *kyusho* because we find a *kyusho* chart in his book *Karate Do Kyohan*. Masatoshi Nakayama (中山正敏, 1913–1987), in his book *Dynamic Karate* (Kodansha, 1966), also makes reference to

Funakoshi's work by including two pages (302 and 303) with the same diagrams (photo right). If these two masters considered these vulnerable points to be so important as to show illustrations of them in their books, then why do we seem to ignore them and fail to study them? I believe there are at least two major reasons.

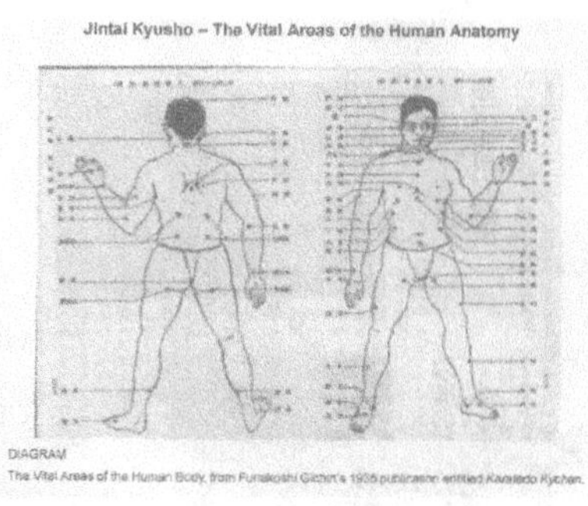

The first reason is the popularity of sport karate. In tournament *kumite*, there are only two targets: *jodan* and *chudan*. Generally speaking, in a *kumite* match, as long as you throw a punch or a kick to the general *jodan* or *chudan* area, you get a point. Therefore, for those who are focused only on scoring points, there is no need to learn the specific locations of the *kyusho* as this will not increase their score. This attitude, unfortunately, is spreading to dojo *kumite* training. For instance, does your sensei approve of attacks or counterattacks to the groin in *ippon kumite*? I am sure he does not allow that. How about if you counterattack the opponent's eyes with *nihon nukite* during *ippon kumite* training? Is this technique widely accepted in your dojo? Groin kicks and eye jabs are very effective techniques, but aren't they (and possibly many others) sort of banned or disapproved of?

The second reason is more complex and can be controversial. Shotokan is a long-distance fighting method, unlike Goju Ryu or Uechi Ryu. In other words, most of the techniques in Shotokan are designed for fighting from a distance that is greater than an arm's reach. In Goju Ryu and Uechi Ryu, practitioners focus on short-distance fighting methods, including *kakie* (カキエ or 掛け手, 'sticky-hand' or 'pushing-hand') training (photo left). They also train to harden their body to withstand the impact of punches and kicks. Students typically stand in *sanchin dachi* (サンチン立ち, '*sanchin* stance'), which is shown at the top of following page, while the instructor strikes or kicks their leg, back, belly, etc. In Shotokan, we do not have this type of

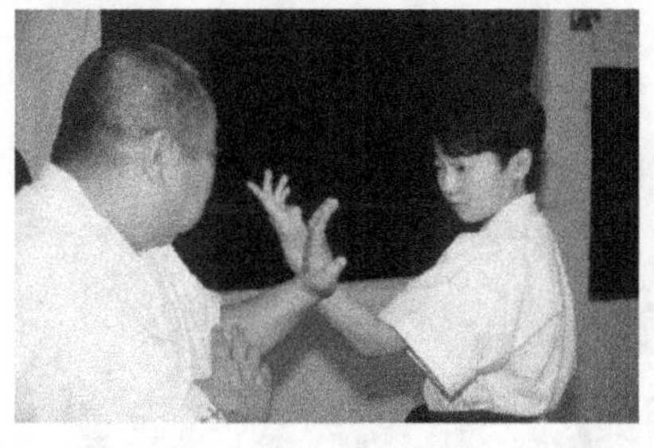

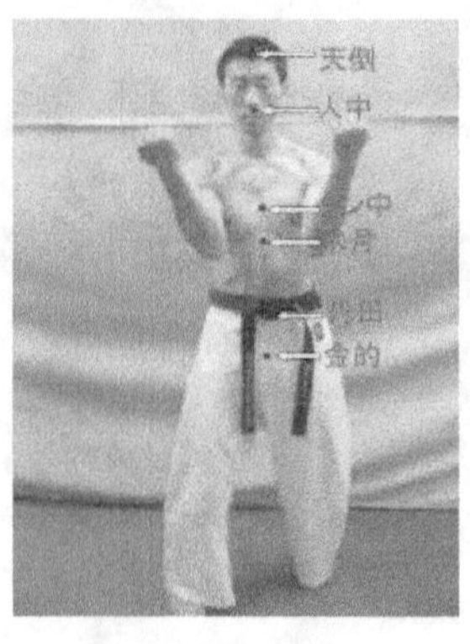

exercise as we keep all of our training very noncontact.

Some of the *kyusho*, such as the ones in the groin and the eyes, need no explanation. However, some of these points can be very small (as described before). Thus, to be able to use them effectively, we must learn their precise locations through experimentation by frequently hitting or pressing some of them. Recently, *bunkai* training has become more popular, which is a good trend in general. *Bunkai* contains *tsukami uke* and *nage waza* (投げ技, 'throwing techniques'), which can be leveraged with *kyusho*, *tenketsu*, and joint attacks. So, this type of training provides us with a rare opportunity to work on these aspects. Unfortunately, however, I have not seen these specific leverage applications enjoy the same growth in popularity as what *bunkai* training has in general.

Now that you have a better understanding of the challenge presented by these critical points, isn't it about time you begin to study them more closely and possibly incorporate this knowledge into your karate training? If you are interested in seeing a list of the pressure points in the human body, here is the URL for the previously referenced article on the *Livestrong* website: www.livestrong.com/article/158577-list-of-pressure-points-in-the-human-body.

Below is the original list of the eight striking points and eight nonstriking points along with a translation for each:

八打

一打　眉頭雙睛
二打　唇上人中
三打　穿腮耳門
四打　臂後骨縫
五打　脇内肺腑
六打　撩陰高骨
七打　合膝虎頭
八打　破骨千金

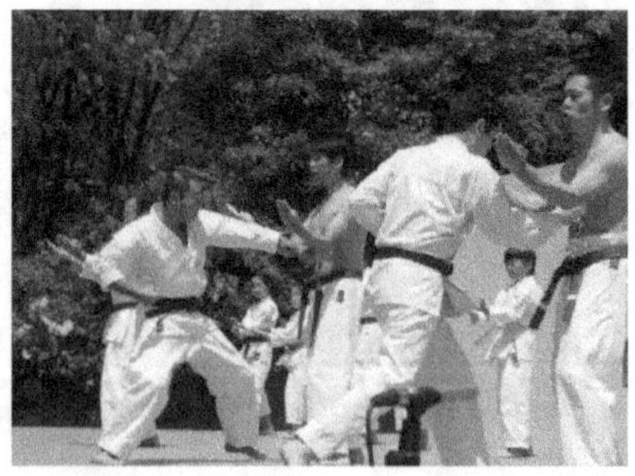

Eight Striking Points

1. Eyes and surrounding area
2. Philtrum [area between the upper lip and the nose]
3. Ears and area in front of the ears [near the jaw joints]
4. Back of the elbows
5. Sides of the trunk over the rib cage
6. Front of the pelvis
7. Knees
8. Shins

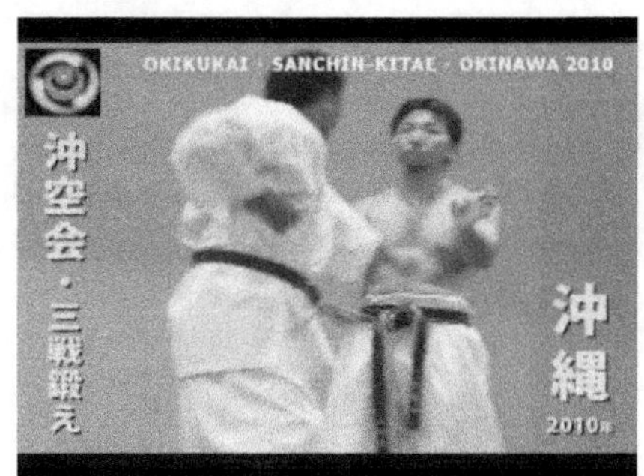

八不打

一不打　太陽為首
二不打　正対鎖口
三不打　中心両腕
四不打　両脇太極
五不打　海底撩陰
六不打　陵腎対心
七不打　尾呂縫府
八不打　両耳扇風

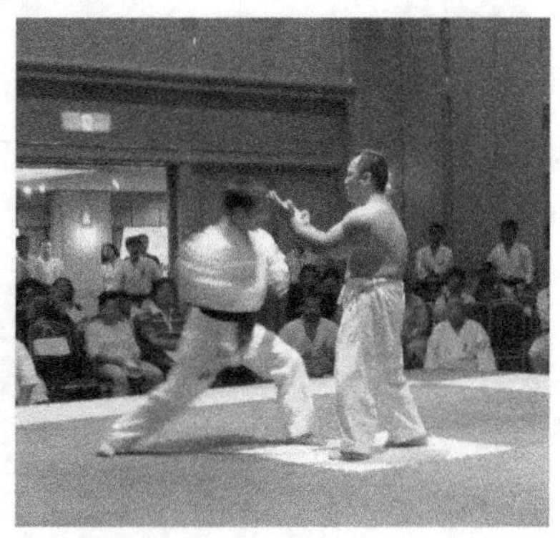

Eight Nonstriking Points

1. Temples
2. Throat and neck
3. Solar plexus
4. Armpits
5. Perineum [area between the anus and the scrotum or vulva]
6. Back of the trunk over the kidneys
7. Tailbone
8. Ears

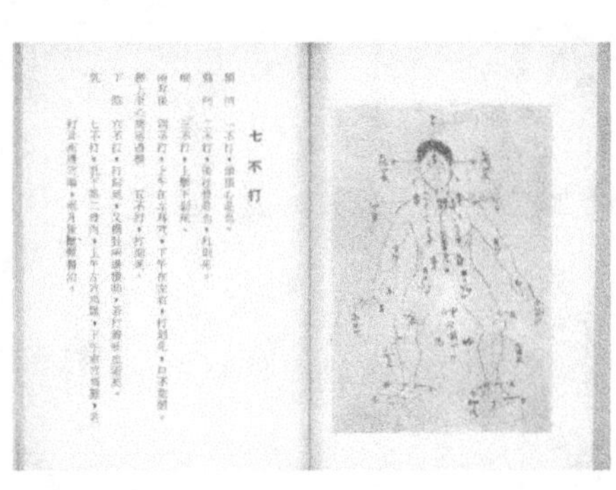

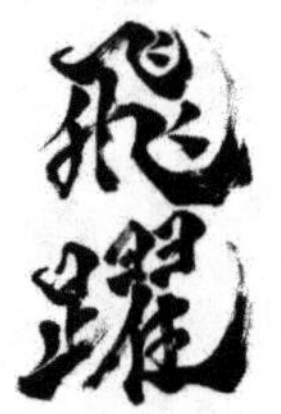
飛躍

Chapter Nine
第九章

Ip Man's Wing Chun Rules of Conduct
葉問詠春祖訓

Ip Man (葉問, 1893–1972) was a master of Wing Chun (詠春) kung fu and was best known for one of his students, Bruce Lee. In fact, Wing Chun was an unknown kung fu style until Lee became world famous and mentioned that his martial arts background was in this style.

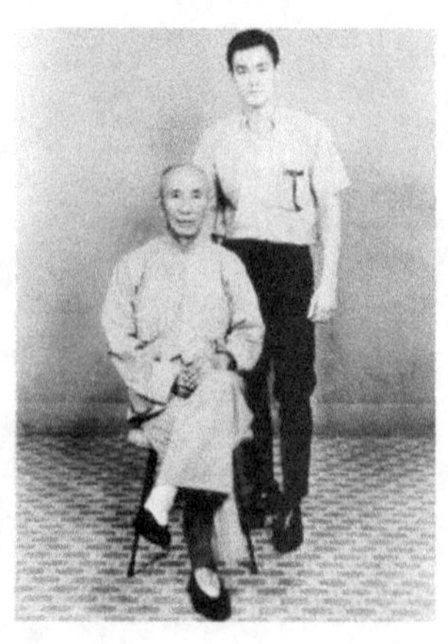

I am not going to write about Ip Man or Bruce Lee here as their biographies have been published by many others who are probably much more qualified to write about them. What I want to write about is Ip Man's greatest contribution to the martial arts world: the introduction of the *Wing Chun Jo Fen* (詠春祖訓, '*Wing Chun Rules of Conduct*'). Unless the reader has practiced this style, the *Wing Chun Jo Fen* should be new to you. We have studied Funakoshi's *Niju Kun* (二十訓, '*Twenty Principles*'), and I believe it is interesting and educational to learn about and study these codes of conduct.

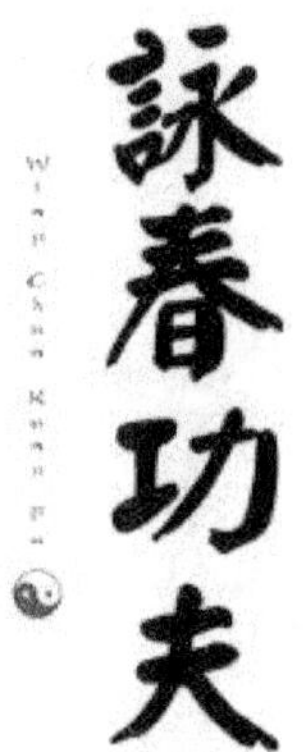

First, I would like to touch on the origin of Wing Chun and a little of its history. The exact date of the origin of this style is not historically documented. Due to the particular period when this fighting art was created, which was during the middle of the nineteenth century, I suspect it was impossible to create and keep such a document. The creation of Wing Chun is said to have occurred during the period after the army of the Qing dynasty (清朝) attacked and burned the Southern Shaolin Temple. According to legend, the originator is believed to be the young woman Yim Wing Chun (嚴詠春). She had supposedly learned a fighting style from the Buddhist nun Ng Mui (伍枚), who was one of the Shaolin Monastery survivors.

This fighting style is said to have been inspired by the nun's observations of a fight between a snake and a crane, so you can easily guess the techniques of this style. Wing Chun is a striking art that utilizes kicks, punches, elbow strikes, knee strikes, and open-handed techniques primarily for close-range combat.

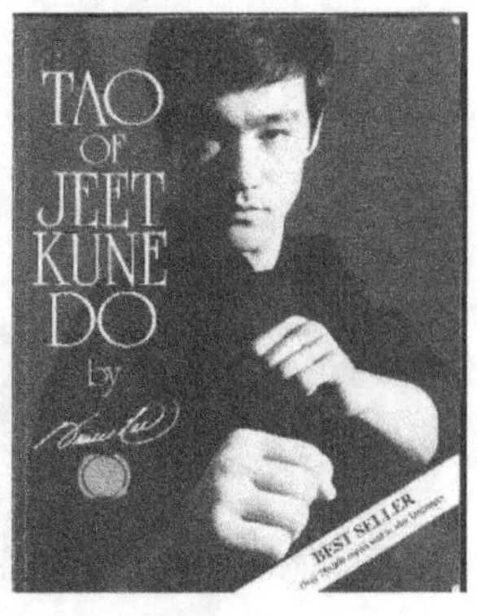

It is very interesting to examine the style Bruce Lee created, Jeet Kune Do (截拳道 [*jiéquándào*]), and compare its techniques to those of Wing Chun. You will find that there is very little resemblance to his original art. As this is not a chapter about Lee or Jeet Kune Do, I will not go any further than to make just one statement. I know there are many blind followers of Bruce Lee, and my statement may not please them, but I dare to reveal this because of the great respect I have for Ip Man. Lee's deviations were not based on technical discovery or improvement as he would have us believe. They were made mainly because he needed to adapt the style to look good on the screen. I am not blaming Lee for having done this as he was a movie actor before he was a martial artist. It was a very natural thing to do, and he was very successful at it. He should receive the credit he is due for what he did, which was to popularize Asian martial arts around the world through the movies he starred in. But, I must stress that we should never inflate his image above what he really was and create a god.

OK, let us look at Ip Man's *Wing Chun Jo Fen* (詠春祖訓, '*Wing Chun Rules of Conduct*'), which consists of nine rules.

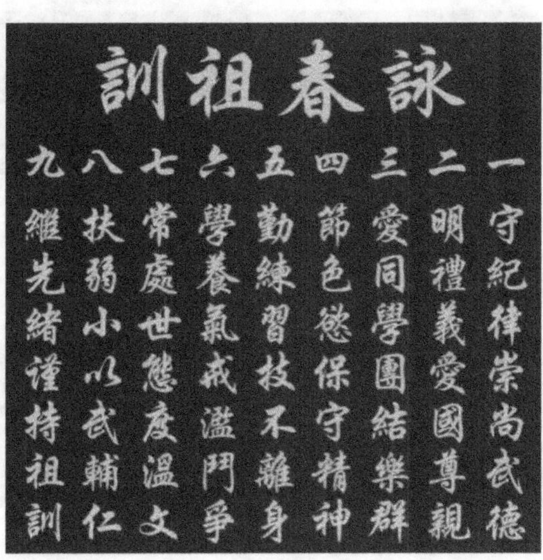
詠春祖訓

一 守紀律崇尚武德
二 明禮義愛國尊親
三 愛同學團結樂群
四 節色慾保守精神
五 勤練習技不離身
六 學養氣戒濫鬥爭
七 常處世態度溫文
八 扶弱小以武輔仁
九 繼先緒謹持祖訓

I will examine each rule by listing the original Chinese text and then including the translation underneath. The rules are fairly straightforward, so there will be little explanation added beyond the translated text.

Rule 1

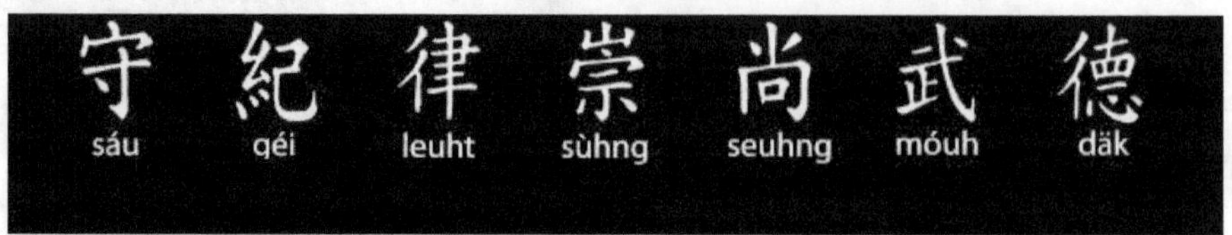

Remain disciplined and uphold yourself ethically as a martial artist.

Rule 2

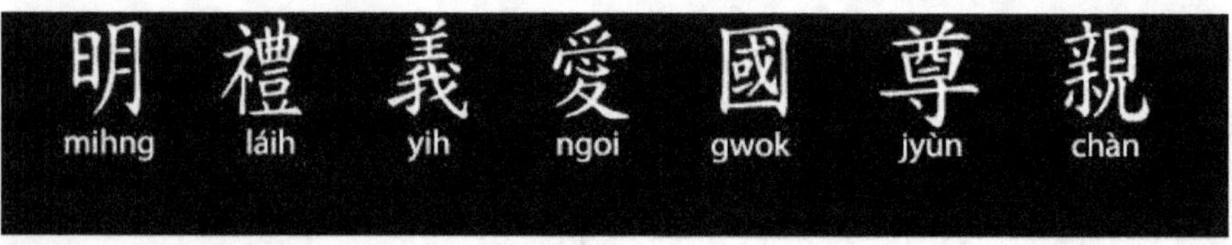

Practice courtesy and righteousness, love your country, honor your family, and respect your parents.

Rule 3

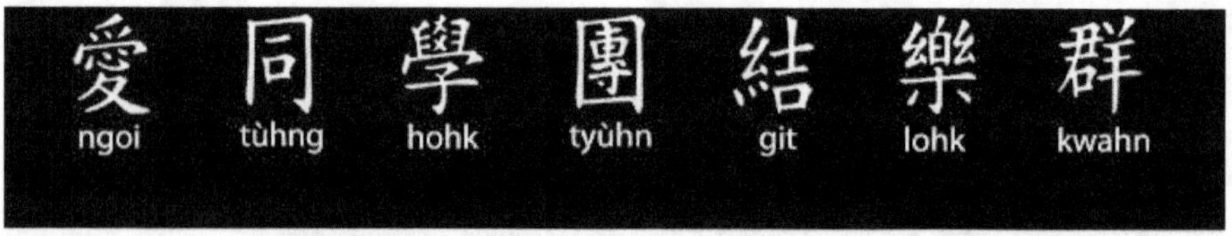

Love your fellow students, be united, and enjoy working together in harmony.

Rule 4

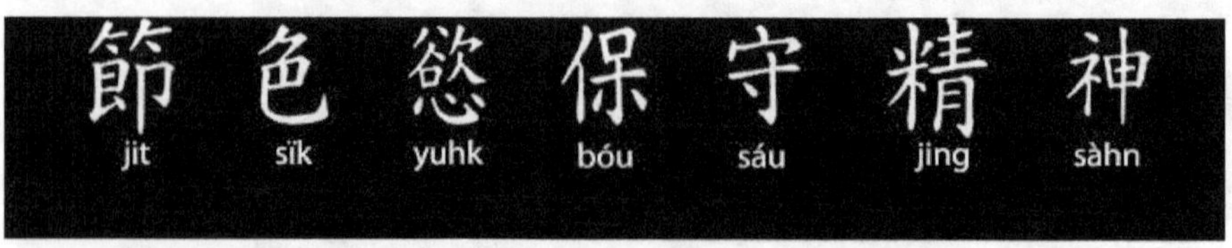

Control your bodily desires, preserve a sound spirit, and stay healthy.

Rule 5

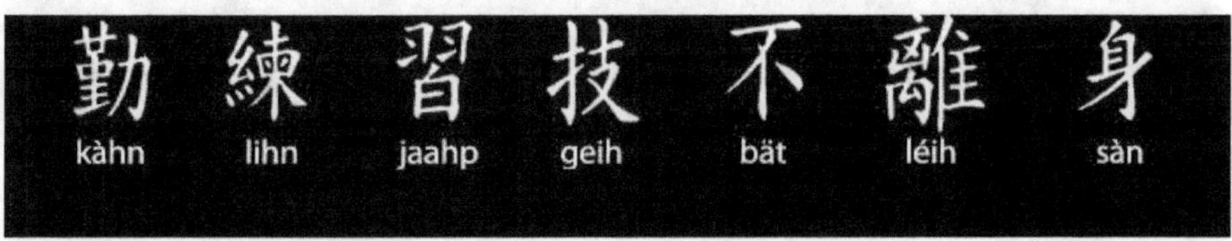

Train diligently, keep practicing, and maintain your skills throughout your life.

Rule 6

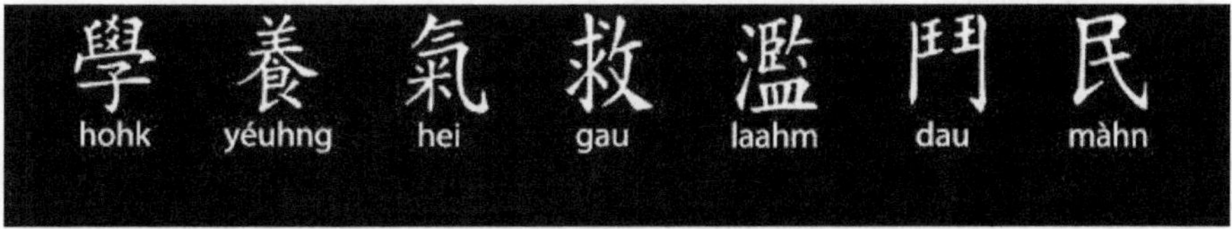

Learn to develop your ki and avoid the attitude of arguments and aggression.

Rule 7

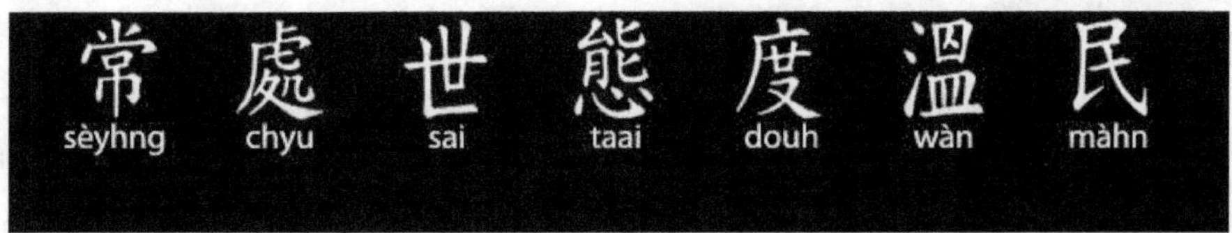

Your character in your daily life should always be moderate, kind, and gentle in manner.

Rule 8

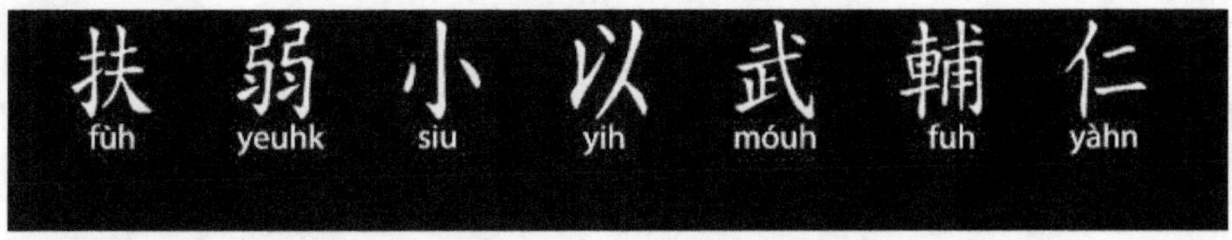

Help the weak and disadvantaged (young and old) and use your martial skill to keep justice.

Rule 9

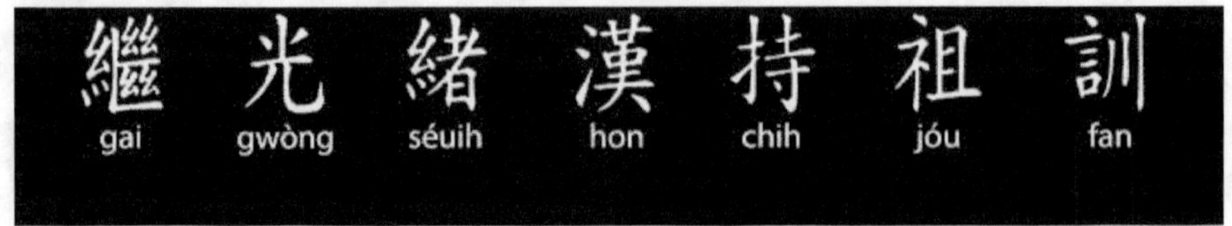

Pass on the tradition and preserve and uphold these rules of conduct.

In addition to these nine rules, there are three things martial artists must refuse or avoid. I found them to be interesting, so I will list them here:

1. Refuse to teach government officials.
2. Refuse to teach local bullies (gangsters).
3. Refuse to accept disreputable employment.

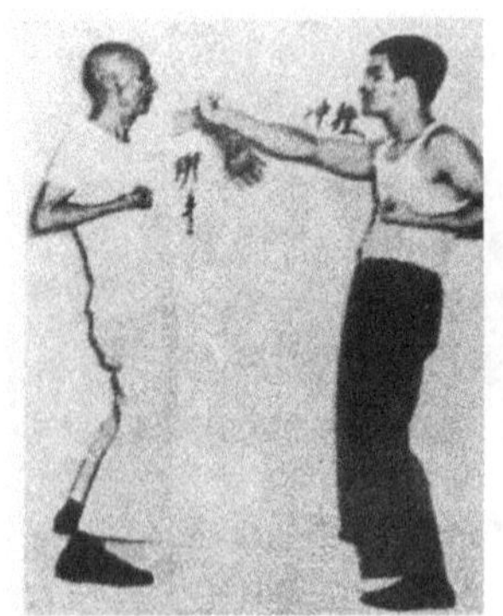

Ip Man died from throat cancer in December 1972, which happened to be just seven months before Bruce Lee died, in July 1973. It is very true that Ip Man became a legend and made Wing Chun a well-known style. I also consider the *Wing Chun Jo Fen* to be a valuable teaching, and we must all respect it, even if we are not Wing Chun practitioners.

Despite all of this, however, I must end this chapter with the sad fact that Ip Man was addicted to opium. One of his former students revealed that he used tuition money to support his opium addiction. He had many students, and Wing Chun became famous, but I wonder how he could be at peace with his deviation from the rules of conduct, particularly of Rule 4. Regardless, do you not agree that we can learn some important lessons from the *Wing Chun Jo Fen* that we may want to incorporate into our karate discipline?

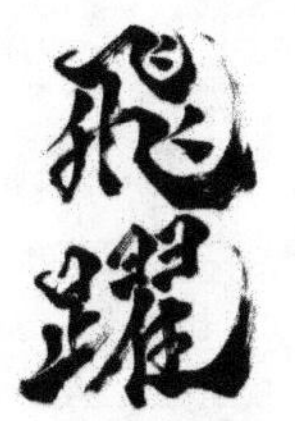
飛躍

Chapter Ten
第十章

Bruce Lee's One-Inch Punch Examined
ブルース・リーの寸勁を科学的に検証する

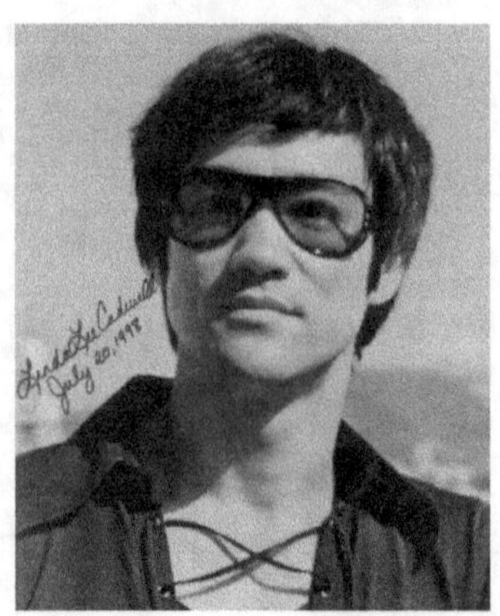

This is probably the first biomechanical evaluation of the martial arts skills of Bruce Lee, so let me start by introducing him. Even though he is well known, there are a few things that most people ignore or do not know.

Bruce Lee (李小龍 [read as *Lǐ Xiǎolóng* in Chinese]) was the professional name of Junfan Lee (李振藩 [read as *Lǐ Zhènfān* in Chinese]). He was born in Chinatown, San Francisco, California, U.S.A., on November 27, 1940, and died in Hong Kong on July 20, 1973, at the age of thirty-two. In addition to being an actor, he claimed to be a martial arts expert and the founder of his style, Jeet Kune Do. He is widely considered by commentators, critics, media, and other martial artists to be one of the most influential martial artists of all time and a pop-culture icon of the twentieth century. He is often credited with helping to change the way Asians were presented in American films.

The name *Bruce Lee* is still very famous and popular among not only kung fu movie buffs but also karate practitioners. It is amazing that many people still idolize him and say he was the greatest kung fu expert since he died forty-five years ago. I decided to write this chapter to shed some light on the real ability of Bruce Lee because many karate practitioners believe that is what they see in the movies. What I will attempt to do is evaluate his real martial arts performance (that is, his performance without choreography) scientifically to give it a fair shake.

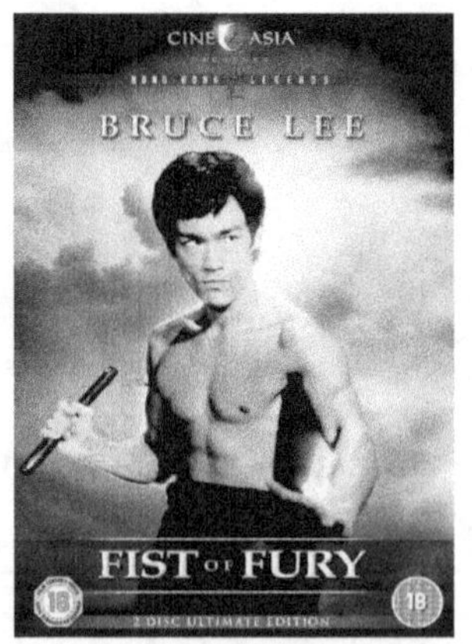

I am aware that what I am trying to do here is controversial and that many Bruce Lee lovers and admirers will not be happy that I am questioning his martial arts expertise. I want to emphasize that the real objective of this chapter is not to bad-mouth Bruce Lee but rather to give his real performance a fair evaluation. Before getting into the evaluation, though, I would like to give him the credit that he deserves.

I consider Lee's greatest contribution to the martial arts to be the fact that he was the first Hollywood actor to introduce the American public to Asian martial arts and ignite their popularity throughout the world through his kung fu movies (even though most of them were made in Hong Kong). There were other Hong Kong kung fu movies before those of Bruce Lee, but those movies were cheaply made, the action was poorly choreographed, and the dubbed English was so bad that it was almost comical. Lee was a good actor with experience in the film industry who knew how to excite American audiences. He worked with Hong Kong director Raymond Chow (鄒文懐 [read as *Zōu Wénhuái* in Chinese], 1927–) to produce his first kung fu movie, *The Big Boss* (唐山大兄 [Golden Harvest]), in 1971. Then, he gained more popularity with his next film, *Fist of Fury* (精武門 [Golden Harvest]), in 1972.

Lee became an almost instant hit around the world with his kung fu movies, and his fame only grew with each successive film. His fighting style was unique, and he had a long, peculiar *kiai* that sounded like the scream of a cat or bird, but the audience loved it. He died suddenly one year later, in 1973, which was strange as he looked very fit and was so young. There were many rumors and controversies surrounding his death, but I will not go into that subject as it is not our main concern in this chapter.

Having said all that, when it comes to his martial arts ability, that is another story. When we watch movies about superheroes such as Superman, Spider-Man, The Hulk, etc., we do not believe the actors can actually fly or break through walls. It is very strange that we want to believe that the actors in kung fu movies can also be martial arts experts. It is true that some martial artists have become movie actors, such as Jet Li (李連傑 [read as *Lǐ Liánjié* in Chinese], 1963–) and even one of the JKA instructors, Tatsuya Naka (photo right), who played a major role in

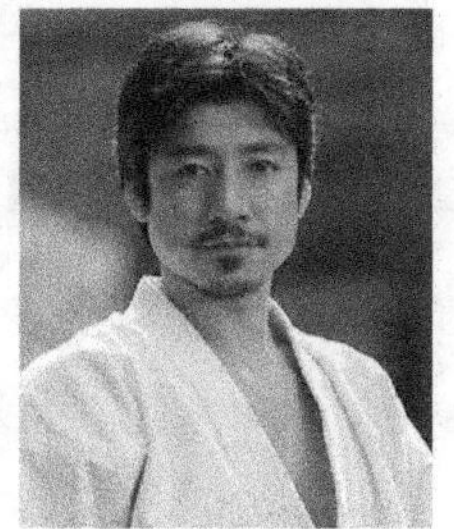

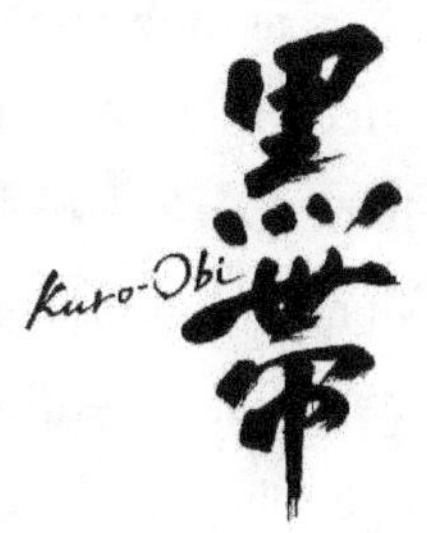

the movie *Kuro Obi* (黒帯 [Toei Company, 2007]). But, remember that they were martial artists before they became actors.

Let's look at who Bruce Lee truly was. He was the son of Hoichuen Lee (李海泉 [read as *Lǐ Hǎiquán* in Chinese], 1901–1965), a Cantonese opera star from Hong Kong. While in Hong Kong, he was introduced to the film industry by his father and appeared in several films as a child actor. He held dual citizenship in Hong Kong and the United States. He was raised in Kowloon (a section of Hong Kong) with his family until his late teens and then moved to the United States in 1958 at the age of eighteen.

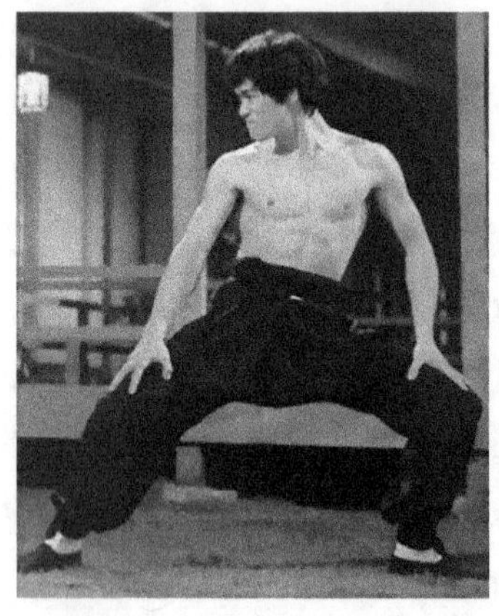

Now I have to bring to your attention the myth that Bruce Lee created. The myth I am referring to is that he was a kung fu expert. Many an audience loved Lee's action and believed—or, I should say, "wanted to believe"—that the skills they saw in his films were real. What I am trying to do in this chapter is evaluate his true skill level and prove that it was only a myth. Some readers may be offended and ask, "Why are you doing this? It is like telling children that Santa Claus is a fairy tale." I agree that my actions would be unwarranted if my audience were just kung fu movie buffs, but I am doing this for the senior karate practitioners who still idolize Lee. I want them to see the reality. I feel strongly that senior karate practitioners must not mix up true martial arts skills with fabricated techniques that look real for the movies.

One cannot fully evaluate Lee's martial arts skills based on the action in his movies as this is choreographed and rehearsed just like the demonstrations performed by JKA masters such as Masahiko Tanaka (田中昌彦, 1941–), Mikio Yahara (矢原美紀夫, 1947–), and Tetsuhiko Asai. His training photos can be evaluated, but this is probably not convincing. What I need to do is conduct a biomechanical, scientific evaluation of his real action. By "real," I mean that it must not be rehearsed and also that it must be shown in public.

Demonstration 1

In Photo 1A, you can see that Lee is standing sideways in relation to his partner in the white uniform. This is the big telltale sign of a push instead of a punch. If he were going to throw a real punch, he would be facing straight toward his partner.

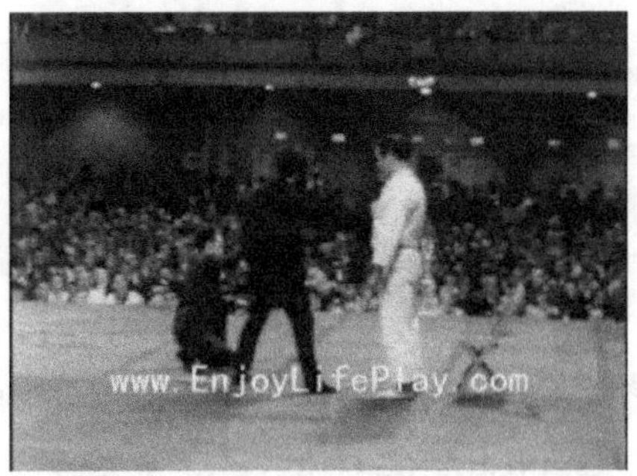

1A

Photo 1B shows some proof that Lee is pushing his partner. Notice how much he leans into him and that his left foot is lifted. This clearly shows that he is not generating this punch (or push) from the hips. He must have pushed about ten inches, judging from the photos. Note that this photo may not be related to the first and third photos. I just used it to show his punch more clearly.

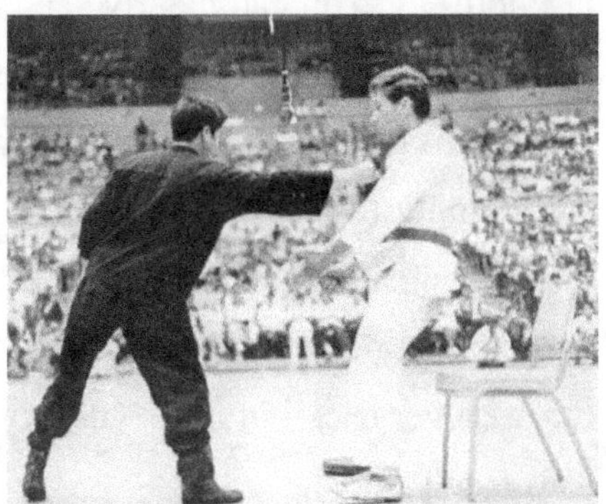
1B

Photo 1C shows how the perfect prop, a chair right behind his partner, can make his "punch" look effective and powerful. Why? If there were no chair, the partner would just take a few steps back instead of collapsing from the punch. With a chair so close, this guy has no choice but to tumble and fall. If this were a real one-inch punch with its full effect, the partner might take a few steps back but, at the same time, would probably bend over from the pain in his chest. You can get a better look at how he punched in this video: www.popmech.tumblr.com/

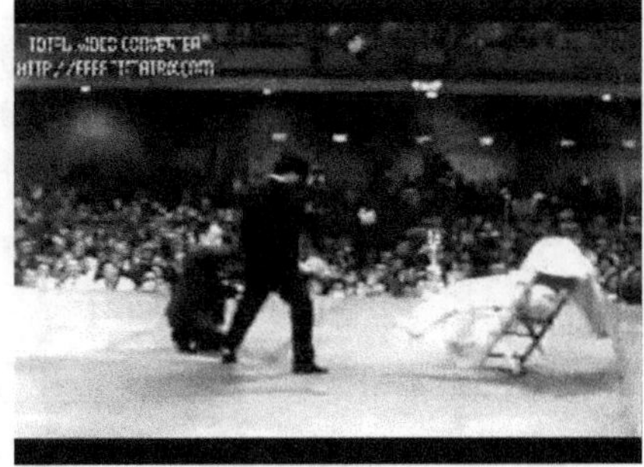
1C

post/109674670789. Now that you have read my explanation, you should be able to detect that he is pushing instead of punching his partner.

Demonstration 2

Here is another video that shows some of Lee's feats, such as his one-inch punch, six-inch punch, and board breaking: www.youtube.com/watch?v=btl3tp91sQc. Go to about the seven-second mark to see his one-inch punch in slow motion.

Let me explain what he is doing in this demonstration. I have to point out that he uses another trick. Check out his right hand in Photo 2A. You can clearly see that he is using an open hand in front of his partner's chest. This gives you the impression that he is not going to use much power. However, it really means that he has an additional two inches once he closes his hand to push. It is a clever trick but is also deceiving, unfortunately.

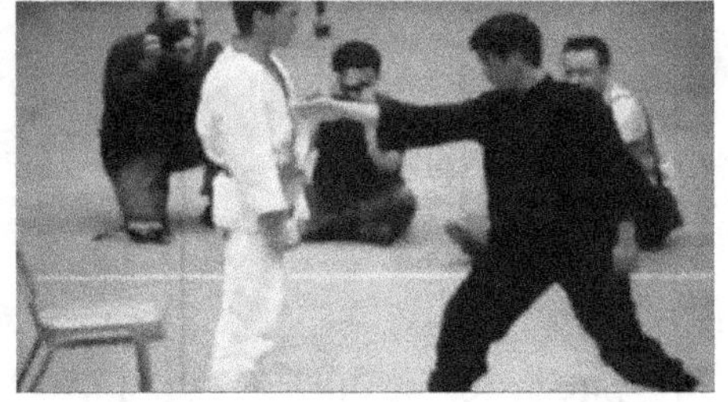

2A

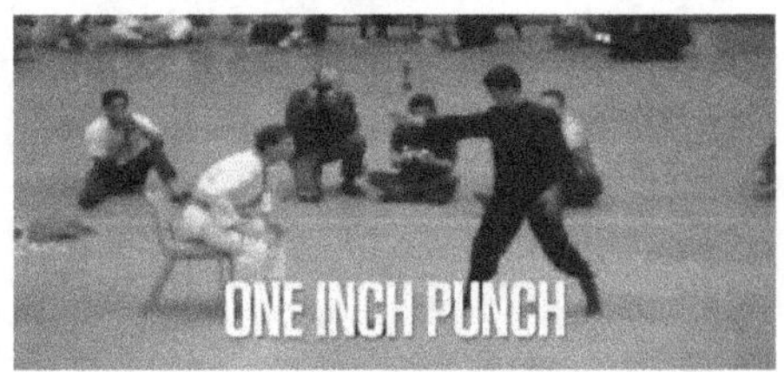

2B

Take a look at Lee's right hand in Photo 2B. He opens it again after the punch, but you can see that he uses his fist to push his partner backward. Why does he open his hand? It is obviously used to make his punch look soft but powerful. This may impress amateurs, but I am sorry to say that it certainly is a poor trick he uses here.

Demonstration 3

In a video clip with the title "Six-Inch Punch," Lee demonstrates his short-distance punch, which you can see at this URL: giant.gfycat.com/BigImprobable-

Bullfrog.gif. I am sharing this clip because it shows his punch in slow motion, so you can see how he moves his upper body about two or three feet to push the guy. Where he positions his fist when delivering this punch is irrelevant as he is using a leaning motion with his upper body to generate power.

The start is the same in Photo 3A. He positions himself sideways. You can see his partner leaning slightly backward, though I do not know if he is doing this intentionally or unintentionally. Since his partner's center of gravity is behind his heels, it is easy for Lee to push him backward.

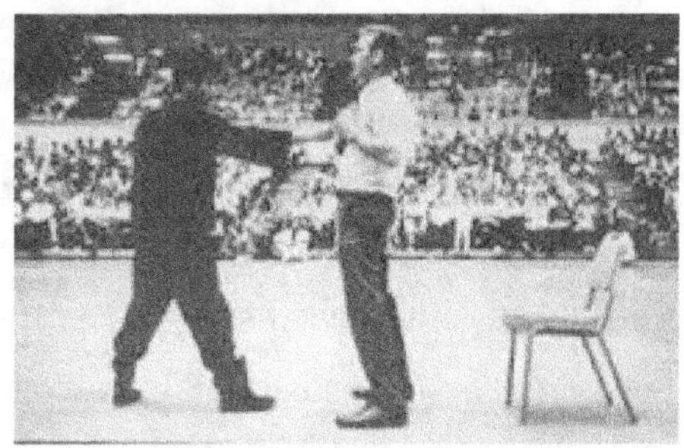

3A

In Photo 3B, the prop is the same. The partner has a chair right behind him. One thing I need to mention is that the chair slides backward many feet once he sits in it. If the chair had had rubber feet, it couldn't have done this. I could be wrong, but I am assuming Lee wanted to have this visual effect simply to impress the audience. He was a movie actor, but, at the same time, I have also heard that he was heavily involved in the choreography and visual effects of his action scenes. This is the reason I suspect that he purposely set this up. Just think, if you really wanted to show a one- or six-inch punch, why would you need a chair? Below is a set of three photos showing the sequence.

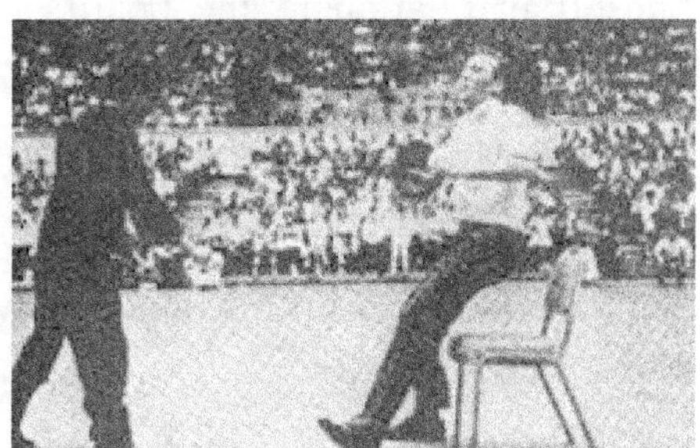

3B

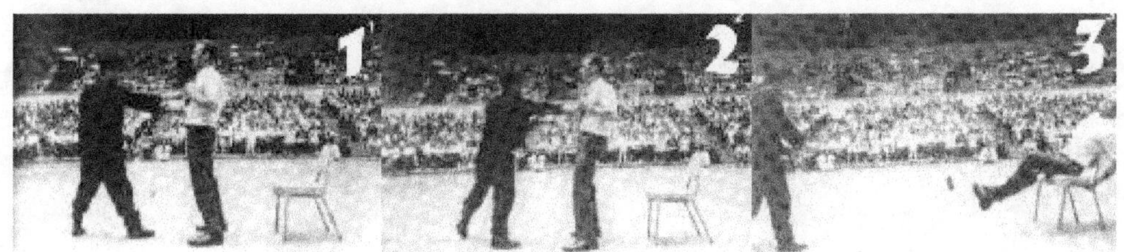

Demonstration 4

The last demonstration is his board breaking, which he did on TV in Hong Kong. I will evaluate how he did this performance.

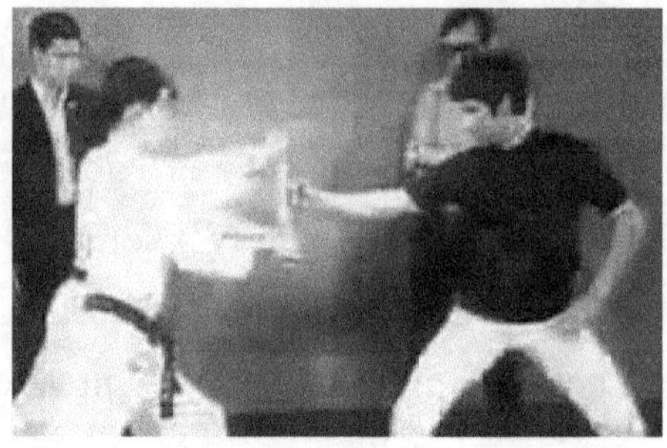
4A

Since Lee has to break the board, he is standing in a straddle stance as shown in Photo 4A. This means he can lean in with his upper body instead of using only his hips.

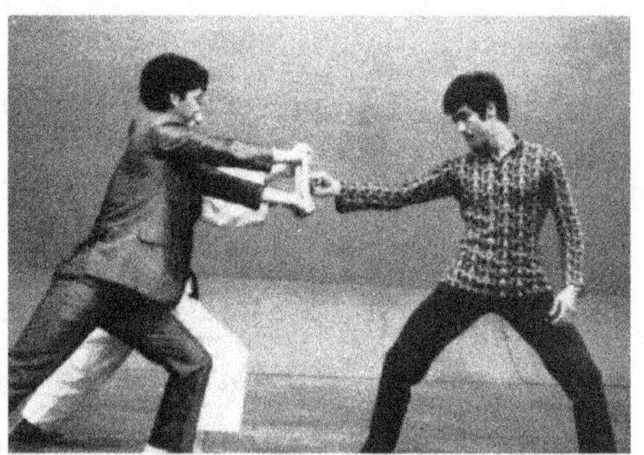
4B

Photo 4B shows how Lee positions himself in relation to the board. This is from another TV program in Asia.

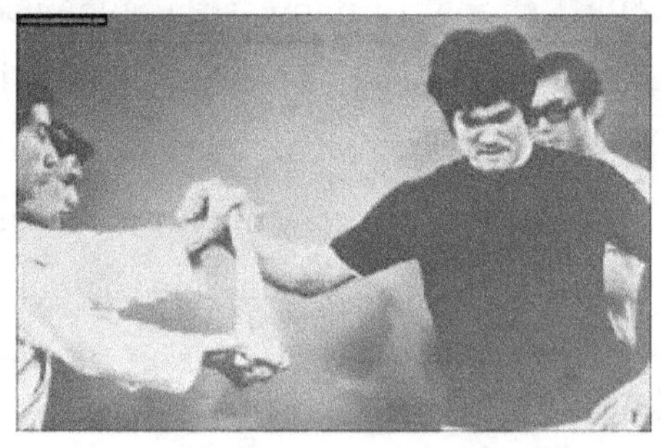
4C

Photo 4C shows the position after the break, and I consider this to be proof that he has leaned in with his upper body. Notice that his punching arm is now bent. This proves that he has leaned so much to break the board that his arm bent back as a reaction. If he had used only his hips to punch, his arm would be straight. If the wood is soft, anyone can break one or even two boards with a push like this. Just try it and you will see how easy it is to break a board. But, try to stand in a natural stance as you would in the *yoi* (用意, 'ready') position and extend your arm to touch the board before you break it. This way is much harder.

Conclusion

I conclude that Bruce Lee's one-inch punch was not a real one-inch punch at all but rather a one- or six-inch push with several props to make it look impressive. Once again, the intention of my evaluation is not to degrade Lee in any way. What I have done in this chapter is evaluate his martial arts skill level from a biomechanical perspective.

Lee was a great movie actor and should receive credit for this. He also promoted Asian martial arts and made kung fu and karate known around the world. He should receive credit for this, as well. On the other hand, his impressive on-screen action should not be automatically interpreted as martial arts expertise. He used all the cinematic tricks and techniques available to make the action faster and more dynamic. Truly, he was very successful at this, and I do not blame people for wanting to believe he was a kung fu master.

This was indeed impressive as the one-inch punch was almost unheard of in the sixties, particularly in the Western world. If you are as old as I am, you remember that Japanese karate (mainly Shotokan) was the mainstream martial art in the U.S.A. Lee brought something new and different, so I give him a lot of credit for doing that. His well-planned performances impressed not only the members of the audience who were not involved in the martial arts but also those who were martial artists themselves.

I do not know exactly why he carried out those performances. My guess is that he needed to generate some credibility for his acting career. Being an Asian in Hollywood was a handicap in the sixties, so he was probably struggling and was unable to get a lead role at that time. The Long Beach demonstration was in 1964, at which time he was almost unknown.

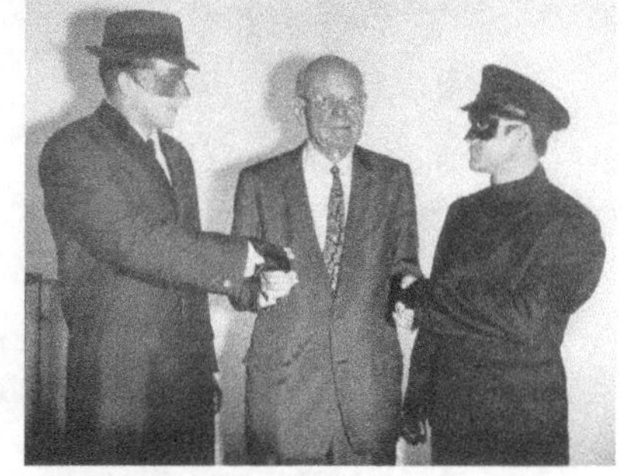

He finally got a break in 1966 when he captured a role in *The Green Hornet* (Greenway Productions, 1966–1967), which only ran for one season. It was a big role, but he was the sidekick (no pun intended), Kato, which was not the lead role. I have heard that he auditioned for the hit TV series *Kung Fu* (Warner Bros. Television, 1972–1975) in 1971 and that management chose Caucasian actor David Carradine (1936–2009) to act as a mixed-race (Chinese and Caucasian) Shaolin monk instead.

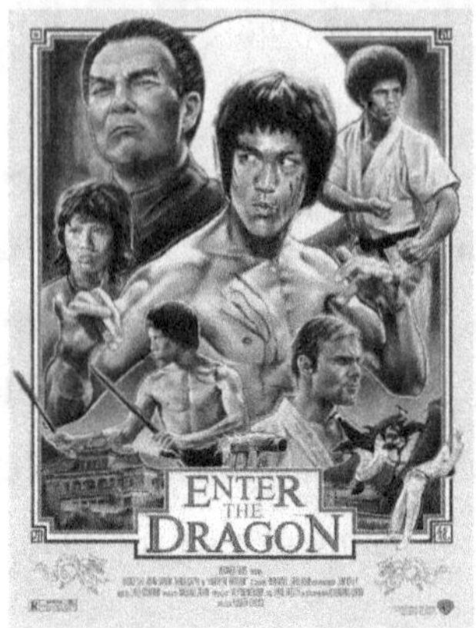

So, Lee had to go to Hong Kong instead of Hollywood to make himself known in the movie world. As previously mentioned, he teamed up with Raymond Chow, the founder of Golden Harvest, and created *The Big Boss* in 1971 and *Fist of Fury* in 1972. Then, his dream came true when he starred in *Enter the Dragon* (龍爭虎鬥 [Warner Bros., 1973]), the first Chinese martial arts film to have been produced by a major Hollywood studio. The rest is history, but, unfortunately, Lee was never able to fully enjoy his fame from *Enter the Dragon* as he died even before it was released in 1973.

The true irony is his one-inch punch demonstration. The footage of this demonstration is now widely available with Internet technology, so although it may have given him some credibility in the martial arts of the sixties and also helped his movie career, the long-term consequence is that his martial arts skills have been fully exposed and now haunt his fame over fifty years later.

The reader will note that I did not explain or elaborate on the real one-inch punch in this chapter. My demonstration of the real one-inch punch is available for you to see at Karate Coaching (www.karatecoaching.com).

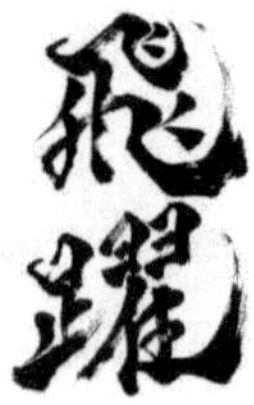

Chapter Eleven
第十一章

What Is Ueshiba's Teaching of San Go Ichi?
植芝の参合一の教えとは？

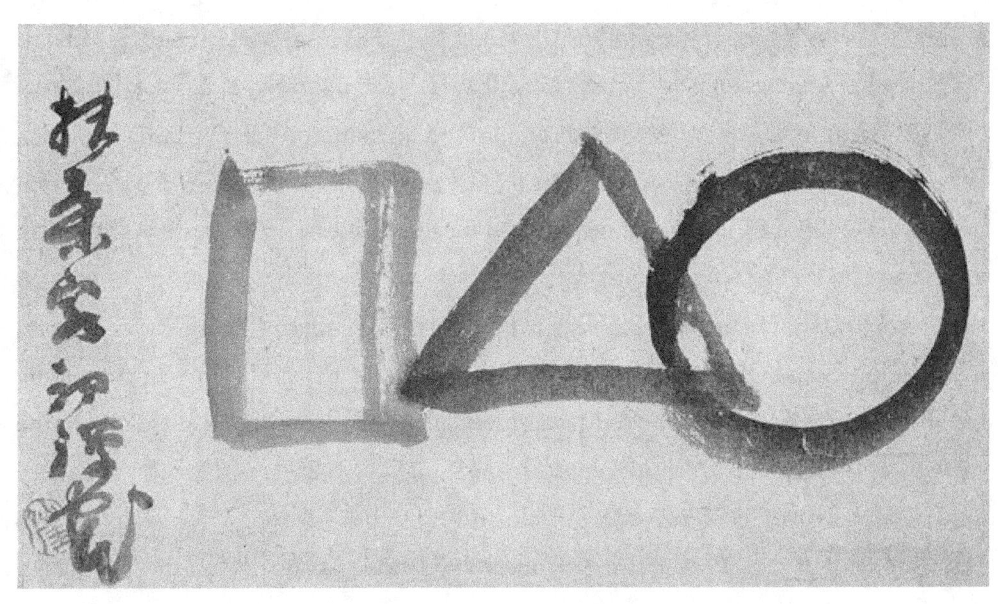

Uchu (宇宙, 'The Universe')
A brush painting by Zen Buddhist monk Gibon Sengai (仙厓義梵, 1750–1837)

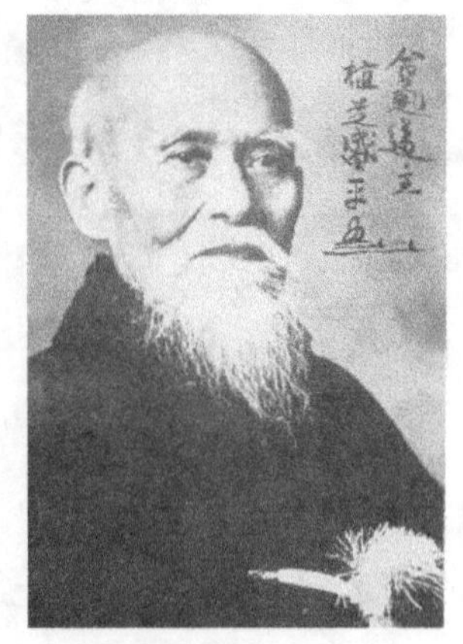

In the past, I have given explanations of Funakoshi's *Niju Kun*, Ip Man's *Wing Chun Jo Fen*, and Goju Ryu's *Kenpo Hakku* (拳法八句, 'Eight Verses of Kenpo'). Here, I would like to bring up another martial arts concept that was uniquely used by Morihei Ueshiba (植芝盛平, 1883–1969 [photo right]), the founder of aikido.

The concept Ueshiba used to describe aikido techniques is called *san go ichi* (参合一). *San* (参 or 三) means 'three', and *ichi* (一) means 'one'. Since the first and last words are *three* and *one*, and the pronunciation of the middle word, *go*, is similar to that of the number five in Japanese, this word can easily be mistaken for the number five. However, the character used for 'five' is 五, whereas the one used for *go* here is 合, which means 'combine', 'become', or 'unify'. This same character is pronounced as *ai* when used as the first character in the word *aikido* (合気道), which means 'the way of unifying ki'. Therefore, *san go ichi* literally means 'three combined into one' or 'three unified into one'.

So, what are these three things? Ueshiba used three figures to illustrate them: a circle, a triangle, and a square (as shown on the introductory page of this chapter). What did he mean by this? And, what is the "one" that comes from the combination of these three figures? The answers to these questions are exactly what I wish to investigate and try to find out.

Before we jump into this subject, I believe we should have a basic idea of what aikido is and who Ueshiba was. As I mentioned earlier, aikido was created by Ueshiba, who was often referred to as *Osensei* (大先生, 'Great Teacher'), in the early twentieth century. Aikido came from jujutsu, which is one of the Japanese martial arts. However, I consider aikido to be unique because Ueshiba made his *budo* more than just a standard martial arts method. According to the *Wikipedia* entry on aikido, it is

> a synthesis of his martial studies, philosophy, and religious beliefs. Aikido is often

translated as 'the way of unifying (with) life energy' or as 'the way of harmonious spirit'. Ueshiba's goal was to create an art that practitioners could use to defend themselves while also protecting their attacker from injury.

The uniqueness of aikido definitely comes from the combination of the martial art itself with a type of Shinto (神道) religion called *Oomotokyo* (大本教, 'Great Origin'). Below are some resources for additional reading:

Aikido: www.aikikai.or.jp/eng/aikido/index.html
Morihei Ueshiba: www.aikidofaq.com/history/osensei.html
Oomotokyo: www.oomoto.or.jp/English/enFaq/indexfaq.html

Aikido came from jujutsu, but what kind of jujutsu did it originate from? Now we have to touch on Daito Ryu Aikijujutsu (大東流合気柔術), a style that has a controversial history. This martial art first became known in Japan in the late nineteenth century and was introduced by Sokaku Takeda (武田惣角, 1859–1943 [photo right]). Takeda had extensive training in several martial arts, including jujutsu, kenjutsu, sojutsu (槍術, 'spear arts'), naginatajutsu (薙刀, 'halberd arts'), kyujutsu (弓術, 'archery'), horse riding, and sumo. What is interesting about his style, Daito Ryu, is that there are no known documented records of it before Takeda despite the fact that it is supposed to have a long historical lineage.

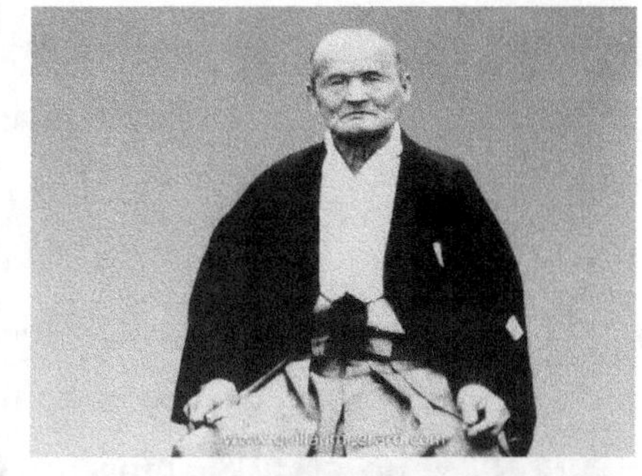

In addition to the background of his style, I wish to share some other interesting facts about Takeda himself as he was a unique martial artist. He was well known in Japan as a great jujutsu master in the late nineteenth and early twentieth centuries. One of the unique things about him was that he never owned a dojo where he could train or teach his art. He also did not live in his own residence until he got married at the age of fifty-one. This was not because he was poor—his teaching fees were actually extraordinarily high—but because he chose to do so. What he did was stay at various students' houses as he taught them the art. So, if a student wanted to learn from Takeda, he had to not only pay the high tuition but also provide a room in his house for Takeda to stay in for a period of anywhere from a few months to half a year.

Another interesting story about him is that he was quite short (just under 5 feet [150 centimeters] tall) but was very strongly built. Some students reported that his arms were as thick as his legs. There are many other interesting stories about Takeda, but I will not go into them in this chapter. Below are some resources for additional reading:

Daito Ryu Aikijujutsu: www.daito-ryu.org/en
Sokaku Takeda: www.daito-ryu.org/en/takeda-sokaku.html

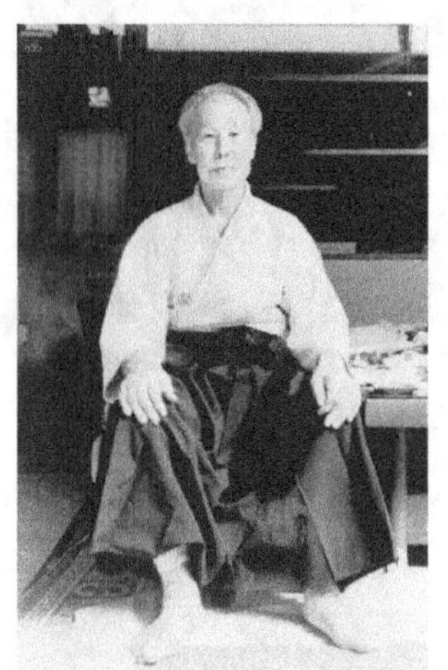

It is well known that Takeda created two famous masters in the twentieth century. One is, of course, Morihei Ueshiba; the other is Yukiyoshi Sagawa (佐川幸義, 1902–1998 [photo left]). After studying their arts, I found it very interesting that these two masters were both excellent in their jujutsu skills, yet their approaches were quite different. This chapter is not about comparing these two masters, so I will keep my analysis to a minimum.

I must say that Sagawa was totally physical in his approach. He emphasized physical training and the importance of hip and leg strength. Here is a well-known quote from him: "Building the legs and hips is the way to progress. This is a conclusion that I have reached through more than fifty years of training." His skill level was considered by many martial artists to be better than that of Ueshiba. He lived to be ninety-six years old and trained and taught aikijujutsu right up until the very last week of his life.

Sagawa is not a well-known jujutsu master in the Western world since he did not advertise his dojo or his art as Ueshiba did. He also did not allow any video recordings (as far as I know), so we can only guess how skillful he was based on photos and experiences written by his students. I am thoroughly impressed by the fact that he maintained his superhuman skill until the last days of his life. I do not expect that you would believe anyone could throw a strong young opponent as soon as the latter touched—not grabbed, just touched—his sleeve or foot, but Sagawa demonstrated this (photos below).

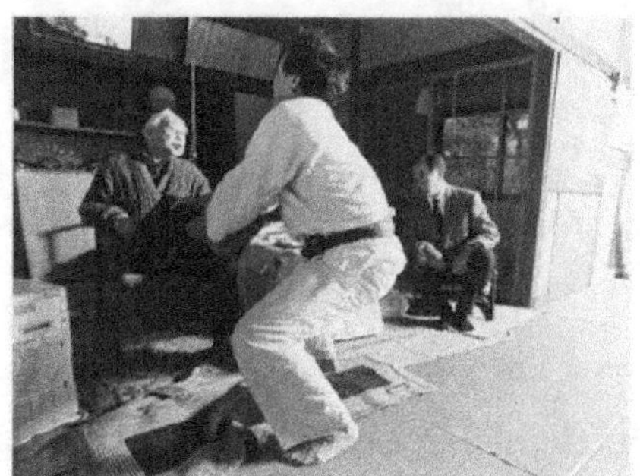

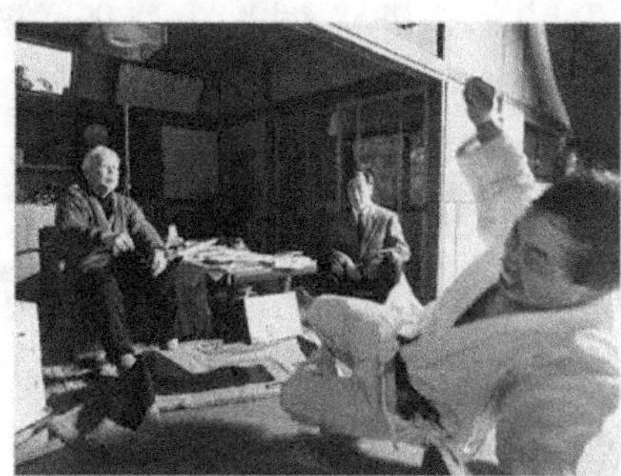

Here is an excellent article by Kiyokazu Maebayashi published in *Aikido Journal* on July 11, 2015, which shows how capable Sagawa was: members.aikidojournal.com/public/yukiyoshi-sagawa-daito-ryu-master. If you are interested in learning more about his life and training, you can find it in the book *Transparent Power* (透明な力 [Kodansha, 1995]), which was written by one of Sagawa's senior students, Tatsuo Kimura (木村達雄, 1947–). The English version of this book, published by MAAT Press in 2009, is available from *Amazon* at the following URL if you wish to purchase a copy: www.amazon.com/Transparent-Power-Tatsuo-Kimura/dp/1893447103.

I must emphasize that Sagawa believed in physical strength, which he said was the necessary foundation for jujutsu techniques. Here is another quote from him: "People who think they can ignore training their bodies and only work on techniques are amateurs. You cannot do a technique if your body is not developed.

Actually, if you don't prepare your body properly, you have no hope of ever perfecting your technique." I believe this statement clearly describes the main principle of his teaching.

Ueshiba's approach, on the other hand, was quite different. I am sure he also encouraged practitioners to train their body, but he used a unique approach by adding in religious concepts. Thus, I agree with those who claim that Ueshiba's art was half *budo* and half Shinto.

To understand how aikido came about, we must touch on an unusual mystical experience that Ueshiba is reported to have had when he was forty-two years old. I have a copy of the book *Takemusu Aiki* (武産合気 [Byakko Press, 1986]), which was written by Hideo Takahashi (高橋英雄, 1932–). This book is a collection of Ueshiba's quotes. I found an English version of this book, entitled *The Heart of Aikido: The Philosophy of Takemusu Aiki* (Kodansha, 2013), available from *Amazon* at the following URL if you wish to purchase a copy: www.amazon.com/Heart-Aikido-Philosophy-Takemusu-Aiki/dp/1568365144. Unfortunately, I do not have a copy of the English text, so I will translate some of the original Japanese quotes about this incident in 1925.

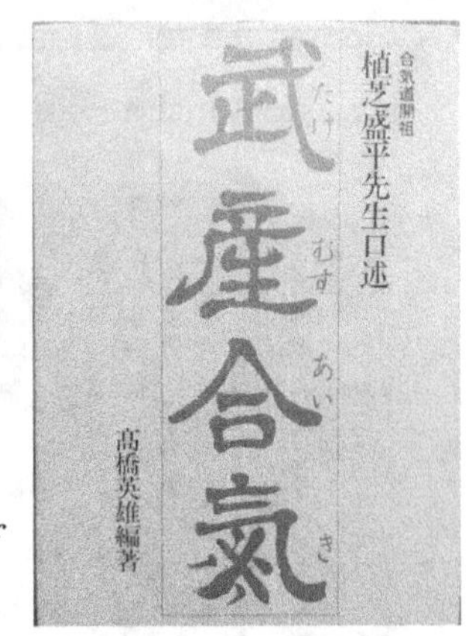

The text is rather long, and the context is incredible, so I am not sure if the reader will believe what Ueshiba wrote. Despite these facts, I think it is important to share his experience in his own words so that you might be able to understand where he is coming from and the concept or philosophy aikido is built on. What is written below is my own translation of Ueshiba's quotes, so I take full responsibility for its accuracy.

> I believe it was the spring of 1925. It happened when I was taking a walk alone in the backyard. All of a sudden the earth and heaven shook, and I saw the golden air [ki] spewing out of the ground. This air wrapped around me, and I felt that I also became a golden body. As soon as it happened, my body and my mind became very light, and

> I understood everything around me, including what the birds were saying. At that moment, I realized that I had a clear understanding of the will of the God who created the universe. At the same time, I received the enlightenment that the foundation of *budo* is God's love and the spirit of universal love. When I realized that the message was from heaven, it moved me so greatly that I could not stop the tears from falling from my eyes. Ever since that moment, I consider the entire earth to be my home and all the stars in the universe to be my family. As a result, I totally lost interest in and desire for not only material goods but also status, honor, and even winning in a fight.

Ueshiba also explained human beings and what we are:

> Human beings do not exist separately as we see with our eyes. Instead, we are all connected in the ki or spirit world as all of us are created with the ki that fills the universe.

I do not know if the reader will believe what Ueshiba wrote, and there is no way to prove or disprove his experience. I can only say that it was similar to the experience of opening or connecting a chakra as reported by yoga experts or that of enlightenment as reported by religious people. The above information may help give the reader some understanding of the philosophy and beliefs behind Ueshiba's art. With this understanding, let us now look at the term *san go ichi*.

First, I need to mention that I had great difficulty understanding the full meaning of Ueshiba's explanation of these figures, even though I read the book many times. Of course, the reason is not the language as I am a native Japanese speaker. Rather, his explanations and descriptions are deeply tied to the concepts and beliefs of his religion, which are unfamiliar to me. I will do my best to decipher these messages filled with religious terms and hidden meanings. I hope the reader, especially if you are not an aikido practitioner, can understand what Ueshiba was trying to teach through this text.

I have already mentioned that the first word, *san*, means 'three'. I must mention here that the number three has a religious and mystical meaning in Japan. The number three is considered to be a lucky number in Japanese culture and religion. In the Western world, the number seven is commonly considered to be a lucky number. If you are interested in the belief in the divine or mystical nature of figures, there is an independent school on this concept called *numerology*. Check out the article "Numerology: Discover & Understand Your Life Path Number" by Felicia Bender published on the *Astro Style* website: www.astrostyle.com/numerology. You may find some interesting points, though you may not believe any of them.

I will not go any more deeply into the subject of numerology in this chapter except to say that the number three is believed to have the character of creation and production according to the Japanese religion, Shinto. Interestingly, the triangle is commonly used to represent the number three as this figure shows how one point splits (or grows) into two points.

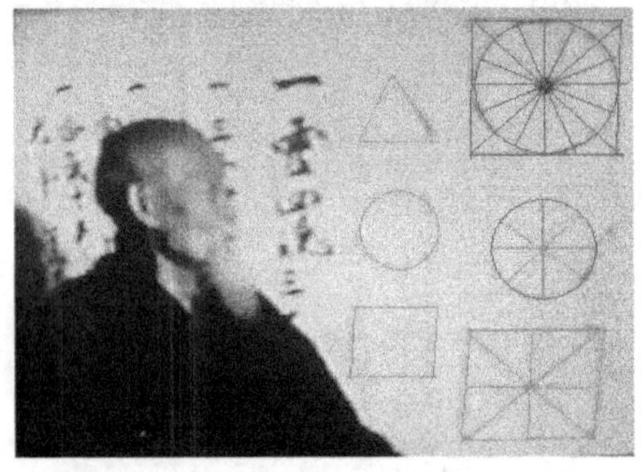

So, the first figure in Ueshiba's concept of aikido techniques is the *sankaku* (三角 or △, 'triangle'). This is followed by the *maru* (丸 or ○, 'circle') and then the *shikaku* (四角 or □, 'square'). It is known that Ueshiba used these figures to represent the three principles and to illustrate the techniques of aikido so that practitioners could better understand. However, if we just look at the figures without further explanation, they remain a mystery. To explain these principles, I will use quotes from the book *Takemusu Aiki* instead of describing them just by guessing. I will translate each of Ueshiba's messages and then add my own comments where necessary.

合気道の技という動きを表すものになっています。
[These three figures] illustrate the movements of aikido techniques.

三角（△）に入り身し、丸（○）く捌いて、四角（□）に納める。
You move into the opponent with *irimi* (*sankaku*/triangle), block or avoid the attack using a circular technique (*maru*/circle), and complete the defense with a throw (*shikaku*/square).

I need to comment on the *irimi* technique. As discussed in Chapter 5: "Five Practical Training Ideas to Improve Kata and Kumite," *irimi* refers to the act of entering straight into the technique as opposed to *taisabaki* (also mentioned in Chapter 5), which uses a more indirect entry. Direct responses to an attack are often excellent and very effective as they can easily knock the opponent off-balance. To learn more, check out the article "Irimi and Tenkan: Aikido's Demonstration of Yin and Yang" published on www.mainlinebudo.com on October 15, 2015: www.mainlinebudo.com/?p=1054.

> 合気道とは大自然の絶対愛を基として、体を△に象り○を中心に、気により△□の変化と気結び、生結びを身体に表わし、生み出しつつ気魂力を養成し、皆空の心と体を造り出す精妙なる道である。
> Aikido is based on the absolute love of the natural order. Make your body into the shape of the triangle. Make the shape of the circle your center. Connect the changes of the triangle and square using your ki. Your body must show the connection at the same time so you will develop the power of ki. As a result, aikido is a precise way to build the spirit and the body of total *ku* ['emptiness'].

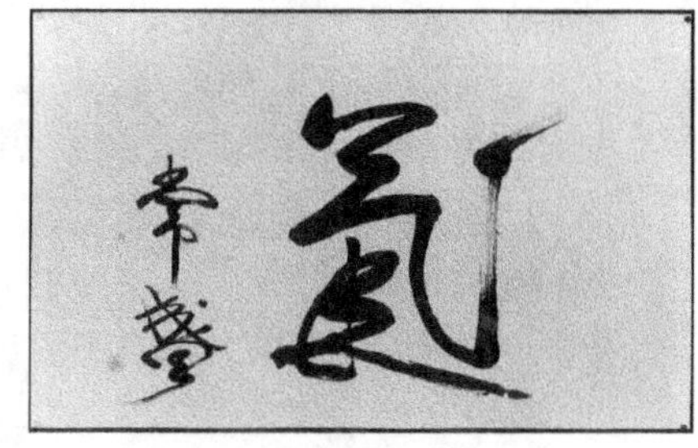

I am not sure what the reader thinks, but I am afraid this explanation sounds like a riddle to me. Since this statement does not quite make sense, we need to continue with the other explanations in the book and hopefully gain a better understanding of the teachings as we move on.

> 相手とムスビを作るまでの半身（三角体）の構えが△で、造化三神を象ったものです。
> The *hanmi kamae* (triangular posture) you assume before connecting to the opponent is a triangle and is a representation of Zoka Sanshin [a god of the number three].

I understand the posture of *hanmi*, so I understand that the triangle shape is a half-facing position. Unfortunately, I just do not understand why it is a representation of a god. I guess we just have to take it as his belief and simply consider it to be a name for this *kamae*.

> 宇宙を和と統一に結ぶの「和」が○、「統一」が□で表されています。
> *Wa* ['harmony'] and *toitsu* ['unity'] must be linked in the universe. *Wa* is represented by the circle, and *toitsu* is represented by the square.

I can understand the symbolism of the circle, which is harmony; however, I do not understand at this time why the square is unity. We need to read on and see if we can find the answer to this question.

> △○□が一体化となり、それが気の流れとともに円転してスミキルのが合気道。
> All three figures, △○□, become one body. Then, this body rotates along with the flow of ki and results in *sumikiru* ['being serene'], which is aikido.

I can understand conceptually how these three shapes could combine into one form. I can also understand that one rotates his body with the flow of ki. The most challenging word is *sumikiru*. *Sumi* means 'clear', and *kiru* means 'complete'; thus, the combination of these two elements means 'completely clear' or 'serene'. Ueshiba says that this serene mental and physical condition can be compared to the state of a fast-spinning top. When it spins very quickly, the axis is very steady, and the whole top looks as though it is still. So, as the body rotates, the practitioner's mind must be spinning at high speed. With this established, his body looks steady but, at the same time, has a lot of energy inside it. Ueshiba says this state of mind and body, *sumikiru*, is a *gokui* (極意, 'essential point', 'secret teaching', or 'ultimate understanding') of aikido.

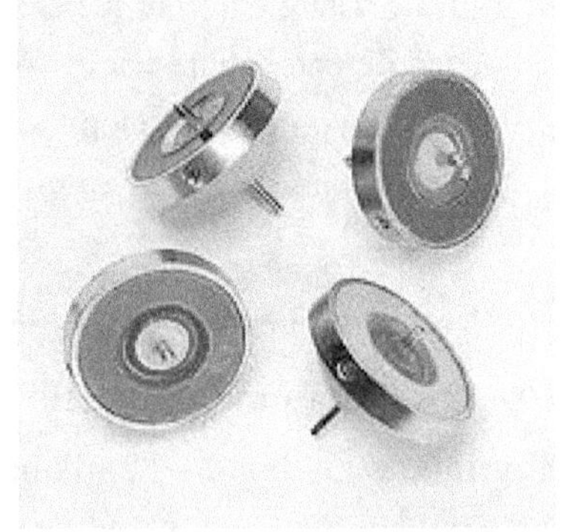

△○□が（一体）となって、これがまた丸く円になることが、合気道の実行である。

Aikido technique is illustrated by these three figures, △○□, which combine into one and form a circle.

Here is the religious symbolism of *sangen no hosoku* (三元の法則, 'the law of the three elements'), which is shown with the figures △○□. This could lead to more mysticism and confusion, but, hopefully, it will give us some idea of the complexity that is associated with these three figures. I will not translate all the characteristics and personalities of these three, but I will list some important ones that may be related to what we are discussing here.

表1　三元の法則（三光の原理）

△	○	□
気体	液体	固体
☆	☾	●
星	月	太陽
使命	生命	宿命
剣	玉	鏡
未来	現在	過去
真	善	美
智	仁	勇
塩	水	米
青色	赤色	黄色

The triangle (△, 三角, or 流) represents heaven and fire. It is a flowing material such as a gas. It flows with and by ki, which is the nature of animals. It is also a symbol of the stars, the sword, the future, and salt. Its color is blue or green.

The circle (○, 丸, or 柔) represents a flexible material such as a liquid, which is the nature of plants. It is also a symbol of the moon, jade, the present, and water. Its color is red.

The square (□, 四角, or 剛) represents earth. It is a hard, solid material, which is the nature of minerals. It is also a symbol of the sun, the mirror, the past, and rice. Its color is yellow.

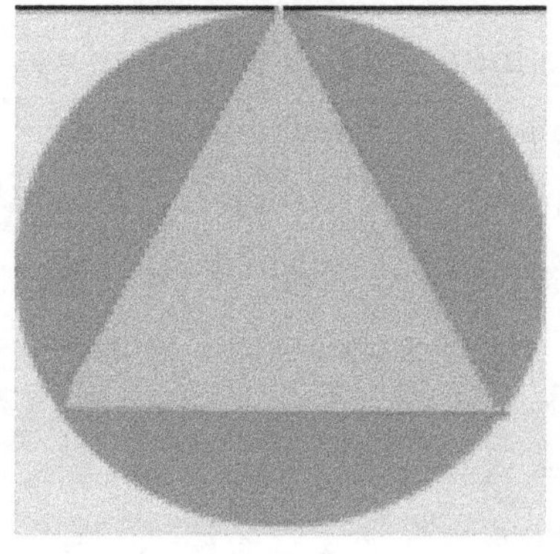

After reviewing these characteristics, I now understand why the square is unification. I believe it is the symbol for the final movement, such as a throw or an arm lock. It is the result of the unification of the body and mind (ki) with the opponent and the universe. As shown in the illustration to the left, you start with the triangle, which is then linked and covered by the circle. Finally, these are unified and positioned within the square.

Let me share some interesting information about the one-body format after the three figures are all combined within the square. Where do you think this design came from? Believe it or not, it is widely used as a part of an amulet of a very famous and highly prestigious Shinto shrine, Tsubaki Okami Yashiro (椿大神社), which you can read about at this URL: www.japanhoppers.com/en/kansai/tsu_suzuka/kanko/2376/.

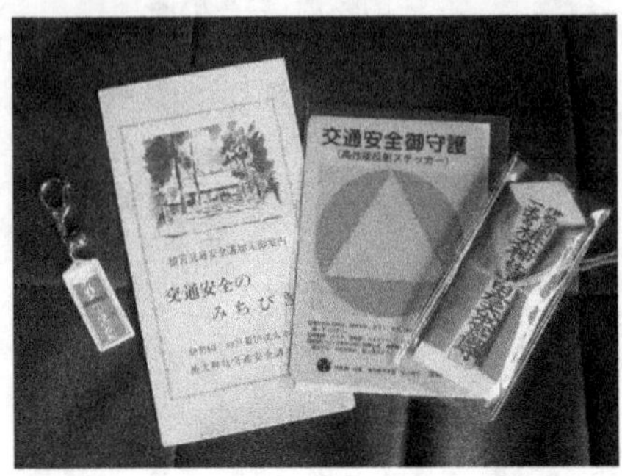

This amulet (photo left) is supposed to protect your car from traffic accidents. That is why the colors are red, green, and yellow to signify the colors of a traffic signal. Most likely you do not believe in the effect of this amulet, but this is not a joke. Many thousands of Japanese people who visit this shrine every month buy these amulets and hang them in their cars.

Next time you visit Japan, check and see if you can find one in a taxi or a bus as many taxi and bus companies buy these amulets to "protect" their vehicles and their passengers. In fact, passengers appreciate this very "responsible" act by the taxi and bus companies when they see an amulet in the vehicle they are riding in. The interesting thing is that if you were to ask those Japanese people if they really believe in the effects of the amulet, I am pretty sure ninety-nine percent of them would say no. They say they do not believe in superstition but also say it is better to have one in a taxi or a bus just in case.

Let me further explain these three figures. The idea of the three figures was not, in fact, originated by Ueshiba or aikido. Of course, this statement is not meant to belittle aikido's concept or its originality. The concept of the triangle, circle, and square has been around for hundreds of years in Japan and has been handed down to the present day. The photo shown on the introductory page of this chapter is of a brush painting of the three figures that was created in the eighteenth century by famous Zen Buddhist monk Gibon Sengai (仙厓義梵, 1750–1837). The title,

Uchu (宇宙, 'The Universe'), was given to it later by Daisetsu Suzuki (鈴木大拙, 1870–1966), a famous author of books and essays on Buddhism and Zen. You can read more about him at this URL: www.britannica.com/biography/D-T-Suzuki.

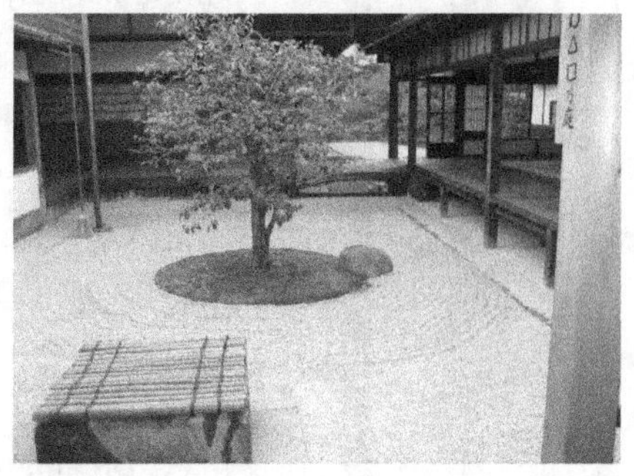

Also, next time you visit Kyoto, Japan, you may want to visit the famous Zen temple Kenninji (建仁寺), which you can read more about at this URL: www.kenninji.jp/english/index.html. In fact, this is the oldest Zen temple in Kyoto, and it is worthwhile to visit such a historic site. In addition, you can also visit its special garden, *Maru Sankaku Shikaku no Niwa* (○△□乃庭, '○△□ Garden' [photo above right]).

So, it is interesting to note that the idea of these three figures can be found not only in Shinto teachings but also in Buddhism, or at least in the Zen sect of Buddhism. Let me continue with my translation of a few more of Ueshiba's quotes so we may have a better understanding of his philosophy and understanding of martial arts.

> この私の中に宇宙があるのであります。すべてがあるのであります。宇宙が自分なのであります。宇宙そのものでありますから、自分もないのであります。また自分が宇宙であるから自分一人のみがあるのであります。
> The universe exists within my body. All matter exists within me. In other words, I am the universe. Since I am the universe, my individual existence does not exist. At the same time, I am the universe; thus, I exist alone.

This one is a little riddle but is also very interesting.

> 私は武道を通じて肉体の鍛錬を修行し、その極意を極めると同時に、より大いなる真理をもかちえたのである。すなわち武道を通じはじめて宇宙の真髄をつかんだ時、人間は〈心〉と〈肉体〉と、それをむすぶ〈気〉の三つが完全に一致し、しかも宇宙万有の活動と調和しなければいけないと悟ったのである。
> Through the physical training of *budo*, I attained its *gokui* ['ultimate understanding']

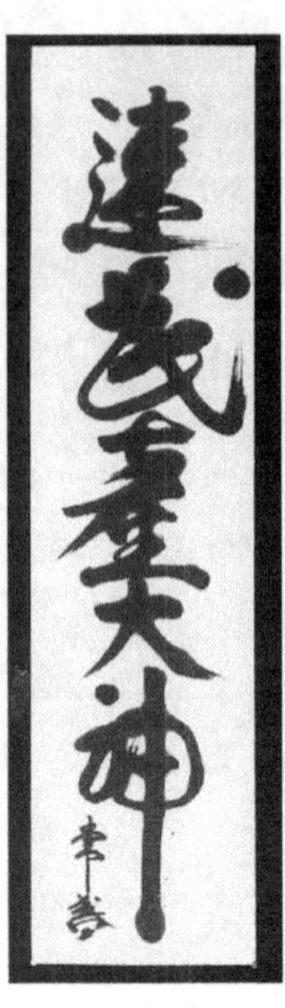

as well as the greater truth. In other words, when I first grasped the quintessence of the universe through *budo*, I came to understand that the three elements of the spirit, the body, and ki must completely unite and simultaneously harmonize with the actions of the entire universe.

つまり「気の妙用」によって、個人の心と肉体とを調和し、また個人と全宇宙との関係を調和せしめるのである。合気道は、真理の道である。合気道の鍛錬とは真理の鍛錬にほかならず、よく努め、よく実践し、よく究めつくすところすなわち「神業」を生ずるのである。
In other words, by using the "mysterious effect of ki," we can harmonize the spirit and body of the individual, and the relationship between the individual and the whole universe can also be harmonized. Aikido is the way of truth. Aikido training means nothing but the training of truth. Only by hard training, good application, and complete mastery will you be able to attain "superhuman feats."

合気道は、次のごとき三つの鍛錬を実行してこそ真理不動の金剛力が己の全身心に喰い入るのである。
一、己れの心を宇宙万有の活動と調和させる鍛錬。
一、己れの肉体そのものを宇宙万有の活動と調和させる鍛錬。
一、心と肉体とを一つにむすぶ気を、宇宙万有の活動と調和させる鍛錬。
Upon training in the following three disciplines, one can attain true and immovable supernatural power within his whole body and spirit.

- Train one's spirit to harmonize with the actions of the entire universe.
- Train one's body to harmonize with the actions of the entire universe.
- Train one's ki, which combines his body and spirit, to harmonize with the actions of the entire universe.

この三つを同時に、理屈でなく、道場において、また平常の時々刻々の場において実行しえた者のみが合気道の士なのである。
Only those who have been able to carry out these three disciplines, not just in theory but in the dojo as well as all throughout their daily lives, will be aikido practitioners.

かくのごとく熱心に稽古の徳を重ねるに至らば、相手と相対した時にいまだ手を出さぬうちに、すでに相手の倒れた姿が見える。そこでその方向に技をかけると、面白く投げられる。

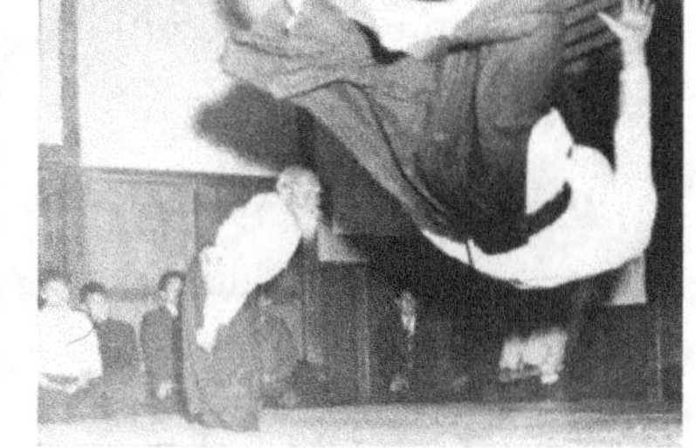

If you continue to attain the benefits of training to the level mentioned above, when an opponent confronts you, you will already be able to see his fallen figure before you start the fight. Once that happens, you can throw him without any effort whatsoever.

I conclude that these three figures represent the three stages of a typical aikido technique as shown below:

Stage 1 (triangle [△]): *irimi* (入り身, 'entry')
Stage 2 (circle [○]): *enten* (円転, 'rotation') or *tenkan* (転換, 'diversion')
Stage 3 (square [□]): *nage* (投げ, 'throw') or *katame* (固め, 'lock')

Ueshiba concludes with the following statement, which I find interesting:

三合一の真理や呼吸、合気の理解なくして合気道を稽古しても合気道の本当の力は出てこないだろう。
I suspect that unless you understand breathing, *aiki*, and the truth of *san go ichi*, you cannot achieve the true power of aikido, even if you practice aikido.

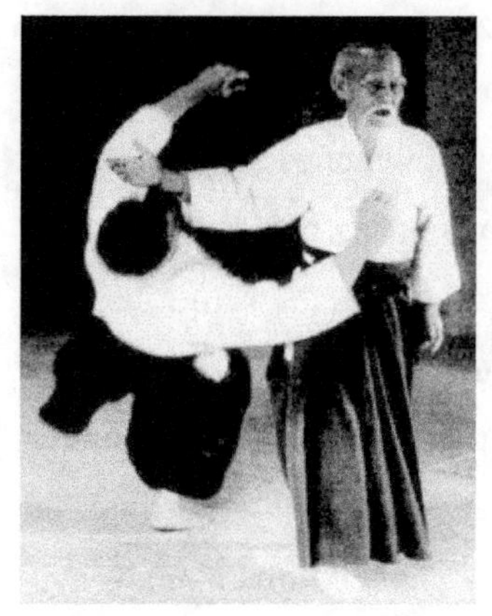

As a conclusion, he is saying that without understanding breathing, *aiki*, and the religious concepts, one cannot acquire true aikido. I can see and understand how with correct breathing methods and throwing techniques, one can execute aikido techniques. On the other hand, I also know that one can attain such power and develop excellent jujutsu techniques without *aiki* or religious understanding. Take a look at Ueshiba's teacher, Sokaku Takeda, and other jujutsu experts, such as Yukiyoshi Sagawa. They attained similar, if not greater, abilities without getting into the religious beliefs and concepts. At the same time, I am not disputing the legitimacy of his claim.

In the Western world, martial arts such as fencing and sword fighting have developed without including any religious concepts. On the other hand, it was very common in sixteenth- and seventeenth-century Japan for sword experts, such as Sekishusai Yagyu (柳生石舟斎, 1529–1606), Nobutsuna Kamiizumi (上泉信綱, c. 1508–c. 1573), Bokuden Tsukahara (塚原卜伝, 1489–1571), Ittosai Ito (伊東一刀斎, c. 1560–c. 1653), and many others, to tie their swordsmanship to religious concepts and beliefs. This is a very unique part of kenjutsu. We say, "*Satsuninken o katsuninken ni shoka shita*" (殺人剣を活人剣に昇華した, 'They turned the killing sword into a saving sword'). In other words, these sword experts turned their killing skill into a higher moral concept that would save rather than kill people. They say that once one achieves the highest level of swordsmanship, he can easily avoid killing his opponents in unnecessary fights as he wins before the fight starts. This is exactly what Ueshiba was saying when he stated that he could see his opponents already fallen on the floor before they even touched him.

Interestingly, Sagawa also attained a similar power that his students called *transparent power*, which became the title of the book I mentioned earlier. These students were thrown by Sagawa like a piece of cloth but could not figure out how the power was being generated. For instance, an opponent would be thrown backward as soon as he touched Sagawa's foot or sleeve as the latter would sit comfortably and totally relaxed in an easy chair. (The photos on page 119 show him carrying on a casual conversation with someone as he watches the incident.)

I have never practiced aikido or received any lessons on its philosophy in the past; therefore, I may not be qualified to make any judgments on the religious part. On the other hand, I will say that, as a martial artist in general and a *karateka* specifically, I can make some judgments on the technical part of aikido. The concept of the three stages (i.e., *irimi*, *enten*, and *nage*) makes sense and can work. In other words, by stepping in close to the opponent, you can off-balance him. Then, by using body rotation, you can position him so that he has to fall on his own. The final move is a small one that helps the opponent fall down. To outsiders, this looks like a throw, even though the person doing the throwing hardly puts any strength into the technique at all.

I can picture the karate version of these stages. *Irimi* is the same, so you step in as your opponent comes in with *jodan oi zuki*. You use one hand to block the *oi zuki* with *jodan nagashi uke*, and you use the other hand to counterattack. You do not need to put any strength into this counterattack at all. In fact, all you have to do is stick your fist out in front of the opponent's face and he will literally slam into it.

This combination of *uke waza* and *kaeshi waza* will work even more effectively if you add *tenshin* (転身, 'body rotation'). Since this is not a how-to chapter, I will not explain the details, but you execute the *tenshin* footwork simultaneously with the *uke waza* and *kaeshi waza*. With a *tenshin* movement, you end up facing the opponent at a forty-five- to ninety-degree angle, which is much more advantageous than being directly in front of him. Once you become proficient at *tenshin* movements, you can even position yourself behind the opponent with one step and a turn.

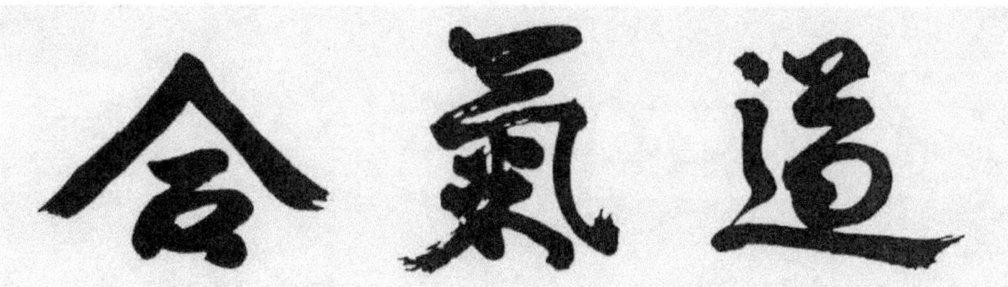

As I close this chapter, I wish to add that I consider karate to be my religion and my dojo (or wherever I train) to be my shrine or temple, so I do not feel uncomfortable with Ueshiba's approach. But, there are two main differences. One is that I do not have any ties or connections to any of the Shinto or Buddhism sects. The other, which may be a bigger difference, is that Ueshiba had a mystical experience that took him to the ultimate level of martial arts. So far, I have not had any mystical experiences to enlighten me. This must mean that I am still far away from the ultimate level; thus, I will simply continue my daily training.

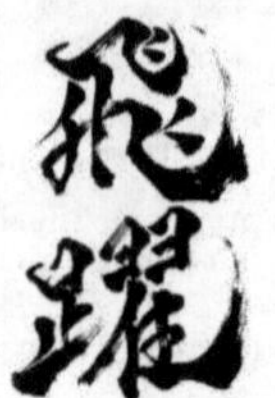

Chapter Twelve
第十二章

Do Not Explain in Karate Training
稽古での説明は悪効果

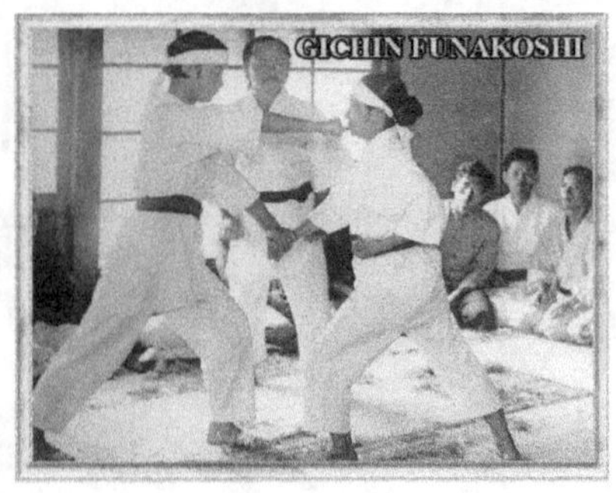

I am sure you were shocked and maybe even offended by the title of this chapter. Of course, I chose this title to catch your full attention. I expect I will get a lot of pushback from it, but give me a chance to explain why I think it is better not to explain when we teach karate.

If you happen to have a Japanese sensei or have had one in the past, I suspect you have noticed that your sensei does not or did not explain too much in his karate class. Many people may blame this on the language barrier. While it is true that many Japanese sensei are not fluent in the local language, whether it be English, French, Spanish, or whatever, I emphasize that this is the basic attitude of Japanese instructors in general, regardless of language ability. I can say this because of my personal experience not only as a student but also as a teacher, but here I wish to present a very good logical reason for it.

Before I go into the explanation of this logical reason, I would like to share a little background about the Japanese word *manabu* (学ぶ, 'learn'). This word's origin is *manebu*, which means 'imitate'. So, the original concept of learning something for the ancient Japanese was that of imitating the teacher. This is why we have the concept of *shuhari* (守破離). Many readers may already know the meaning of this, but it is a concept that describes the stages of learning to mastery. To explain this concept, let me quote aikido instructor Seishiro Endo (遠藤征四郎, 1942– [photo right]).

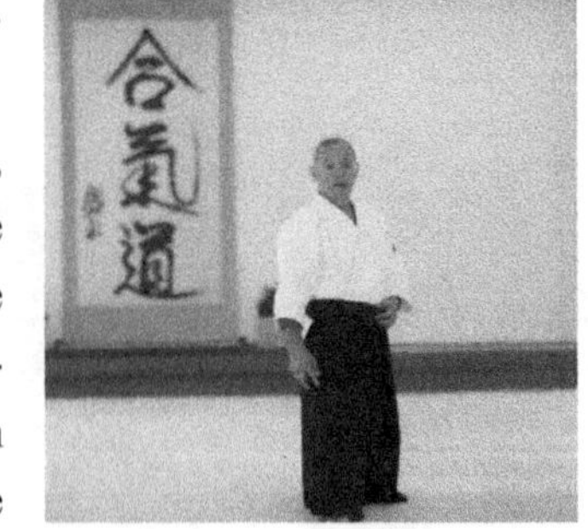

> It is known that, when we learn or train in something, we pass through the stages of *shu*, *ha*, and *ri*. These stages are explained as follows. In *shu*, we repeat the forms and discipline ourselves so that our bodies absorb the forms that our forebears created. We remain faithful to these forms with no deviation. Next, in the

stage of *ha*, once we have disciplined ourselves to acquire the forms and movements, we make innovations. In this process, the forms may be broken and discarded. Finally, in *ri*, we completely depart from the forms, open the door to creative technique, and arrive in a place where we act in accordance with what our heart/mind desires, unhindered while not overstepping laws.

So, the main idea is that while you are learning in the *shu* stage, all you are expected to do is repeat and imitate. This means you repeat the same thing without thinking or trying to be different. In fact, this idea was even more prevalent when I was in school some fifty to sixty years ago. I remember that we, as karate students, never asked our sensei or our senpai any questions. We knew that we were not supposed to ask any questions during the training session. Without exaggeration, the only word we could use was *osu* (オス). If we dared to ask any questions about techniques, *kata*, *kumite*, or anything else, they never gave us any answers. Instead, they would come back with a sharp statement such as "Keep your eyes open," "Watch more carefully," "Practice more," etc.

When we had a question that we believed was important, we, only once in a while, dared to ask. However, it was important to pick the right moment, which always had to be after the class was over. We would wait until we had gone to a restaurant or a café after training if we wanted to ask something. In a casual environment, while we were talking about social subjects, we used to slip a question or two into the conversation. Regardless, I remember it was awfully difficult to ask our sensei a technical question.

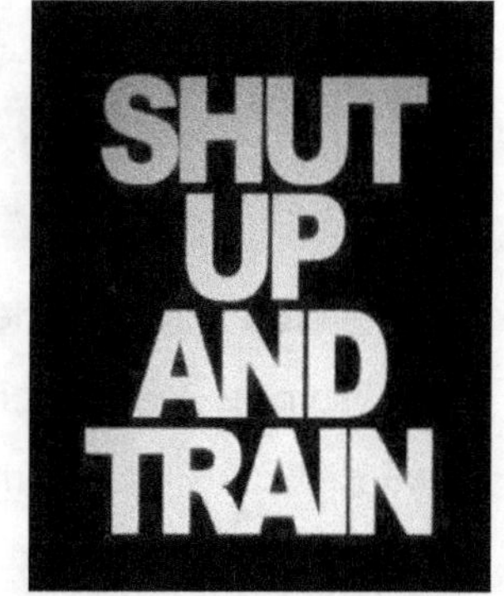

Even though this situation may have changed somewhat since those days, I am pretty sure that this basic concept has not changed much in Japan. I suspect that you consider this to be a terrible learning situation. You are half right but have missed the point on the other half. Let me explain further.

Do you think this "barrier" prevents students from learning or at least slows them down? I suspect this is considered to be the case in countries outside of Japan. If you are a karate instructor—I imagine many of you are—I am sure you try to give a lot of explanation on the key points of the techniques and many things about karate. I have watched many classes taught by both Japanese and non-Japanese instructors in classes outside of Japan and have found that the latter spend much more effort and energy on verbal communication.

Japanese instructors tend to speak less and demonstrate more. This is partially due to their weakness with foreign languages. Regardless, we Japanese instructors feel uncomfortable when we see non-Japanese instructors spend so much time explaining technical matters, especially difficult subjects, with great enthusiasm. It is not my intention to bash these instructors, but I feel they are almost in love with themselves or ecstatic about showing their own knowledge. I apologize if I have offended anyone, but this is my true impression, and I am pretty sure many other Japanese instructors would agree with me.

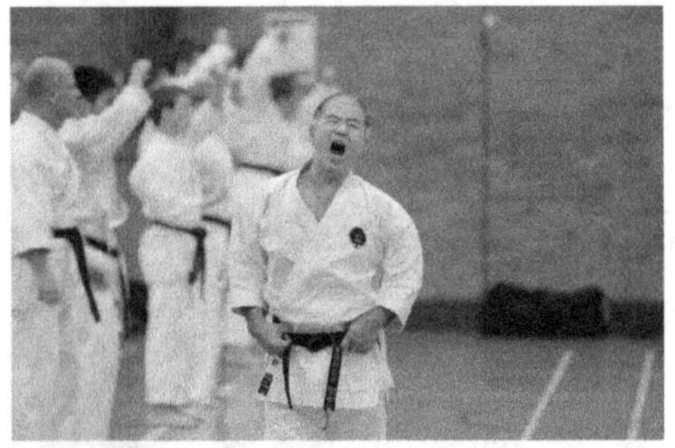

OK, we must agree that there is a difference in teaching styles because of the difference in culture. In fact, many Japanese instructors believe that giving too much explanation is bad for learning. As I have already mentioned, many of them lack language ability, but this is still the same even in Japan, where we have no difficulty with language. It is probably a big mystery to the reader to find out that Japanese sensei do not believe in giving much explanation. You may have noticed this before but most likely did not know why and probably ended up guessing it was just because of the language problem.

Let's investigate why Japanese instructors prefer to explain less. First of all, the most important reason comes from culture. Believe it or not, we do not value verbal explanation too much when it comes to learning anything, but this is especially true when it involves a physical or technical skill. This comes from the belief that words are imperfect and are unable to describe anything fully and adequately.

Further—and this is probably shocking to Westerners—we do not believe too much in logic. We avoid people who like to argue. In fact, have you noticed that most Japanese people are poor at giving speeches and presentations? We never learn how to speak eloquently in school. Using a joke to help the students relax during a karate lesson is almost unthinkable and impossible for a Japanese sensei (with the exception of those who have lived abroad).

We consider it almost impossible and unrealistic for the student to fully understand a physical thing (something that happens inside the body, which is very personal) through verbal explanation. Japanese instructors feel that he must learn physically with his own body by repeating the technique thousands of times. In other words, he must feel it and know it with his body.

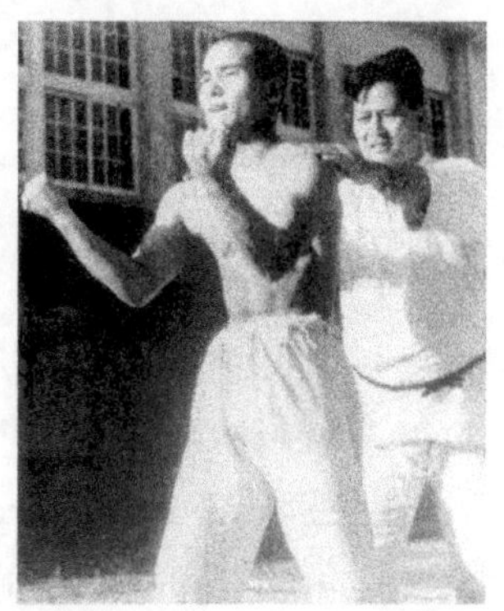

Japanese martial arts instructors tend to give little explanation during their classes because they also believe explanation results in a long period of time of not doing anything, which is not good for the student, either mentally or technically. Since they ascribe less value to thinking, they encourage the student to keep moving and repeating the techniques.

In addition, these instructors do not expect most students to understand not only karate techniques but also concepts related to *kata*, *kumite*, *bunkai*, etc., in the initial phase or even during the first few years. In fact, they consider this to be a necessary stage.

Think of a situation where an instructor spends a lot of time and energy explaining something difficult, such as ki, breathing methods, *gamaku*, *muchimi*, etc. The student may gain some understanding on this subject, so what's wrong with that? If the student understands something, hasn't the teacher fulfilled his duty? Yes, that is how it will be regarded in countries outside of Japan. Japanese instructors, however, think that even though the student may feel as though he has gained some understanding, it is not a true or full understanding. In fact, the student is unable to demonstrate that "something," even if he thinks he has understood it. We consider a purely mental understanding to be a dangerous state as it does not coincide with a physical understanding in most cases. We fear that the student is not ready and that a premature "understanding" will only harm the natural development of his karate skill.

Let's look at another easy example. How about swimming, which is also an acquired skill? You cannot swim unless you learn how, especially if we are talking about a difficult swimming method such as the butterfly stroke. Let's take a student who happens to be such a novice that he does not even know how to float and is afraid to put his face in the water. If he is impressed with Michael Phelps (photo left), he may ask his swimming instructor how to do the butterfly stroke like him. Of course, the instructor does not want to crush the student's excitement or interest, but a Japanese instructor will not spend time explaining how to do a dolphin kick, etc. He will tell him, "Yes, Phelps is great. I will teach you how to do a dolphin kick once you learn how to float." Once the student learns how to float, he may realize he has to learn other important things, such as how to do a dog paddle, how to hold his breath with his face in the water, etc.

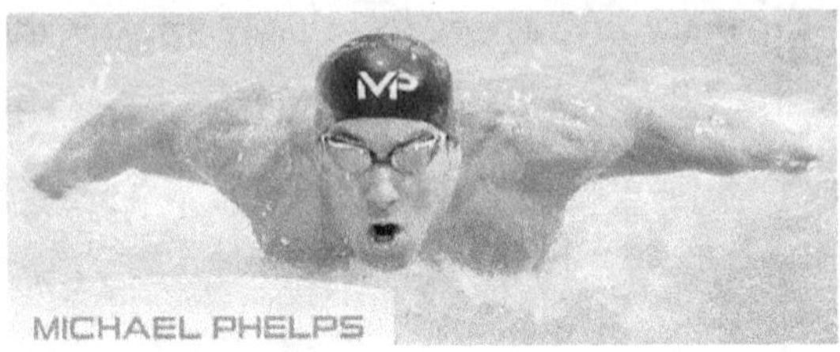

MICHAEL PHELPS

As you know, karate skill requires much more complex physical and mental techniques. In the water, as long as you can float, you can save yourself, even if you cannot do the butterfly stroke. However, in a life-or-death situation (or even in a street fight), failure to perform a technique could result in serious injury, possibly even death.

As I mentioned earlier, we Japanese instructors do not rely too much on verbal communication and understanding when it comes to learning a skill. Instead, we ascribe value to physical understanding. This is exactly why we demand that our students look closely and imitate us as much as possible. This is true not only in the martial arts but also in other arts. You can find the same teaching method in carpentry, cooking, brushed calligraphy, Zen study, etc.

When you become an apprentice to a master carpenter, your boss will not teach

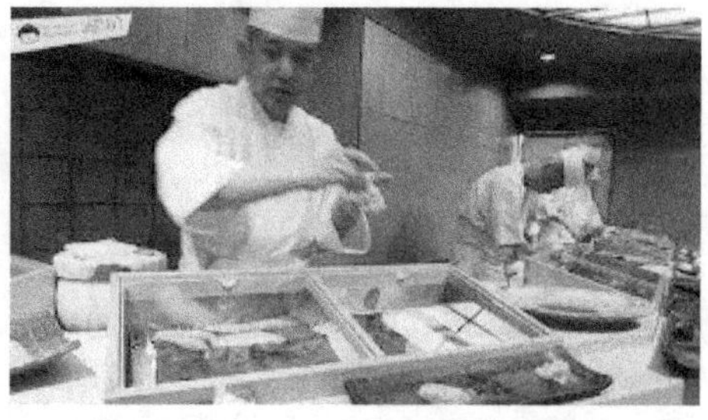

you any carpentry skills, at least for several years, if ever. It is your job to "steal" such skills by watching your boss. The same goes for culinary arts, such sushi preparation (photo right). Why does sushi taste better in Japan? It is not because the fish or rice is better. It is because the sushi chef has been properly trained for at least several years before being able to begin preparing food and serving it to customers.

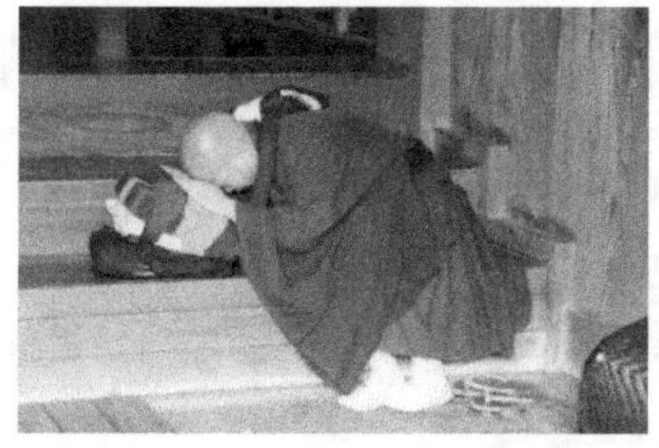

Another good example is found in a Zen monastery, where monks are trained through a daily schedule that is very strict and harsh (from a secular point of view). First, candidates must beg to be admitted by waiting at the temple entrance in a half-sitting position (photo left). This challenge is called *niwazume* (庭詰), which literally means 'staying in the garden' (photo right). If a candidate wishes to join the Zen temple, he must arrive at the gate in the early morning and stay there in a half-sitting position, bowing down to show his desire to join. He continues in this position for nine to ten hours that day. During that period, the monks in the temple will ask him to leave and will sometimes even gently drag him out of the gate. However, this is a part of the ritual, so he must not give up if he is determined to become a monk at this temple. He has to continue his request to be admitted by sitting at the front entrance all day long. After a long day of sitting, the monks will allow him to come in to eat dinner and stay overnight. But, this does not mean the candidate has been admitted. He must restart the waiting process at the front entrance at 4:00 or 5:00 the next morning.

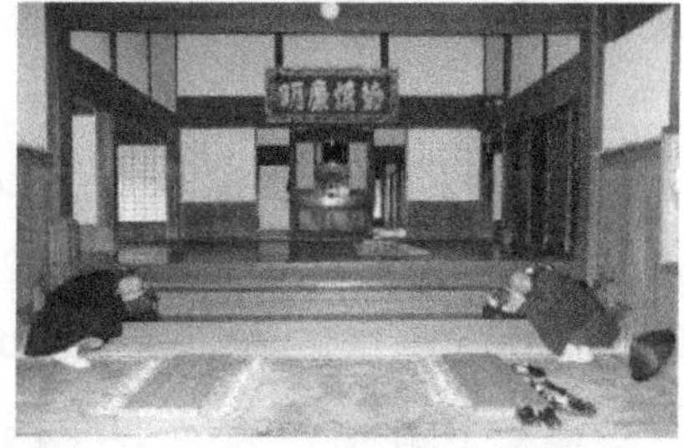

This harsh patience-testing ritual lasts two or three days. However, this is only the first step of the entrance examination. If the candidate can sustain the few days of waiting at the front entrance, the monks will invite him in and ask him to show his interest in joining the temple by sitting in Zen meditation about twelve hours a day for one week. After succeeding at these two tests, the candidate can finally be admitted to the temple as a regular monk in training. After this, he starts a Zen monk life that is filled with Zen meditation and work around the temple. Here is a typical daily schedule at Sogenji (曹源寺) in Okayama Prefecture (岡山県):

3:40 AM:	Wake up
4:00 AM:	Morning service (sutra recitation)
5:00 AM:	Meditation (*zazen* [座禅])
7:00 AM:	Breakfast
8:00 AM:	Daily cleaning (*nitten soji* [日転掃除])
8:30 AM:	Garden work (*samu* [作務])
10:00 AM:	Meditation
12:00 PM:	Lunch
1:00 PM–2:00 PM:	Bath (first group)
2:00 PM–4:00 PM:	Work
4:00 PM–5:00 PM:	Bath (second group)
5:00 PM:	Dinner
6:00 PM:	Meditation
9:00 PM:	Lights out (*kaichin* [開枕])

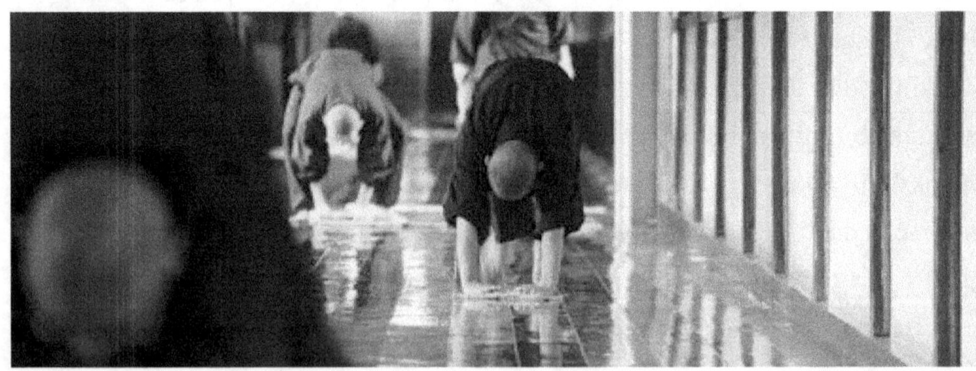

Even though I am writing about karate instruction, I have spent a lot of space explaining Zen monastery rules. This is to show that Zen monks consider actions to be much more important than words. As you know, Zen is a religion whose adherents seek enlightenment. During hours of Zen meditation, a monk tries to reach an enlightened state of mind but encounters many questions, such as "What am I?"; "What is the purpose of my life?"; "How can I be enlightened?"; "Why is there good and bad in this world?"; etc. The monk master of a given temple is supposed to have been enlightened, so a monk in training who is seeking an answer may ask such questions of the master.

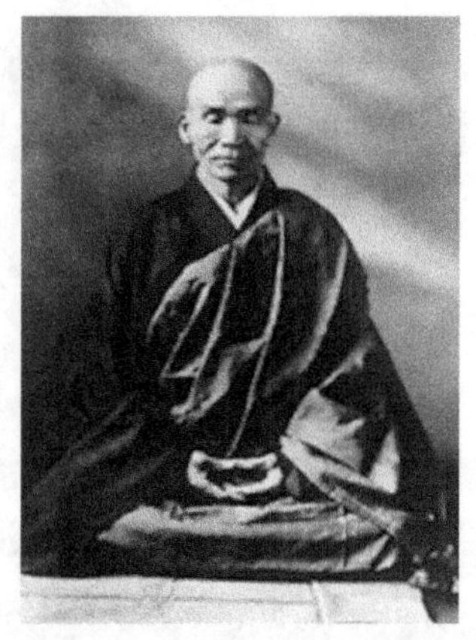

The master will never explain anything. He won't even try. He will simply say, "Do not think," or, "Get busy." He discourages thinking and demands that the monk do things. During Zen meditation, a monk is supposed to empty his mind. This is very difficult; however, he learns how to do it by spending many hours just sitting. He may see the light when he is engaged in garden work, hall cleaning, sutra chanting, etc., rather than when he is thinking during meditation.

So, these examples illustrate that Japanese instructors believe much more in the value of demonstrating techniques with their own body than in that of explaining with words. In Japan, you will see the same tendency not only in karate but also in other martial arts, such as kenjutsu, iaido, kyudo (弓道), aikido, etc.

Lastly, we must consider the fact that karate—not just the techniques but the total structure and system of empty-handed fighting—requires one of the most difficult physical skills. This may sound like a biased statement, but it is logically sound and can be intellectually explained. Thus, Japanese instructors believe it is almost impossible to explain the most critical part of the techniques, so they tell their students, "Practice more."

So, is this approach of not explaining better than the method found in the Western world? My short answer is that it all depends. I believe this practice of not

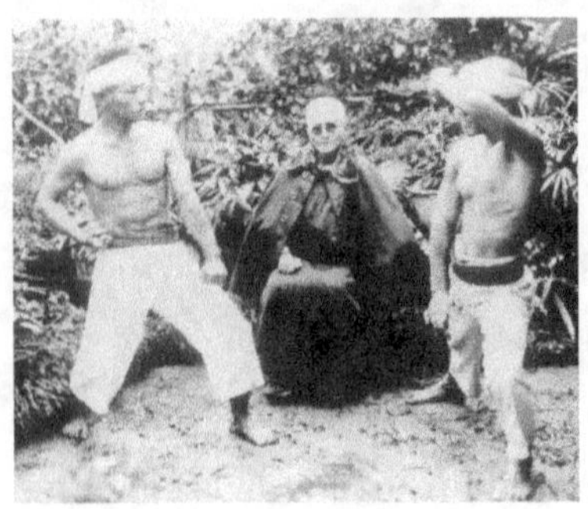

explaining can become an excuse for a Japanese instructor so that he can hide his ignorance or lack of knowledge. If he has to face all kinds of questions, he will be forced to study and learn more. So, in this sense, I like the Western method.

On the other hand, karate skill development is a slow progression that comes in a gradually ascending form. In other words, you need to go one step at a time, which means that your body needs to be trained. Understanding, or believing that you understand, a technique is totally different from being able to execute that technique. Proper understanding comes at the right time, after having repeated the technique thousands of times. Trying to understand these things in your head before the proper time can not only act as worthless self-satisfaction but also become hazardous to your sound karate achievement.

A similar effect is found when a student learns an advanced *kata* before reaching the level at which it is normally taught. I have seen a brown belt run Unsu at a tournament. The instructor of this student is responsible and should be blamed for this ignorant action. We must all know that karate achievement is similar to building a house. If the foundation or the walls are weak, the house will not be able to withstand an earthquake or a storm. Lifetime karate training is more like building a skyscraper of fifty stories or more. The importance of having a solid foundation and a firm structure becomes even more critical.

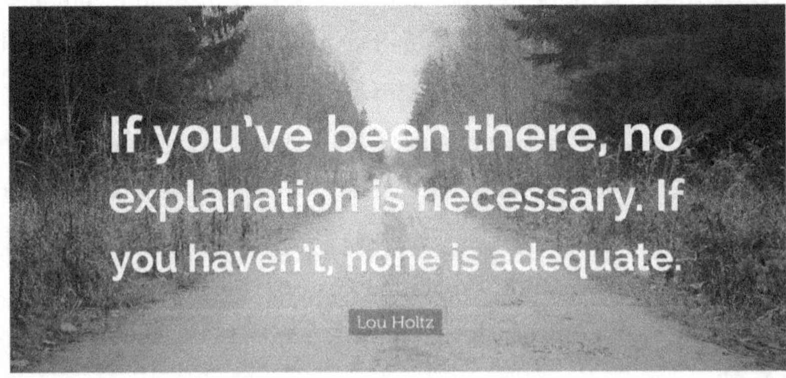

Conclusion

When you teach karate in the Western world, it is important and necessary to include some verbal explanation. Karate training must be truly physical, but, at the same time, thinking must be encouraged. Instructors must remember that they need to be very careful in determining how much explanation is appropriate and necessary. This is because too much explanation can not only waste valuable training time but also be harmful to students who are not mentally or physically ready for it. This can be equated with a situation where an instructor teaches a black-belt *kata* to a colored-belt student or engages a beginner in *jiyu kumite*. The competence of a karate instructor should be determined not only by his karate skill but also by his teaching skill, which includes knowing how much explanation is appropriate.

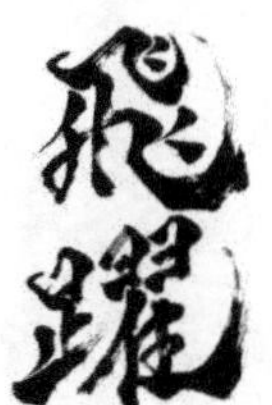

Chapter Thirteen
第十三章

Kuse: the Greatest Enemy of Improvement
癖：上達への最大の敵

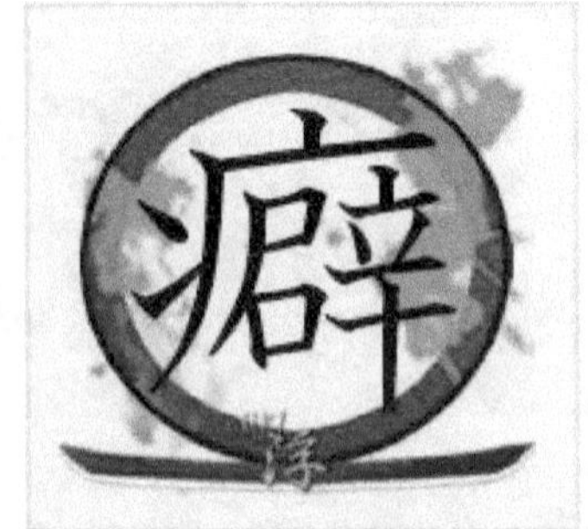

What does the Japanese word *kuse* (癖) mean? Surprisingly, it is not a difficult word, even though the kanji looks complicated. It simply means 'habit'. In this chapter, I will present *kuse* as our greatest enemy.

Since you are a smart reader, you will quickly guess that I am referring to a bad habit, such as getting lazy or sloppy in your training. There are many other bad habits that are not good for your karate improvement, either, but I will not discuss these kinds of bad habits in this chapter.

This may come as a surprise to some since I just mentioned that these bad habits are not good for your karate training; however, these are too obvious, so there is no need to discuss them in depth. If this is the case, I am sure you are asking, "Then, what kinds of habits are you talking about?" To answer this, I wish to touch on a subject that is not so often recognized or discussed not only by karate practitioners but also by instructors.

First, I need to mention that there are two kinds of habits, but I am not classifying them as good and bad. This subject is a little more complex than that, so I need to explain in detail what they are.

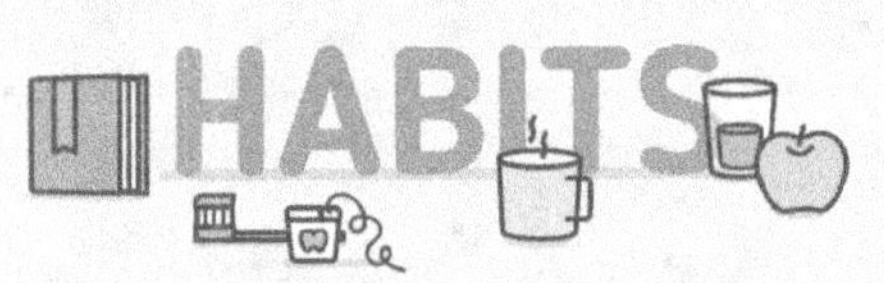

One kind of habit is a popular one that you will know well. It is a routine that is repeated regularly and tends to occur unconsciously. The *American Journal of Psychology* (University of Illinois Press, 1903) states, "A habit, from the standpoint of psychology, is a more or less fixed way of thinking, willing, or feeling acquired through previous repetition of a mental experience."

Examples of this kind of habit are brushing your teeth after each meal, ironing your shirts after doing the laundry, etc. Another example that will be familiar to the reader is your commitment to go to the dojo multiple times every week. This example happens to be a good habit, and this routine certainly helps you in your karate development. There are many routine-type habits that are not so good for you. Examples are gambling or eating junk food.

Even though these routines are habits, they are not called *kuse* in Japanese. We have another word for these: *shukan* (習慣). This literally means 'learned routine' and serves to distinguish these habits from the kind I will explain later.

After repeatedly going to the dojo four or five times weekly for, say, ten years, you cannot think of a life in which you do not go to the dojo at all. You feel uncomfortable going even one week without training during your vacation. Another routine-type habit is eating junk food and drinking soda, which is saturated with sugar. This is also learned after repeating similar behavior but is not good for the *karateka* who wants to stay slim and in shape. So, these types of habits can be good, bad, or even neutral, which I will not explain here. As *karateka*, we must always have a strong will to form and keep good routine-type habits.

Having said that, the very subject I wish to discuss in this chapter is the other kind of habit. This is the one that receives little attention in karate training but should receive more. It can be classified as habitual behavior. It is the unconscious body movements that are developed by repetition but, most of the time, without definitive intentions or self-analysis. People repeat a behavior because it is easy, gives them comforting, or provides a rewarding feeling.

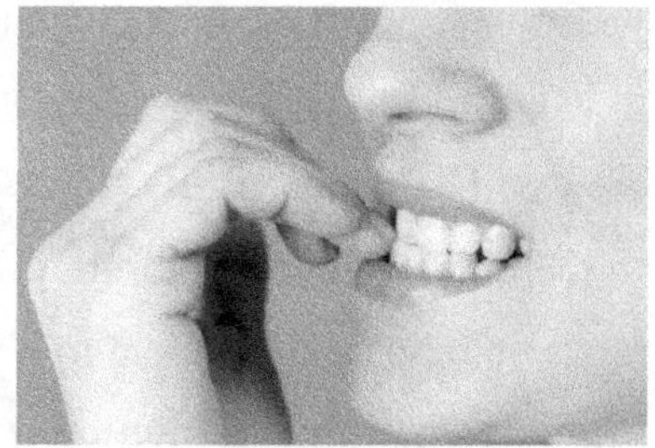

For instance, you are familiar with nail biting, fidgeting, twitching, or tapping the desk with your fingers. There are other examples that you can probably think of that we do when we are nervous, thinking, bored, or deeply upset. But, there are also other kinds of habits that do not come from nervousness or boredom. This is a group of physical movements that are found in your daily life.

For example, you can find this in the way you walk. When you walk, do you know how you step or how your feet move? I am sure most people do not know whether their feet are parallel or are pointing in or out. In fact, most of us would

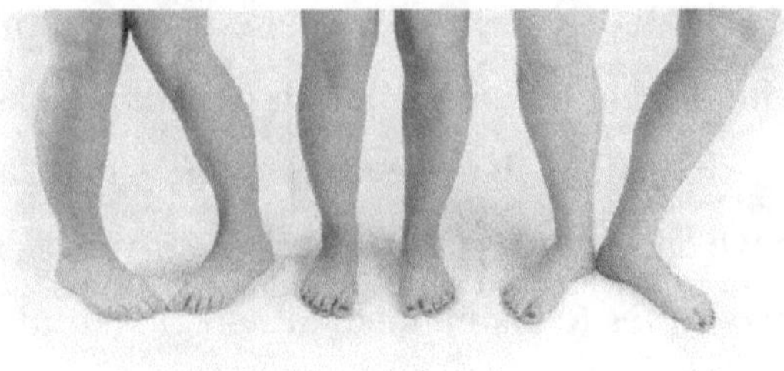

never pay attention to this. How you walk is a habit that is hardly noticed. Thus, this kind of habit is a lot more difficult to modify or get rid of. The way you move your feet is only a part of how you walk. Your posture, how you move your arms, etc., also characterize your walk. In addition, there are other physical movements that are like this, such as how you speak, how you eat, how you sit, and many more.

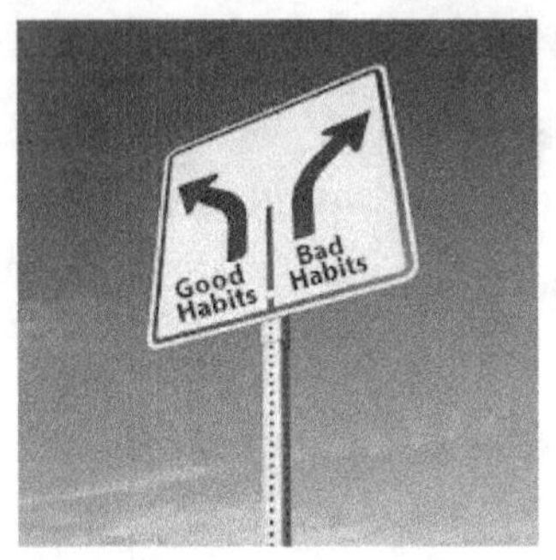

A bad habit is an undesirable behavioral pattern, and not all those habits you have are good or desirable. If you look at your walking habit, you may find yourself slouching and want to correct that. With repetition, you can change it. On the other hand, you must realize that old habits are hard to break, and new habits are hard to form, especially if the old habits were formed many years ago. This is because the behavioral patterns we repeat are imprinted on our neural pathways. The longer the behavioral patterns exist, the longer it takes to change them. You can understand this as you think about the way you walk every day. If you wish to change old habits, it is possible to do so by forming new habits through repetition. However, this process of habit reformation can be slow and demands effort. This is why I say this is the culprit and the biggest barrier to the improvement of karate skills.

You may come back at me, saying, "Wait a minute. The way I walk has nothing to do with my karate improvement." You are partially correct. Even though a martial artist must be able to walk with an excellent method and posture, the habits I am referring to in karate are different. Let me bring up a few examples of *kuse* in karate movements that are quite common. Each practitioner has a different set of *kuse* that need to be corrected, but I cannot cover them all. I wish to share only three situations and a few problem areas that are very common. These errors, however minor they may be, need to be corrected if you wish to reach an advanced level of karate.

Example 1: *Zenkutsu Dachi*

Zenkutsu dachi is probably the most popular stance in traditional karate styles. It is a very versatile stance that is good for both attack and defense. Thus, I am sure you will agree that the development of an excellent, if not perfect, *zenkutsu dachi* is quite critical and necessary for your improvement in karate. You will probably also agree that it is a challenging stance for all of us.

There are many key points and important requirements, such as hip position, pelvis angle, etc. Since the purpose of this chapter is not to discuss correct stance, I will select just three of the most common errors related to the legs and feet in *zenkutsu dachi*.

The first error is not bending the front leg enough (photo below left). I know this requires a strong leg, but the lower leg, that is, the portion between the knee and the ankle, must be perpendicular to the floor.

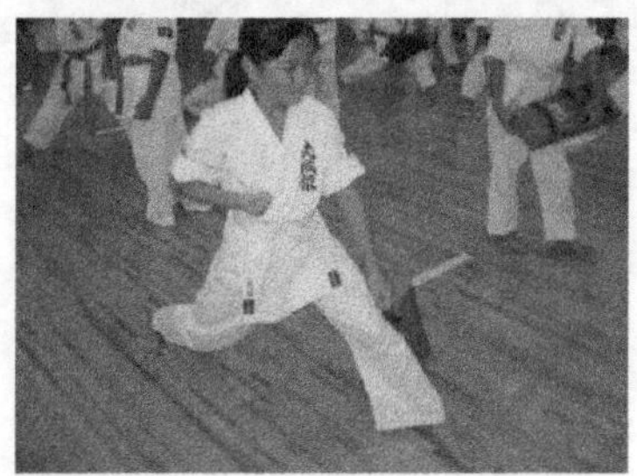

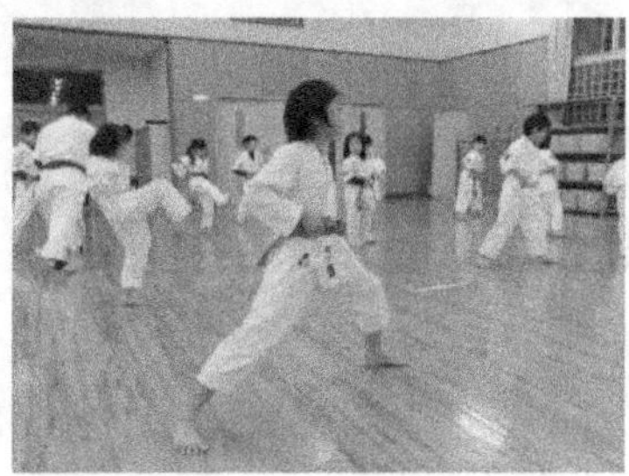

The student in the photo shown above right has a pretty good bend on the front leg. Her error is found in the rear leg, particularly the ankle. This is a very common problem that comes from having either a stiff ankle or a stance that is too long. The rear foot should be pointing forward at an angle of thirty to forty-five degrees.

The *kuro obi* in the photo at the top of the following page has a good bend on the front leg, and the rear foot is also pointing forward at the correct angle. This per-

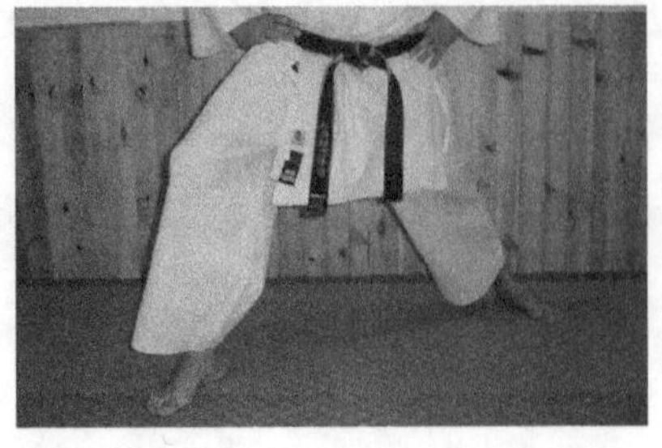

son's error is found in the front foot, which is pointing outward. This makes the stance weak and also slows shifting and leg techniques.

Do you find these errors among the students in your dojo? I am sure you do. If you continue to practice karate with these errors in this stance, they will become *kuse*. That is, they will become fixed, making them very comfortable and natural. Needless to say, it will be very time consuming and challenging if you decide to change them.

Example 2: *Choku Zuki*

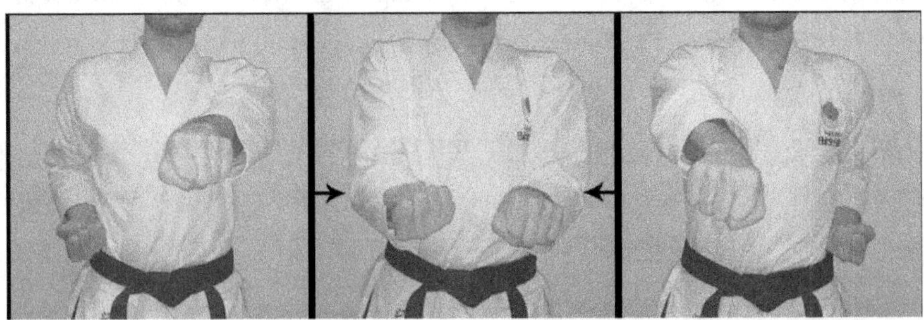

Choku zuki is one of the most popular striking techniques in karate. There are many key points to this technique, too. Once again, I will pick out three of the most common errors.

The first error is swinging the elbow out. *Choku zuki* is probably one of the first techniques you learned. When you first learned it, you may remember that you were told to keep your elbow in as you punched. I am sure you also remember that it was very difficult to do this as your elbow seemed to naturally go out. This arm-swinging punch is frequently used in street fights. In karate, we have a similar punching method called *mawashi uchi* (回し打ち, 'roundhouse punch' or 'round punch'), but the mechanics are somewhat different. Regardless, in karate, *choku zuki* is the most popular, and swinging the elbow out is strongly discouraged. At the same time, this natural body movement is the very reason it was so difficult to keep your elbow in.

You may say that this arm-swinging punch (photo below left) is popularly used in boxing and that the straight punch (photo below right), though it is used, is not too popular. This is true, and it is an important subject, so we must discuss it a little here and try to figure out why.

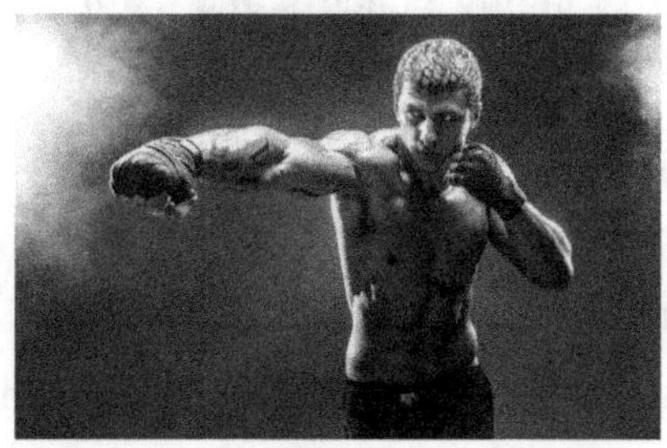

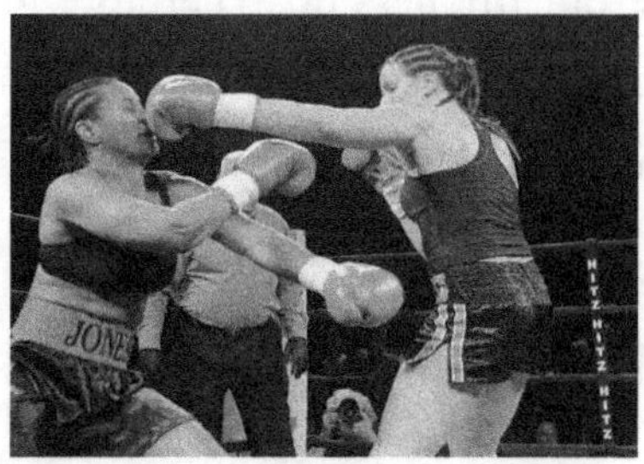

I think there are at least two major reasons. One is the difference in the effectiveness of each punch. In other words, a punch received to the side of the head is much more effective (that is, easier to knock an opponent down with) than a straight punch, especially when delivered with a boxing glove. In general, a person can withstand a strong punch to the chin, or even to the nose. However, when that punch lands on the temple, the shock will shake the brain sideways, which can easily result in a knockdown or temporary unconsciousness. In fact, it is almost impossible to knock an opponent down with a straight punch in boxing. This is the same reason *mawashi geri* is more popular than *mae geri* in full-contact karate tournaments.

The second reason is the way in which the fight takes place. In karate, we are training for a one-punch-one-kill situation. Even though we expect to face a second, or possibly even a third, attack, the ideal situation is to knock the opponent down with one punch or one kick. This means your punch must be almost invisible as such an unexpected punch can have a devastating effect on the opponent (such as a knockout).

In a boxing match, on the other hand, stealth is not the key requirement. The arm-swinging punch is quite visible and takes a little longer to travel in its circular trajectory, but the large boxing gloves make it much easier to block the straight punch. Thus, the arm-swinging punch is more frequently used in boxing despite its shortcomings.

Similarly, although the straight punch is faster and less visible, street fighters have not taken on the pain of going through years of training to master it the way karate practitioners do. Therefore, the arm-swinging punch is the natural choice for street fighters and the one more frequently used by them.

Another error your sensei might have corrected when you were a white belt is your shoulder. The shoulder of the punching side in *choku zuki* tends to come up. This comes from unnecessary tension in the muscles of the shoulder area. Your sensei might have also told you to tense the armpit as you brought the shoulder down. Since the mechanics of *choku zuki* are not natural for a white belt, the muscles of the shoulder area are tense, resulting in a raised shoulder. This is a common *kuse* that persists among beginners.

The third error is found in the fist rotation of *choku zuki*. The mechanics of this movement are new to the beginner and thus difficult to master. It is difficult enough to rotate one fist, but the challenge is even greater than that as you must rotate both fists in opposing directions. Do you remember how many times you had to practice this before it became natural to you?

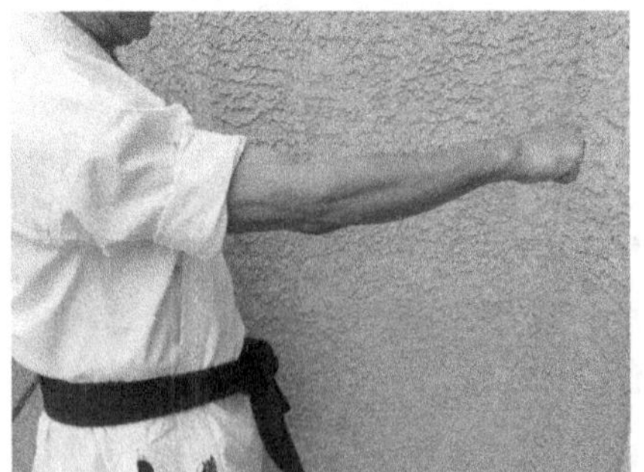

The common problem I would like to present here is not the fist itself but rather the position of the elbow. In order to avoid tennis elbow, you must place your elbow so that it is pointing downward rather than horizontally (photo left). This is a very common problem, but it is not corrected by some instructors, unfortunately. In fact, many instructors do not know that this can lead to serious injury. Being able to keep the elbow pointing downward requires continuous effort and special training of the arm muscles. Otherwise, it is natural for the elbow to turn with the fist and end up positioned horizontally (pointing outward).

This elbow position is also a *kuse* that is extremely difficult to change. It is an important issue that I specifically discuss in Chapter 11: "The Relationship between Choku Zuki and the Elbow Position" of my book *Karatedo Paradigm Shift*.

Example 3: *Mae Geri*

Mae geri is probably the most popular kicking technique in traditional karate. We practice this kick thousands of times to make it perfect. Here are three of the most common errors that are prevalent among practitioners.

The first error has to do with balance. You need to learn how to keep your balance when you kick. It is already difficult to do this while just standing on one leg. If you use the other leg for kicking, the challenge becomes even greater. What beginners do is swing their arms around to keep their balance (photo right). What's wrong with this? Well, there are two major problems.

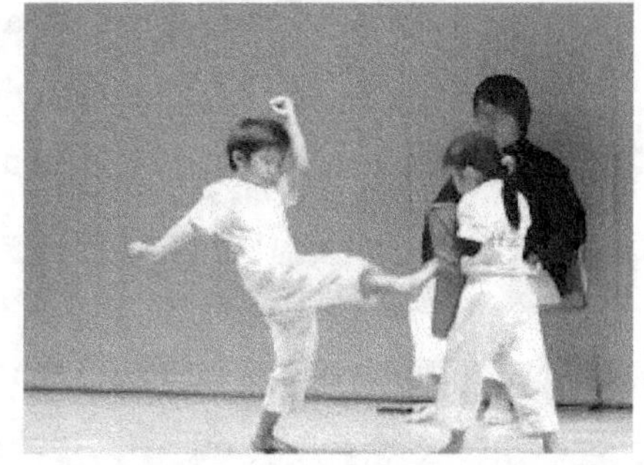

One problem is that these large arm movements become a telegraph for the attack. In the martial arts, our techniques must be stealthy and unnoticeable. The second problem is that the *jodan* becomes open and undefended. The hands must always be ready to be used as a block or an attack, even during a kick.

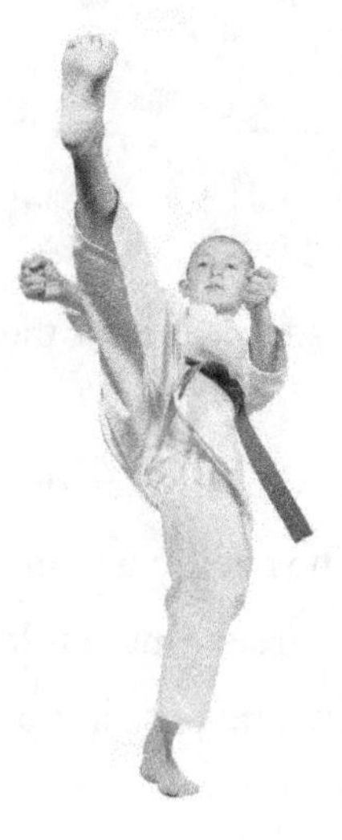

For this reason, we are taught to keep our hands either at *gedan* on both sides of the body or at *chudan* with the fists pointing forward and the elbows held at approximately ninety degrees. As we know, it takes many months, and possibly years, for us to keep our upper body totally relaxed during a kick so that our arms are perfectly under control.

The second error is shown in the photo to the left. This blue-belt practitioner has a very good high kick. His hands are also well controlled and not flying around wildly. So, what is wrong with this kick? This may be a minor error, but take a look at the supporting foot. You can see that it is pointing outward rather than forward. This is a natural tendency when throwing a high front kick as such a kick forces the pelvis to turn. In this case, the left side of the pelvis is pulled back, which forces the left leg to turn slightly to the outside. In order to generate maximum force and speed with a kick, the supporting leg (particularly the foot and the knee) should be pointing in the direction of the kick.

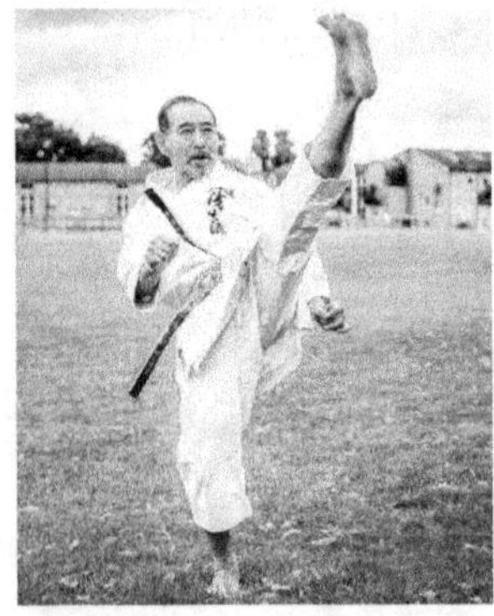

Low-level students should not throw such high kicks. It is better to ask them to kick lower and with better body alignment. Being able to kick high is impressive and desirable, but, at the same time, it is recommended that beginners first learn how to kick correctly.

When I checked some photos of my own kicks, I found this same error in my *mae geri* (photo left). This is a bad *kuse* and is obviously a hard one to get rid of.

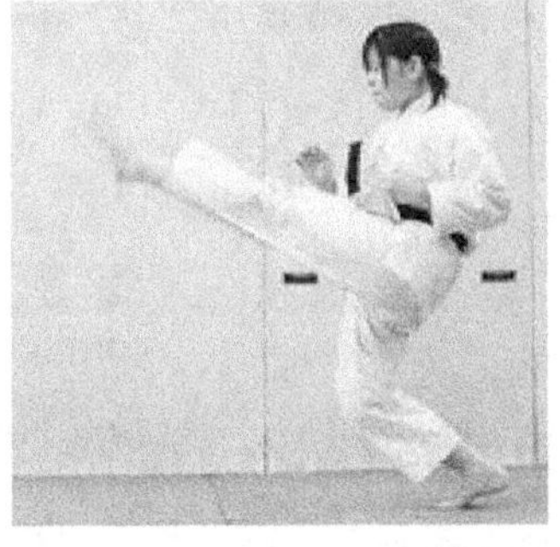

The third error can be seen in the *mae geri* shown in the photo to the right. This looks like a beautiful *chudan mae geri*. She seems to have a very strong kick here. Yes, the heel of the supporting foot is lifted, but is this an error? Well, it depends. If this is a transitional technique while moving forward (especially in a *kumite* situation), it is allowed. On the other hand, when you are practicing *mae geri* in *kihon* or in *kata*, the heel should be on the floor. Why?

As we discussed earlier, standing on one leg makes keeping your balance difficult. You must learn by repeating the most suitable technique. The heel of a white belt tends to come up mainly because he has not learned how to relax the ankle area properly so that the entire foot makes contact with the floor. The position of the standing foot is way out of his line of sight when kicking. In addition, his sense of feeling in the feet (especially on a specific part, such as the heel) is faint and unnoticeable unless he trains his mind during karate training. The kick shown in the photo above is an advanced application that can be used after the practitioner has completely mastered the basic kicking method.

Conclusion

As I have explained in detail, *kuse* is a habit and refers to physical movements that occur unconsciously. In general, these *kuse*, such as how we walk, eat, etc., are formed naturally as we grow up. In other words, these movements have been repeated so many times that we feel very natural doing them.

In Japan, making sucking noises when we drink or when we eat noodles or soup is acceptable. This way of eating is all Japanese people's *kuse*. At the same time, Japanese people know that this is against Western etiquette. As you can imagine, this *kuse* is very difficult for the Japanese to break, so we have an awful time when drinking tea or eating spaghetti or soup while visiting Western countries.

To learn karate techniques, you must, of course, learn new body movements, which is difficult. However, if you really wish to excel at karate, the more challenging task is getting rid of your many *kuse*. These small *kuse* are, in fact, the biggest stumbling blocks that prevent you from achieving an expert level of karate performance. Therefore, I (as well as many *budo* experts) consider *kuse* to be the greatest enemy of *budo*.

It is said that practice makes perfect. This is not a true statement, however. Instead, practice makes permanent. If you practice bad habits, they become permanent. You must always remember that incorrect training makes it more difficult to change back to correct techniques.

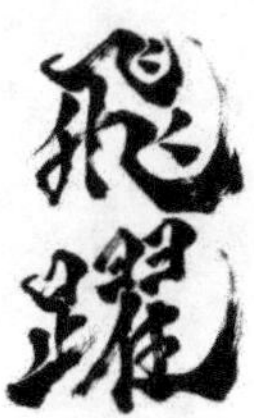

Chapter Fourteen
第十四章

Rethinking the Karate Fist
握りこぶし再考

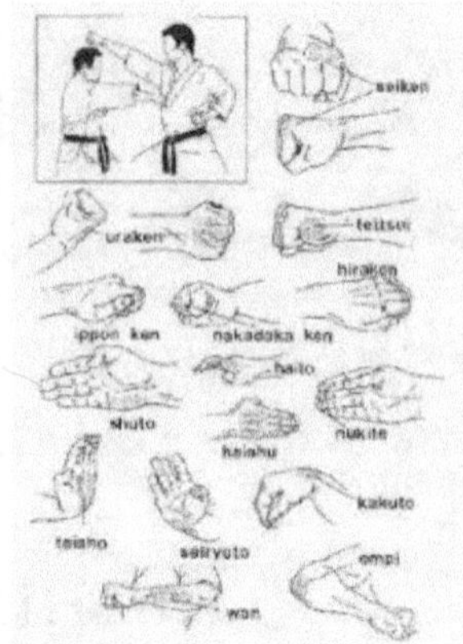

In Western boxing, there is only one way of using your hands: the fist. Of course, this is because boxers are required to wear a pair of boxing gloves. In karate, on the other hand, we have so many different ways of using our hands. Not only can we use both a fist and an open hand but we can also use many different parts of the hand. I am not going to list all of these different parts and methods, but most readers (who are most likely karate practitioners) know most, if not all, of them.

The subject here may come as a surprise to the reader. You might wonder why we are going to discuss such a simple and self-evident subject as making a fist. Yes, it is very true that we *karateka* make a fist every time we train in karate. Therefore, it is almost natural for us. I am well aware of this, yet, despite all of this, I feel a strong necessity to bring this subject to your attention.

My comment may have raised the eyebrows of some readers, but I suspect most practitioners do not know how to make a fist correctly. It is not their fault as I suspect they never learned how to do it from their sensei, who may not have learned how to do it himself. I can almost hear many readers saying, "What is he talking about? How can he say we do not know how to make a fist?" I know how you feel, but wait. You probably believe the way to make a fist is quite simple. Take a look at the photo below. It shows the steps to making a fist.

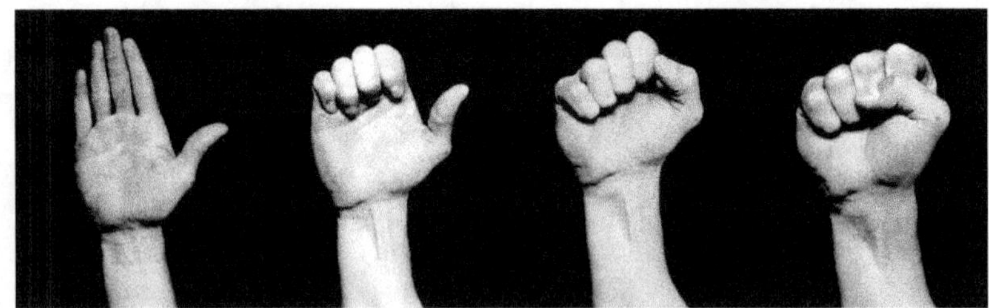

First, we roll in all the fingers except the thumb. By placing the thumb over the index and middle fingers, we now have a beautiful fist, right? Even though the more precise way to make a fist is different—this will be shared in the latter part of this chapter—the general concept shown on the previous page is correct. Well, this is very straightforward, so what is the problem?

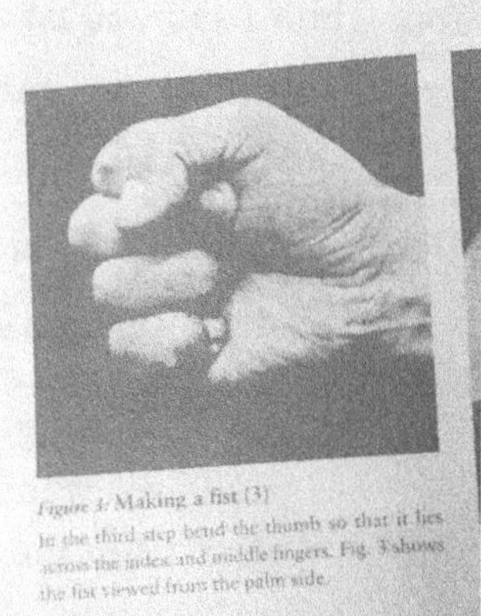

Before I get into my explanation, I wish to share something very interesting. Here are a couple of photos of a boxer whom we all know. Yes, this is Muhammad Ali (1942–2016). Take a look at his fist (photo right). It looks just like the fist we make, even though he wore boxing gloves when he fought. This is nothing unusual, but the next photo (below) is the interesting one. It is interesting not because it is a comical photo of Ali (right) wearing a bathrobe with Sugar Ray Leonard's (1956–) name on it, which happens to be the guy standing in front of him, but because of something else. What is important is not their faces. Take a close look at Ali's right fist under Leonard's chin.

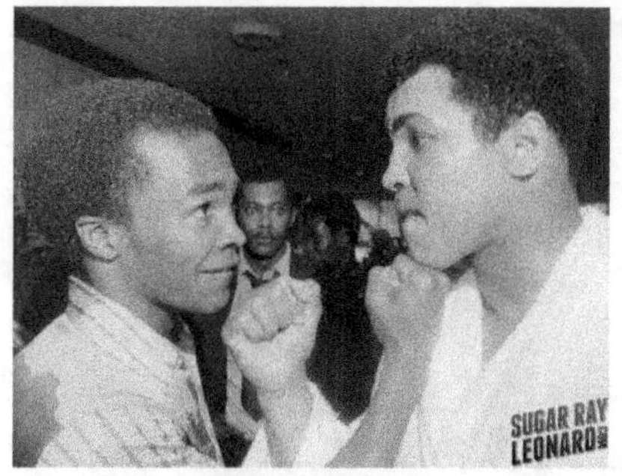

Did you notice that Ali's index finger is extended rather than rolled in? Could this be a freak photo where Ali is just relaxing or being sloppy? No, I can definitively tell you that this cannot be the case. I do not know exactly when this photo was taken, but I am sure he had been training for twenty or closer to thirty years by that time. If this is the case, he would unconsciously make a fist the way he normally did, whether for training or for a photo session. So, I conclude that this is the normal way Ali made a fist. Interesting, isn't it? Well, at least this photo made a strong impression to me.

Before I discuss this interesting fist that Ali is making, let me share another image here to the right. This obviously came

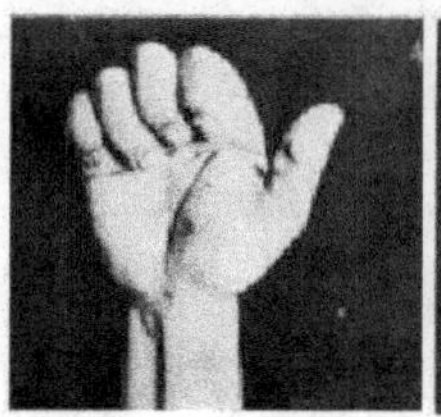
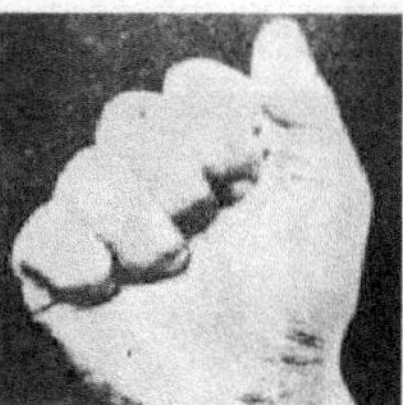
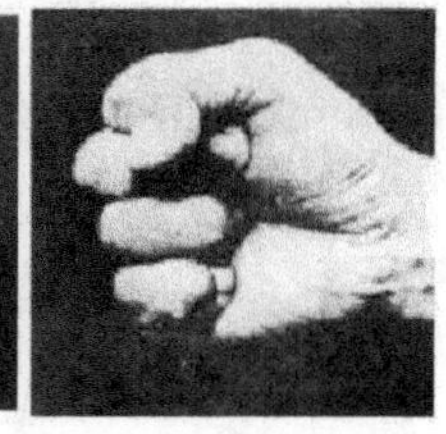

from a book. Do you know which book this is from and who the author is? Some may be surprised to know that this is from page 20 of *Karate Do Kyohan*. So, you know the author. Yes, it is Gichin Funakoshi. Look at the index finger! I wonder if Ali had read this book and seen these photos. This may sound like a joke, but there is a very interesting and important point hidden here. This is another reason I am writing this chapter.

By the way, the photos shown at the bottom of the previous page are actually from page 17 of the English version of the book. Here is the URL for a site where you can download a free PDF of *Karate Do Kyohan* in English (published in 1973): www.freepdf.info/index.php?post/Funakoshi-Gichin-Karate-Do-Kyohan.

In this book, Funakoshi shows the reader how to make a fist with three step-by-step photos. The first two steps look almost identical to the ones shown in the image on the first page of this chapter. However, the last step shows that the index finger needs to be extended. There appears to be a step missing between the second and third photo, so I will add it here (right). Without this, moving from the second to the third photo may be confusing, so this additional photo will supplement the illustration. It is easier to roll all four fingers (from the little finger to the index finger) first rather than rolling only three (from the little finger to the middle finger) and keeping the index finger extended, even though you can do this once you get used to it.

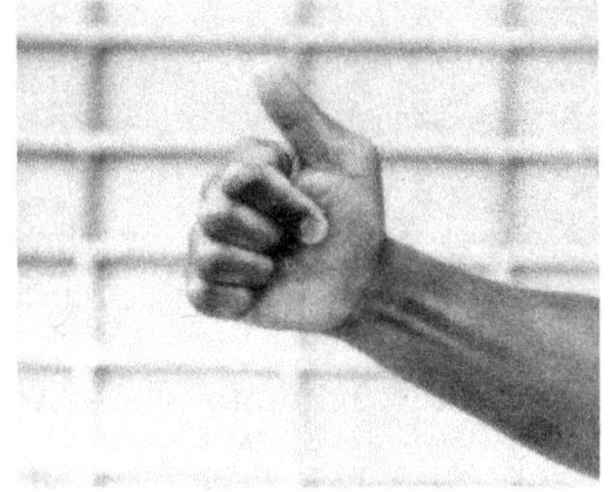

Have you learned this way of making a fist? Most likely you have not. As a matter of fact, when I first learned karate in 1962, I took both Shotokan and Goju Ryu. The teacher at the Goju Ryu dojo in Osaka showed me this method more than fifty years ago. In fact, he showed me two options. One was that of extending only the index finger, which is more popular, and the other, less popular option, was that of extending both the index and middle fingers. I do not know if Goju Ryu practitioners still make a fist this way, but I would like to hear from them about this. As far as I know, this method is still honored in Isshin Ryu (一心流), which is one

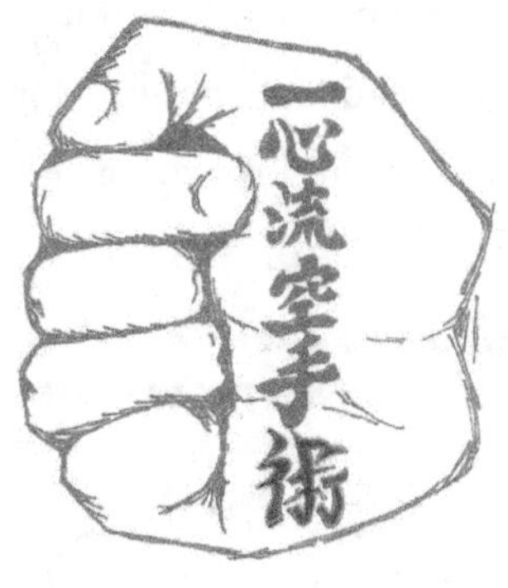

of the Okinawan styles. I can say this because they adopted this fist as their style logo (illustration left).

So, we must assume that this manner of fist making was brought to mainland Japan from Okinawa by Funakoshi and other Okinawan masters. It somehow survived at least until the early sixties (in Goju Ryu). I am not sure how long it lasted in Shotokan, but that may be an interesting research project for me to do in the future.

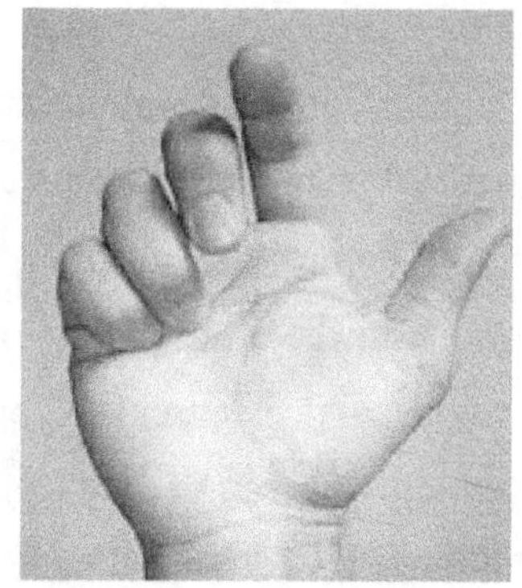

Now that we have touched on the historical background of this fist style, let us get into the meat of the subject. Why did the Okinawan masters use this fist? When I learned how to make this fist in that Goju Ryu dojo, the instructor did not tell me to roll all four, or even three, fingers. He told me to start from the little finger and roll one by one (photo right) but to keep the index finger extended. He also told me to squeeze the little finger the most tightly and then to squeeze the next finger a little less. I was actually told to relax the index finger. You cannot squeeze the index finger because the part of the finger between the second joint and the finger-tip is extended. Try it with your hand, and you will see how it feels. Unfortunately, either he did not explain why I had to make a fist this way, or, if he did, I just do not remember it.

Regardless, I practiced Goju Ryu for one year, and, during that time, I made a fist this way. At the same time, I was attending a Shotokan dojo in Kobe. When I started my karate training, I did not know that I was not supposed to be training at two different dojo that taught two different styles. After one year, my training friend found out and advised me to stop, so I had to choose one dojo. I liked both, but the Shotokan dojo was closer to my house, so I stayed with Shotokan.

At the Shotokan dojo, when my senpai saw my fist, he told me that it was an old way and then told me to roll all four fingers. I do not know exactly when this happened, but I think it was in my first year. I clearly remember that I wondered why it was considered to be an old way. However, in Japan, students are not supposed to ask questions, so I simply said, "Osu," and followed the instruction. For that few months, until I quit Goju Ryu, I used two different styles of fists.

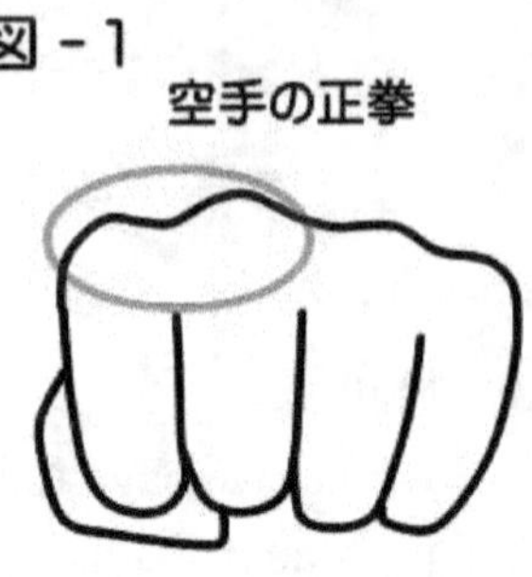

When I started my *makiwara* training, I really had to squeeze my index and middle fingers tightly. If you do *makiwara* training, you know this well. You are supposed to hit the board with the knuckles of the index and middle fingers (illustration right). For many years, I never doubted this method and continued this training. At the age of thirty-eight, I retired from tournaments and started to search for a karate life after competition.

The answer was *budo* karate, in which you train to master the techniques that work in the street, in other words, real fighting techniques for life-or-death situations. After searching for *budo* karate, I found my answer in Asai Ryu karate, which was founded by Master Tetsuhiko Asai. He taught me many ideas that were different from what I had learned in my earlier training in the seventies.

First, you need to keep the elbow pointing downward when you complete *choku zuki*, which is something I talk about in Chapter 11: "The Relationship between Choku Zuki and the Elbow Position" of my book *Karate Paradigm Shift*. In that chapter, I describe in detail why the arm and elbow have to be held in that position, so I will not cover it here. If you are interested in this subject, please get a copy of that book.

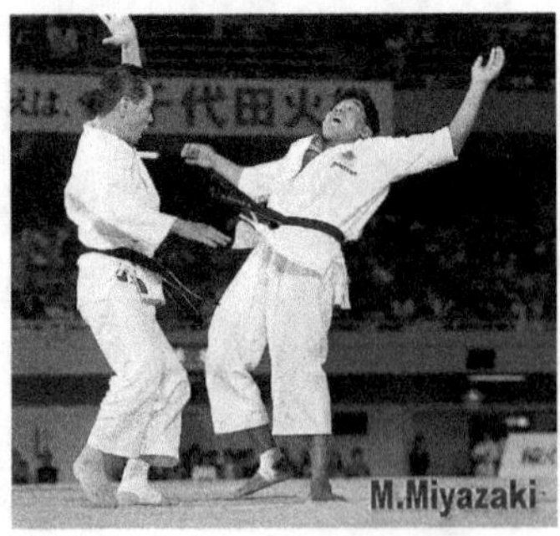

Another important thing I learned is that you have to be totally relaxed. I am talking about the entire body being relaxed. Asai karate is known for its whiplike techniques, such as its whipping-arm strikes (photo left) and whipping-leg kicks. In order to generate this type of body movement, you must learn to relax all of your muscles, and your body must turn into a flexible tube, so to speak. Two flexible branches stick out from the top area of this main tube, which, of course, are your arms. Then, two flexible branches, that is, your legs, support the whole tube from the bottom. One of these two lower branches supports the body while the other is used for whiplike kicks.

This is the reason we use a lot of open-handed techniques. The open hand is naturally more relaxed than the closed fist. We also use fist techniques for punching and striking. I learned that you need to relax your fist if you want to punch faster. In other words, you do not want to squeeze your fist when you are delivering a punch. You make a tight fist only for a split second—the shorter the better—when the fist impacts the target.

The benefit of punching this way is that not only is it faster but it also allows you to keep your shoulder down. When you punch, your shoulder comes up if the punching arm (including the fist) is too tense. When I was competing, my sensei used to tell me that I needed to tense my armpit more so that I could keep my shoulder down when I punched. No one told me to relax my fist. I remember that I used to clench my fists during *kumite* matches, which resulted in a raised shoulder when I punched. What is wrong with this raised shoulder is simply that it causes an up-and-down motion in the upper body, which is not smooth and will be detected by the opponent.

So, what I learned was that I needed to keep my fists in a relaxed state instead of having them tightly clenched. These relaxed fists helped me to relax my shoulders, upper body, neck, etc. In other words, I could much more easily keep my entire body relaxed. This body relaxation is needed to have an effective delivery of the whiplike techniques of Asai Ryu.

There are, in general, three ways to relax your fist. One is to have the thumb and the index finger somewhat tight and keep the other fingers very relaxed (though they are rolled up). The second way is the opposite of the first. In other words, you keep the little finger and the ring finger sort of tight and keep the other three fingers relaxed. Again, they should be rolled up in a relaxed manner. The third way is to have all the fingers relaxed and only halfway rolled. Master Asai asked me which

I thought was the best way. I answered that it was the first option; however, I had a strong feeling that the third option was the answer. I knew that many *kumite* competitors would choose the third option since they used a *kumite* mitt or fist protector, so they might be used to having all their fingers relaxed.

What do you think the answer was? Believe it or not, it was the second option. In other words, he told me that it was best to keep the little finger and the ring finger tight at first. At that time, I was very surprised by this answer, even though I am now fully convinced that this is the correct way. So, I asked him why. He brought out Funakoshi's book *Karate Do Kyohan* and showed me page 20. He also showed me another book by Master Funakoshi, *Rentan Goshin Karate Jutsu* (錬膽護身唐手術 [Tokyo Kobundo, 1925]). On the cover, there is an illustration of a fist made in the shape of what looks like a *nihon nakadaka ken* (二本中高拳) position (photo left).

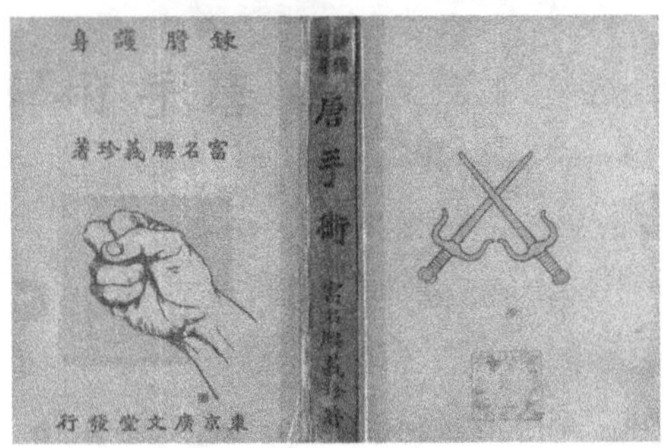

Asai Sensei said that the page from *Karate Do Kyohan* and the cover of *Rentan Goshin Karate Jutsu* made him think about how to make a fist when he was young. Then, he discovered that this method was the best when he started to practice *kobudo* (古武道), especially the *bo* (棒) and nunchaku (ヌンチャク). He practiced many other weapons, as well, such as the *sai* (サイ), *kyusetsuben* (九節鞭, 'nine-section whip'), and *tonfa* (トンファー), and told me he had realized that the best way to hold a *bo* or a nunchaku was the second of the options previously mentioned. Since I had practiced nunchaku and *sai*, I immediately agreed with him on this. It is very true that when holding a stick, you need to squeeze it very tightly with your little finger but not too tightly with your thumb and index finger. If you happen to practice these weapons in an extensive way, I

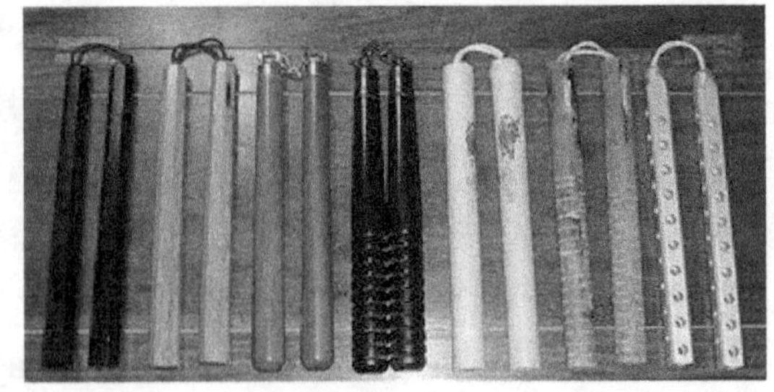

am sure you will see what I am talking about.

He also told me that this was the correct way to hold a katana in iaido (first two photos below) and a *shinai* (竹刀, 'bamboo sword') in kendo (third photo below).

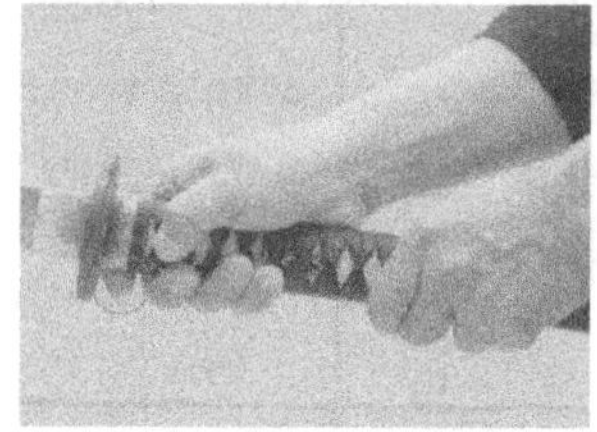
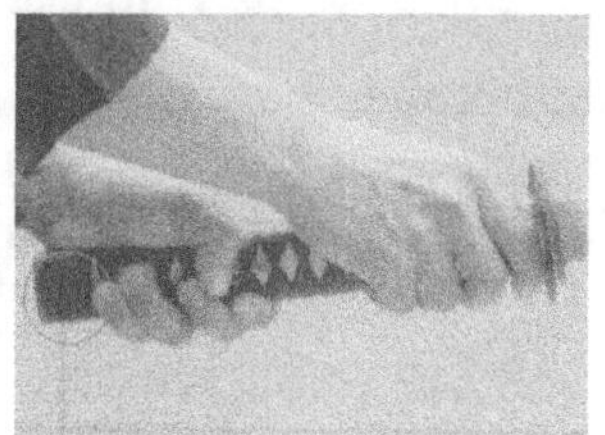
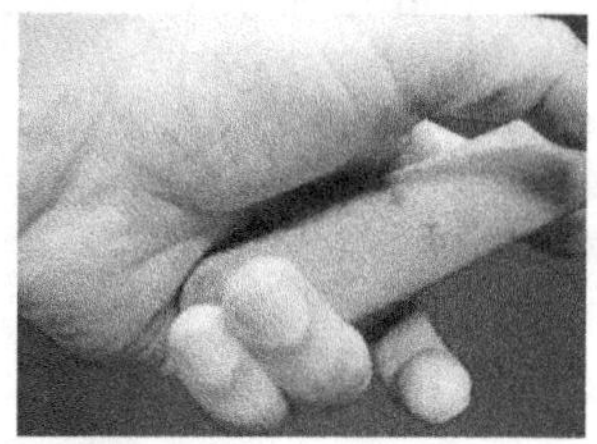

In addition, he said that this way of holding an instrument could be seen in golf (photo below left), tennis (photo below right), or any other sport or art where you need to hold a stick or handle.

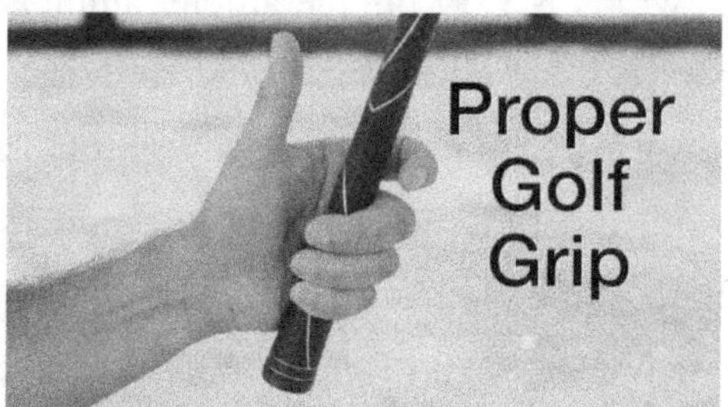

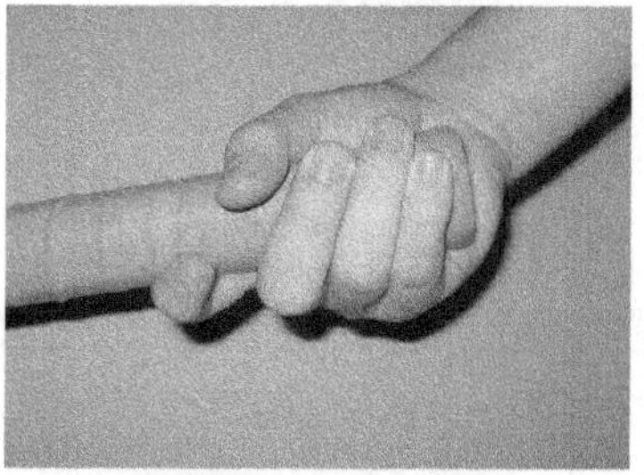

He explained that if you wanted to generate precise movements with a stick, this way of holding was a must. The movement does not need to be large. In fact, a small but accurate movement of a stick requires a relaxed thumb. Why? If you examine the functions of each finger, the answer is self-evident.

Just think about how you would pick up a small item, such as a jelly bean, with your fingers (photo right). Almost all of us would use our thumb and index finger. How about when you turn the page of a book or magazine? Yes, the thumb and the index finger. How about when you pinch someone? Try to do this with your little finger and ring finger.

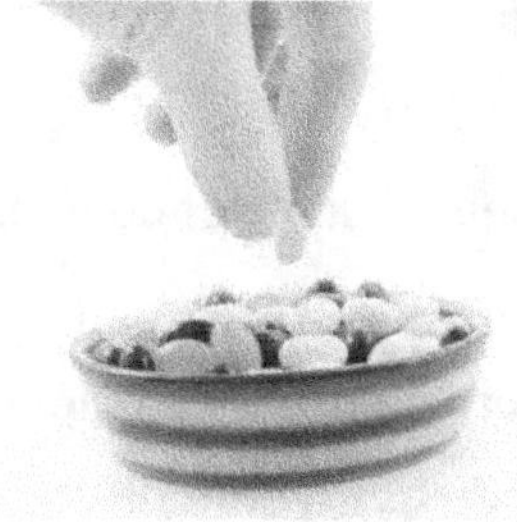

OK, I guess I do not need to answer this or bring up any other examples. Now, do you agree that we need to use our thumb and index finger to do many small and precise activities?

You may say, "Fine, I agree that we need to use our thumb and index finger to do small and precise work, but then why do you say those fingers have to be relaxed when we hold a *bo*, katana, etc.?" That is an excellent question, and the answer is the key to the subject we are discussing here. When you pick up a jelly bean, try tensing your thumb and index finger before you pick it up. Then, try picking it up while relaxing those two fingers instead. Which is easier? It is obviously easier when your fingers are relaxed. The mechanics are the same when you hold or handle a stick or *kobudo* weapon.

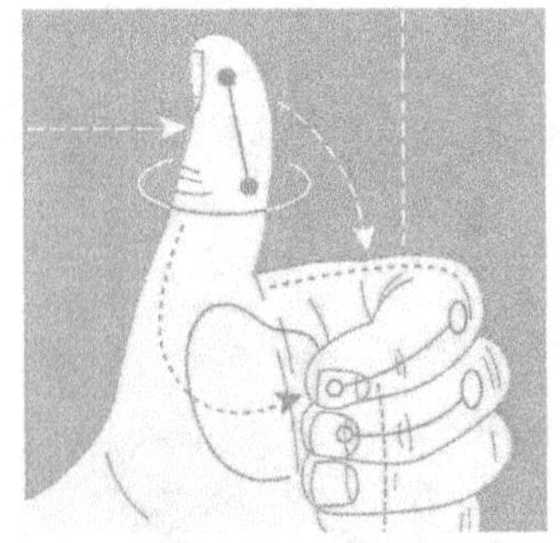

We must pay close attention to the evolution of our thumb, which is very unique among animals, including monkeys and chimpanzees. According to the article "Why Do Humans Have Thumbs," published in the December 2014 issue of the *Smithsonian Magazine*, Suzanne Kemmer of Rice University thinks that "by enabling fine motor skills the thumb promoted the development of the brain" (www.smithsonianmag.com/science-nature/why-do-humans-have-thumbs-180953393). So, we know that our thumb plays a critical role in fine motor skills. By tensing it too much, you hinder the dexterity of the hand or arm. This is why you need to have it relaxed until the moment you really need to tense it. Tensing the little finger, on the other hand, does not have much negative impact on fine motor skills.

This is exactly why Asai Sensei and I recommend that you roll up your little finger tightly but keep the thumb and index finger somewhat relaxed for your arm technique, that is, of course, until it makes contact. Interestingly, this is exactly the fist that is shown in *Karate Do Kyohan*.

Let us look more closely at how a fist with an extended index finger would work. First, I would like to ask the reader to try making this fist. How does it feel?

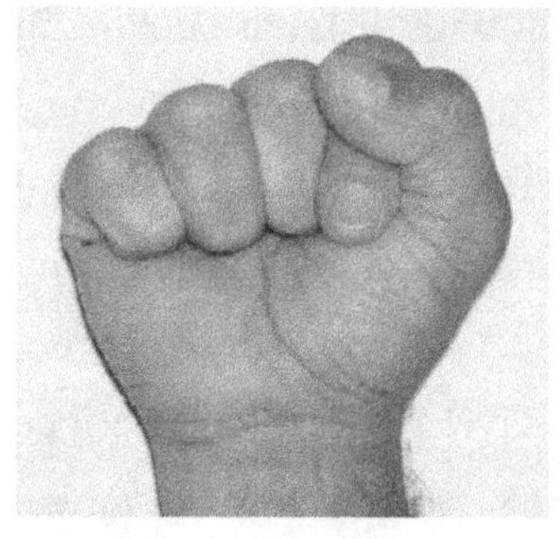

I suspect that you cannot make the part of the fist where the index finger is as solid as when it was fully rolled up. In other words, when there is an impact to the surface of the fist, the half-rolled index finger will give and bend slightly inward. When the index finger is fully rolled up, however, that part of the fist is more solid and seems better for punching. If this is the case, we must think more deeply to find out why the ancient Okinawan masters, including Funakoshi, believed in this type of fist. I am afraid this is one of the secrets that have been lost not only in Shotokan but maybe also in many of the traditional karate styles of Japan.

The major reason I brought this up earlier in this chapter was to de-emphasize the thumb and index-finger area in the arm technique so that you can achieve optimum performance from the hand and arm region. In other words, you can achieve accurate movement and maximum speed from your hand and arm region when your thumb and index finger are semirelaxed or minimally tense.

I also suspect that Muhammad Ali knew this secret. Even though we will never know if he held his fist this way inside his gloves, I have a strong feeling he did. He knew that by relaxing his thumb and index finger, he could achieve the accurate punch that he was famous for. Despite Ali's being in the heavyweight division, he was known for having a fighting style that was light and relaxed, unlike Joe Frazier (1944–2011) and George Foreman (1949–). He himself described his style as "Float like a butterfly, sting like a bee." In order for him to be able to float in a relaxed manner when a strong opponent such as Joe Frazier was coming to knock him down, I would say keeping his fist relaxed was a must.

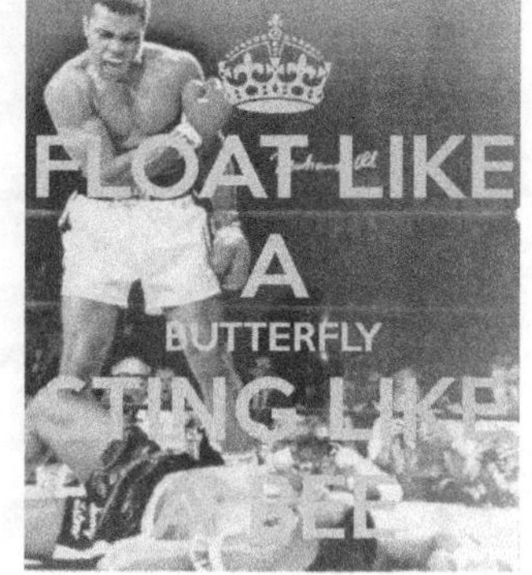

You will also notice when you watch his fighting style that he kept his hands down as he moved around. Most boxers always keep their guard up, but

Ali would judge the distance so well that he could fight with his guard down. To do this, his fists had to be totally relaxed but, at the same time, ready to come up and strike right away if he found an opportunity. Here is a video of some of Ali's matches where his relaxed floating style is very obvious: www.youtube.com/watch?v=jkhpZoPOfZI.

What is more important to pay attention to in his saying is that he described his punch as being like the sting of a bee. Of course, this sting came from movements that were like those of a flittering butterfly. Interestingly, he could have used another analogy if he wanted to describe his punch as being heavy or devastating. That was what Foreman, for instance, was known for. Even though Ali could have used a phrase such as *bite like a cobra* or *ram like a rhinoceros*, he preferred *sting like a bee*.

I find this interesting because his choice of words is very revealing. He knew his punch was light and quick. It was not like *ikken hissatsu*, but that was OK with him. He did not need a heavy punch as he knew how to knock his opponents down by leveraging perfect timing and his own unique rhythm that he had developed. Thus, all he needed was a light but fast and almost invisible punch. So, I conclude that he kept his fist loose around the thumb and index-finger area inside his gloves just as he "accidentally" showed in that memorable photo with Sugar Ray Leonard.

Now, let's get back to the nature of this fist. It is OK for the movements prior to impact, but how about when you actually hit something with it? The downside is that it cannot sustain the impact that comes from hitting a solid target. If you hit a *makiwara* with the index finger extended, you will see that you cannot hit it evenly with two knuckles. In other words, you have to depend more on the knuckle of the middle finger.

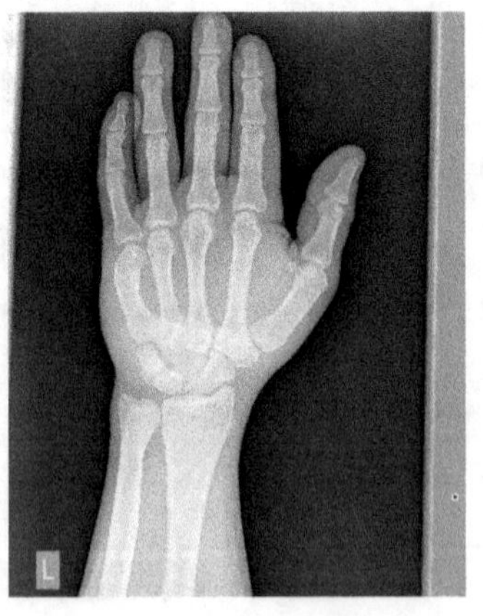

As most people know, there are two bones in the forearm: the radius and the ulna. The radius is thicker and longer and, in fact, acts as the major support for the hand (photo left). You can also see that the middle finger is naturally in the center and receives the most support from the radius.

The subject of which part of the fist should be used to hit a target has been discussed by karate practitioners in the past. It looks as though Shotokan and other traditional karate styles now agree in their belief in using the knuckles of the index and middle fingers (Illustration B). In Shorinji Kenpo (少林寺拳法), on the other hand, the side with the little finger and ring finger is used (Illustration C).

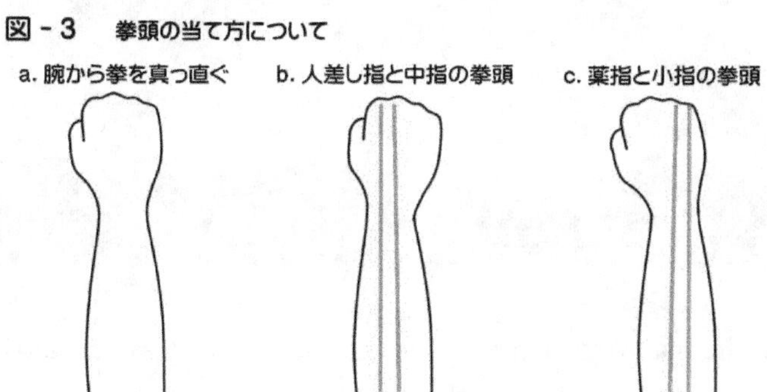

They say it is the most natural as they mostly use *tateken* (縦拳, 'vertical fist' [photo right]) rather than *seiken* (正拳, 'regular [horizontal] fist'). I think the little finger is too delicate to make the full impact, but Shorinji Kenpo's punching concept seems to be somewhat different from that of Shotokan.

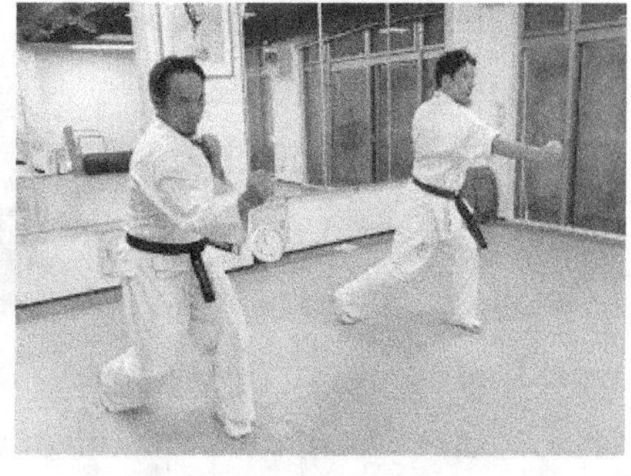

Instead of following the one-punch-one-kill concept, they seem to use the punch as a preparation before a throwing technique. Maybe someone from this style can send me more information on whether or not my understanding is correct. Regardless, I am a little surprised that there is no concept of using the knuckles of the middle and ring fingers. Out of all three choices, I personally like this one the most, and these are actually the two fingers I use.

Asai Sensei and I discussed this and agreed that the karate masters, before karate was introduced into mainland Japan, mainly used just one knuckle when they punched, which was that of the middle finger. However, they must have rarely used the flat fist that we see most modern-day karate practitioners using. Then, what did they use? I believe they used either *nakadakaken* (中高拳, 'middle-knuckle fist' [photo below left]) or *ippon ken* (一本拳, 'index-knuckle fist' [photo below right]).

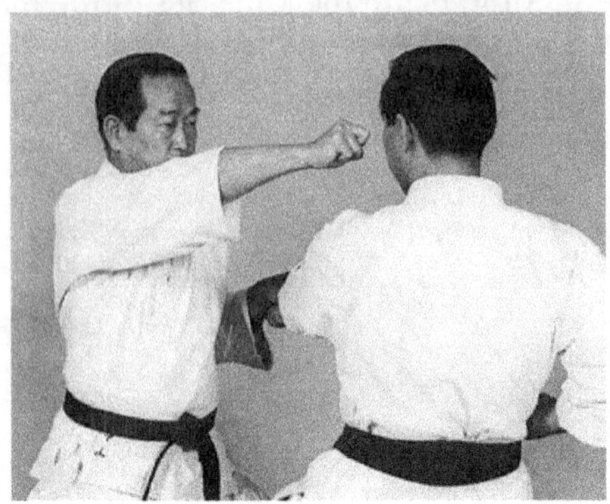

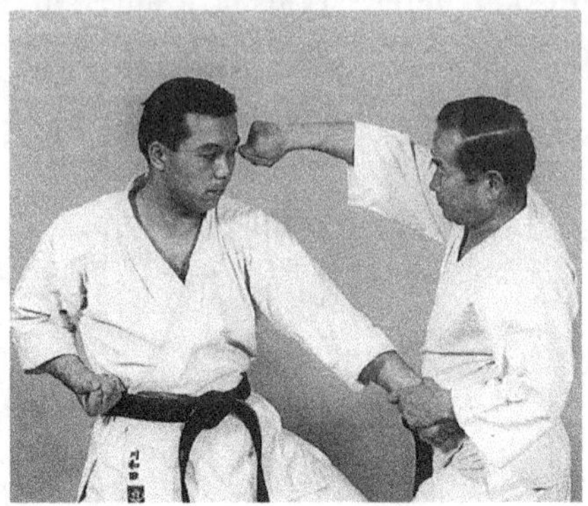

By the way, the fist I use in my *kamae* is almost always *nakadakaken*. As a matter of fact, there are other styles of single-knuckle fists, such as *oyayubi ippon ken* (親指一本拳, 'thumb-knuckle fist' [photo right]). The use of a single knuckle makes much more sense from the perspective of *budo* fighting. If you have studied physics, you know that pressure is inversely proportional to surface area. In other words, the amount of pressure delivered decreases as the surface area increases. So, if you hit a target with the entire surface of the fist, the pressure is much less than if you had hit it with any of the single-knuckle fists. No one can disagree that single-knuckle fists definitely cause a more devastating impact to the opponent.

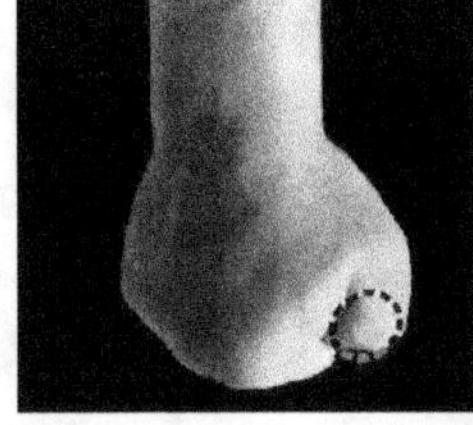

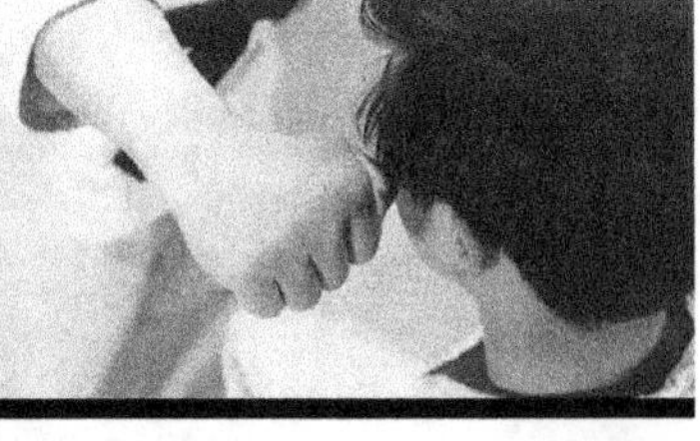

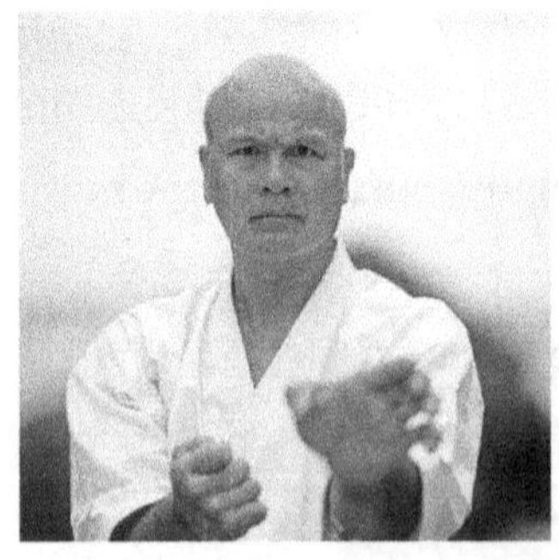

I can see this heritage in one Okinawan style as single-knuckle techniques are commonly used in Uechi Ryu. Interestingly, this style uses an open-handed *oyayubi ippon ken*, which is found in their standard *kamae* (photo left). The way this *karateka* is holding his left hand would be misunderstood by a Shotokan practitioner as an open hand used for *tsukami*. However, this is actually used to strike with the first knuckle of the thumb. In that same photo, the *karateka* is holding his right hand in position for a single-knuckle fist with the index finger. From the looks of it, I consider this to be a very *budo*-like *kamae*. I can also see that his hand technique, whether left or right, could cause a very devastating effect upon the opponent.

I am not going to say that this is proof that Master Funakoshi favored the single-knuckle fist. However, I believe he did. This must be one of the reasons he specifically showed how to make a fist with the index finger half extended in his famous book. Then, why was this sort of lost, or why did he stop teaching this fist? I am guessing it was for two reasons.

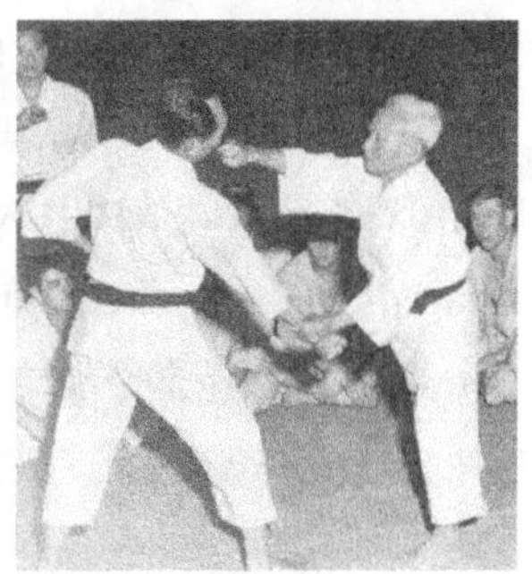

The first reason was that *kumite* training was adopted in his class. As many readers know, his original class consisted of only *kata* training. His students, most of whom were from various universities in Tokyo, asked him to include *kumite*, and some of the students who had experience in kendo came up with the *kihon kumite* ideas. Even though Funakoshi did not allow them to do *jiyu kumite*, he felt that *ippon ken* and *nakadakaken* would be too dangerous if he allowed them even just in *kihon kumite*. Thus, I suspect he recommended that the students use a flat fist for safety reasons.

The second reason is the adoption of *jiyu kumite* in tournaments. The flat fist had to become standard since sport karate has gained such popularity in the last fifty years or so. Obviously, in *jiyu kumite*, single-knuckle fists would be very dangerous and would not achieve any benefit or advantage in sport fighting. When I was competing in the seventies, we did not wear any gloves or fist protectors at all. Even though we were not allowed to hit our opponents, we frequently had some light "touches." Nosebleeds and missing teeth were very common occurrences. I confess that I never thought about forming my fist into *ippon ken* or *nakadakaken* in my competition days.

Conclusion

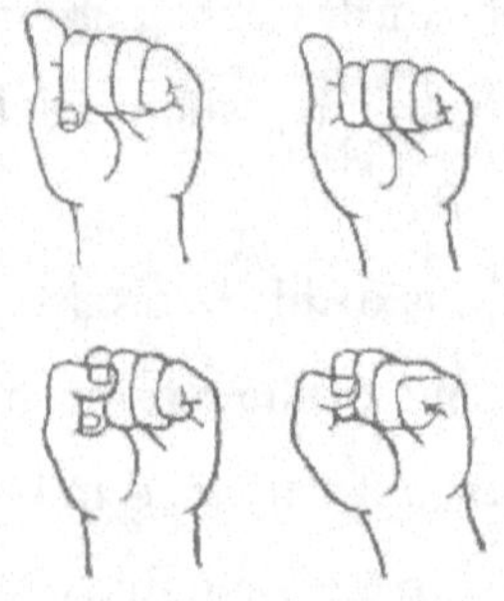

Currently, all of the traditional karate styles of Japan, including Shotokan, use the flat fist with all the fingers rolled in as shown on the right side of the illustration to the left. However, Master Funakoshi, the father of modern karate, is documented by his own published books as having taught a different type of fist with the index finger extended as shown on the left side of the same illustration. This type of fist is now almost forgotten among traditional karate practitioners, but it is still being practiced among some of the Okinawan styles.

I hypothesize that the popularity of sport karate made Funakoshi's fist inappropriate to use, and it was eventually forgotten by practitioners. I believe this fist enables the thumb and index finger to be relaxed, which results in faster and more accurate arm movement. I hope all *budo karateka* will reevaluate this way of making a fist as well as the single-knuckle fists and include them in their daily training if they haven't already.

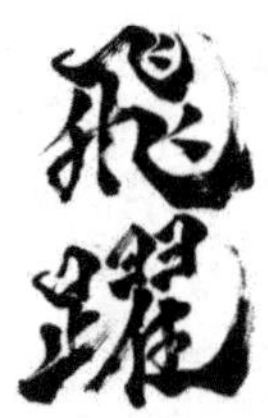

Chapter Fifteen
第十五章

What Is a Spiral Fist?
螺旋拳とは何ぞや？

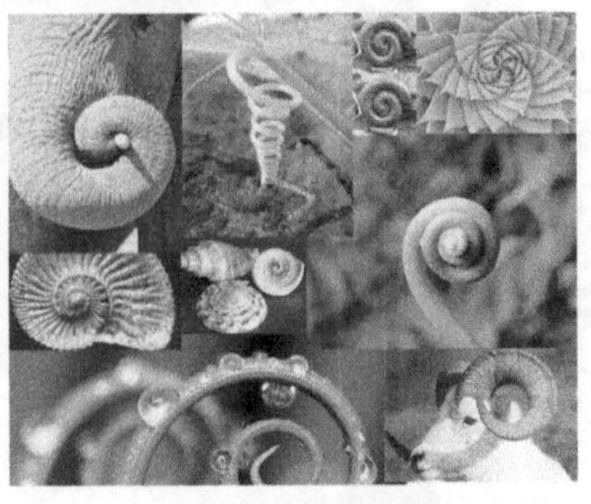

First of all, we should define what a spiral is. *Merriam-Webster's Collegiate Dictionary, Eleventh Edition*, defines *spiral* as "the path of a point in a plane moving around a central point while continuously receding from or approaching it." This can be found in the natural world, such as in some shells, plants, bugs, and even animals.

In this chapter, I wish to share one secret technique of Asai Ryu karate with the reader. The fist used in this style is called *rasen ken* (螺旋拳, 'spiral fist') or *in'yo no ken* (陰陽の拳, 'yin-yang fist'). This fist is taught in Taiwan among White Crane kung fu practitioners, but I am not sure if it is taught on Okinawa. Regardless, I am afraid it is almost forgotten in the traditional karate styles.

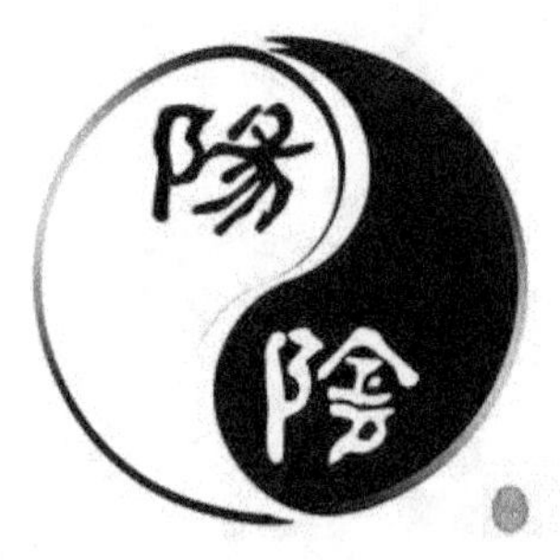

Rasen ken, or *in'yo no ken*, consists of two different styles of fist. In other words, it has an *in* fist and a *yo* fist. *In* (陰 [read as *yīn* in Chinese]) means 'moon', 'shadow', or 'negative'. *Yo* (陽 [read as *yáng* in Chinese]) means 'sun', 'brightness', or 'positive'. Based on this definition, I am sure the reader will have very little idea what this technique is all about.

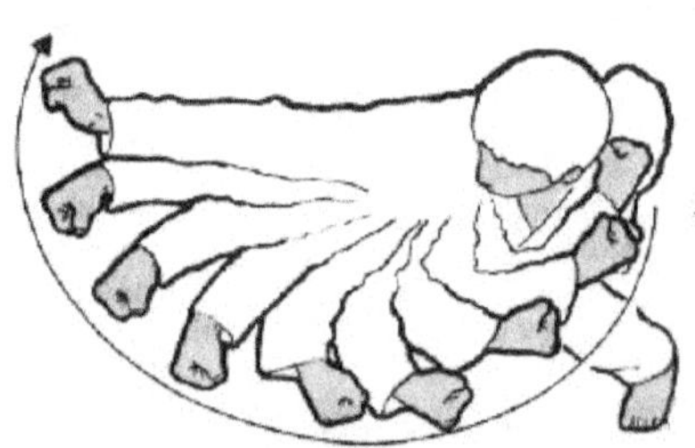

This is one of the *furiken* (振り拳, 'whipping fist') techniques. Most readers are familiar with *uraken uchi* (裏拳打ち, 'backfist' [illustration right]). This technique can be a *furiken* if it is used with a large circular motion. There is another *furiken* technique that you are probably familiar with, which is *mawashi uchi* (回し打ち, 'roundhouse punch' or 'round punch' [top of following page]). In short, a *furiken* technique is defined as a whipping-fist technique with a large circular motion. The arm motion can be horizontal, diagonal, or even vertical. The angles and directions do not matter. The important thing is that the arm swing from the shoulder with minimal bending at

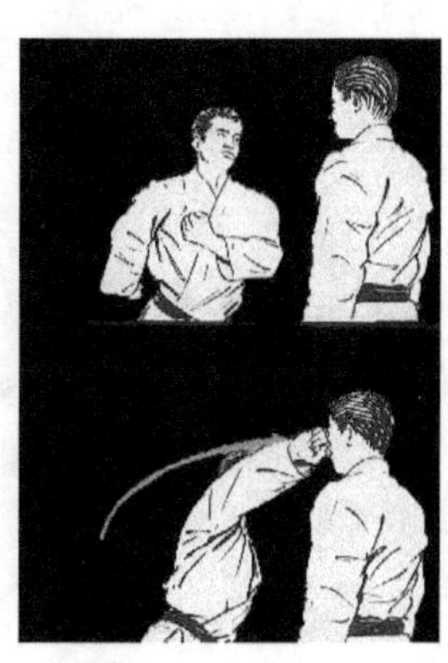

the elbow. This technique also requires the twisting of the shoulders and entire upper body in many cases.

Unfortunately, *furiken* techniques are not too popular among traditional karate styles due to the immense popularity of sport karate. Maybe I do not need to explain why as it is very obvious, but most *furiken* techniques cannot be used to score points in tournament *kumite*; thus, they are ignored or forgotten. On the other hand, these are considered to be key techniques in *budo* karate, including Asai Ryu.

I assume that you now have a general idea of what *furiken* techniques are. OK, then let me explain what *rasen ken* is and how it is used. Before I go into the explanation, I need to mention something. I needed some photos of a fist demonstrating the technique for this chapter, so I looked for some appropriate ones, but, unfortunately, was only able to find one photo of this nature in the public domain. As a result, the fist used in the close-up photos in this chapter is mine.

Yo Ken (陽拳, 'Sun Fist')

OK, as I explained earlier, there are two separate fists. Let us start with *yo ken*, which is the sun fist or positive fist. Look at the two photos shown below. As you can see, *yo ken* looks very similar to *ippon ken*. The photo on the left shows the palm side, and the photo on the right shows the knuckle side of the same fist.

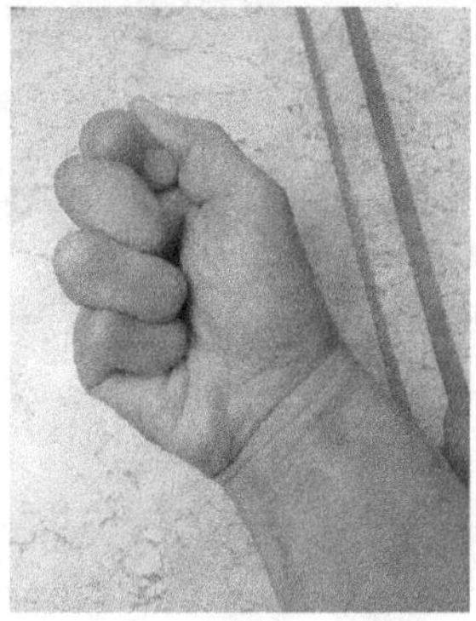

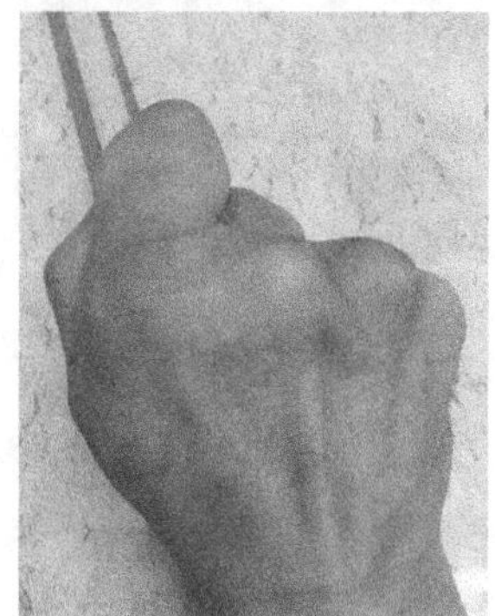

It is difficult to see the spiral shape in the fist forms by looking at these photos. I suggest that you make one with your own hand. If you have the fingers lined up correctly, you can see that the second joints of the fingers (excluding the thumb) are lined up in a beautiful spiral shape. Though it is important to make your fist this way, the form itself is not the ultimate objective of this fist. Just remember that the form is only a by-product.

The key point of this fist is that you need to tighten the little finger the most securely against the palm and then tighten the other three fingers naturally. The third joint of the index finger is not bent, which forms *ippon ken*. Another point to remember is that the base of the thumb should be pressed against the fingertips of the middle and ring fingers.

After having rolled in the four fingers, place the thumb on top of the index finger between the first and second joints. The thumb then presses the index finger down firmly (photo below left). The thumb is fully extended and will line up parallel with the base of the index finger (photo below right). Note that the photos below are used to show the position of the thumb and index finger; therefore, the base of the thumb and the middle finger are not formed correctly in these images.

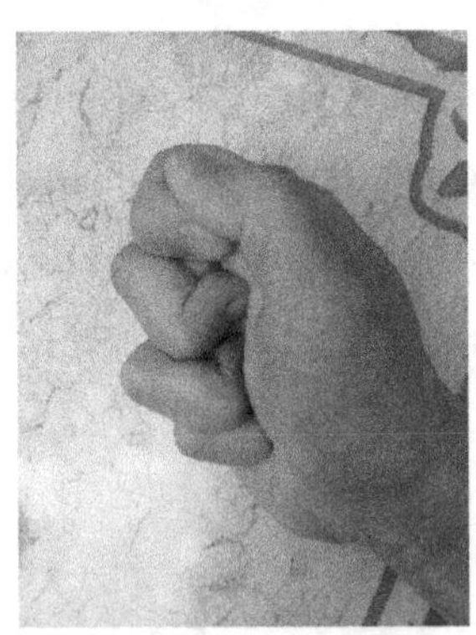

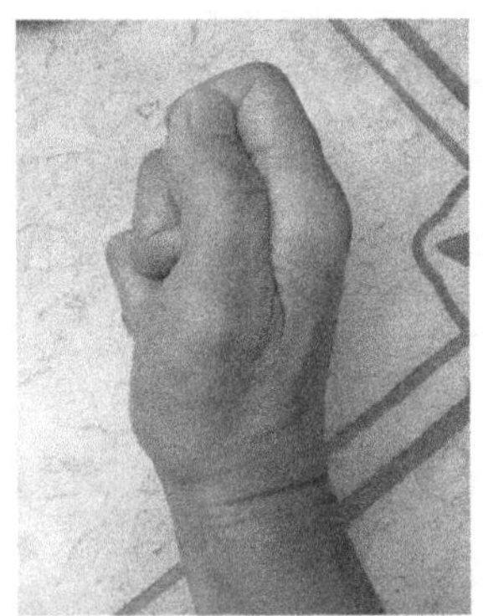

When you strike, there are two methods. One is where the index finger does the striking, and the thumb acts as a support to the *ippon ken*. The other is where the first knuckle of the thumb does the striking, which is called *boshiken* (拇指拳, 'thumb fist') and is a method that is familiar to Uechi Ryu practitioners. The key point for both methods is that the little finger must be tightened the most firmly.

In Ken (陰拳, 'Moon Fist')

The second fist is *in ken*, which is the moon fist or negative fist. The two photos below show this fist from both the palm and knuckle sides. To make this fist, it is important to start from *yo ken*, which was described in detail above. The key point is to maintain the fist and move only the knuckles to change forms between *yo ken* and *in ken*.

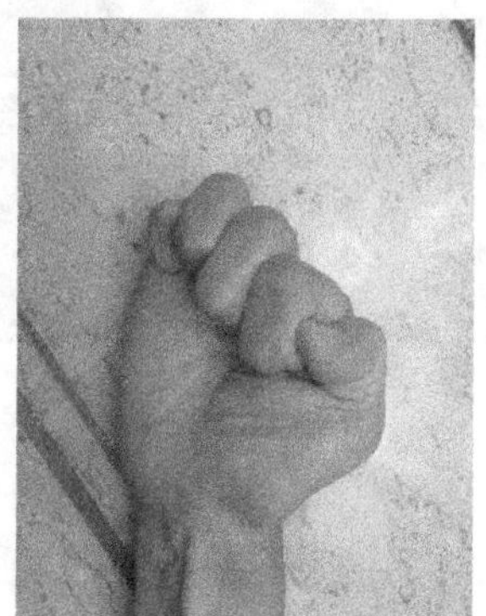

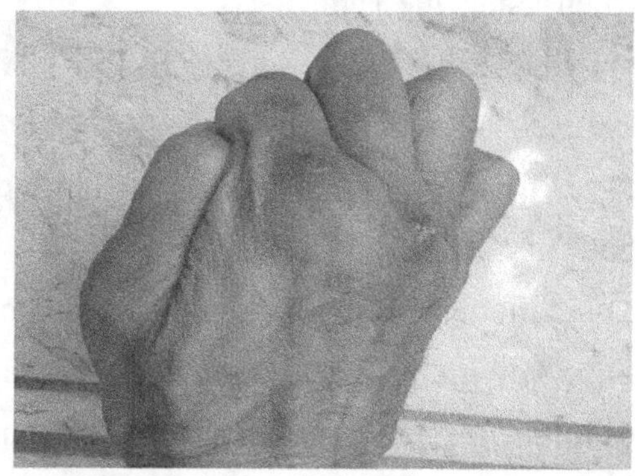

Remember that the fingers must, in general, be touching each other all throughout this process. In other words, do not open the hand or leave any space between the fingers during the process. For *in ken*, you squeeze the thumb tightly against the side of the index finger as shown in the photo above left. You must tighten the index finger the most firmly. The middle and ring fingers are rolled in with a natural firmness, but the little finger is extended at the third joint (photo right).

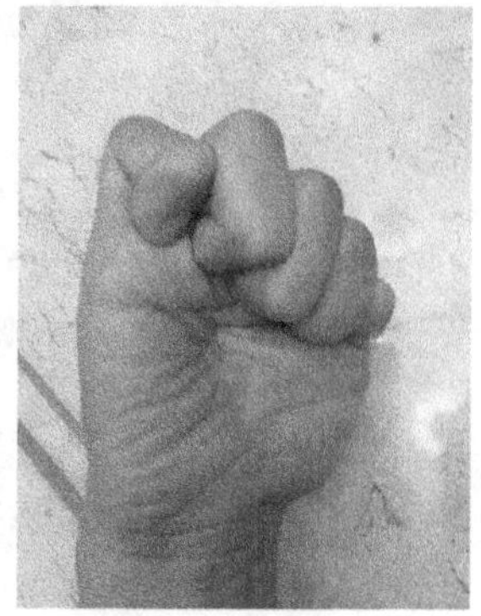

I am afraid the spiral form of the fist is still not too visible in these photos. Though the objective is not to create the spiral form itself, you are welcome to make this fist with your hand if you wish to see the spiral (provided you have the correct form).

What is important here is to know how to use this fist. With *in ken*, you can hit a target with any of the knuckles; however, the knuckle of the little finger is the most frequently used. To use *in ken* with the knuckle of the little finger, you need to swing your arm in reverse. If you are using your right fist, the right arm starts from your left shoulder and swings clockwise. The movement is similar to that of *uraken uchi* except that the striking point is at the second joint of the little finger.

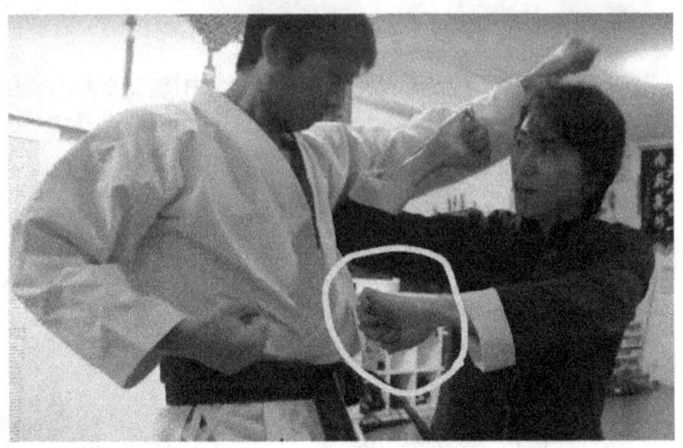

Can *in ken* be used in the regular circular motion of *mawashi uchi* (i.e., counterclockwise when using the right fist)? Yes, it is possible. This fist is not common even among the kung fu styles. Luckily, I was able to find one photo of a Japanese Ba Gua Zhang practitioner demonstrating it (photo above). As you can see, he is delivering *enpi uchi* with his right elbow and simultaneously executing a *chudan* strike with his left *in ken*. His opponent in the karate uniform is the famous Tatsuya Naka of the JKA. Here is a video clip of the demonstration that this photo came from: www.youtube.com/watch?v=NdM_b18AlGk.

Having said all that, it is much more common to use *yo ken* and strike with the knuckle of the thumb or index finger in the regular circular motion. Try these fists and see how they work. Then, you can easily see why one way is much easier and also more practical than the other.

Now you understand how to make the fists and how to use them individually. That is the first step, and now you need to move on to the second step.

What you need to practice is shifting smoothly between these fists. However, at least initially, I assume that the movement of your knuckles and the shifting of your fist may be rough and awkward. You have to repeat this exercise hundreds of times before it can become natural and smooth. Once the shifting becomes smooth, it is important that you be able to do this very quickly. This is because these two fists are often used in the same combination, a typical one being as follows.

Let's assume that you are using your right fist. First, the attacking arm moves in a semicircular movement similar to that of *mawashi uchi* in a counterclockwise direction. The first impact is made with the knuckle of either the thumb or the index finger (*yo ken*). Right after the first attack is completed, the arm direction is reversed (clockwise) and the second impact is made with the knuckle of the little finger (*in ken*). If you keep the fist in *yo ken* position for the second attack, it will become *kentsui uchi* (拳槌打ち, 'hammer-fist strike').

Of course, that is also an option. However, a hammer fist has a large impact area, which means the impact force will be spread over a larger area, resulting in less pressure. Thus, you want to have a small impact point made with a single knuckle. This is why you need to change quickly to *in ken* and stick the knuckle of the little finger out. The arm swings like a windshield wiper. Now you can understand why the form of the fist must change very quickly between the two impacts.

Interestingly, I also found out that this fist is used in one of the kung fu styles, Tong Bei Quan (通備拳 [*tōngbèiquán*]). This style is popular in northern China and is known for being a long-distance fighting method. The fist that practitioners of this style often use is called *garyo ken* (瓦陵拳 [read as *wălíngquán* in Chinese]). Below are two photos of Master Ma of Ma Style Tong Bei Quan demonstrating *garyo ken*, which appear on page 39 of the July issue of *Hiden Magazine*.

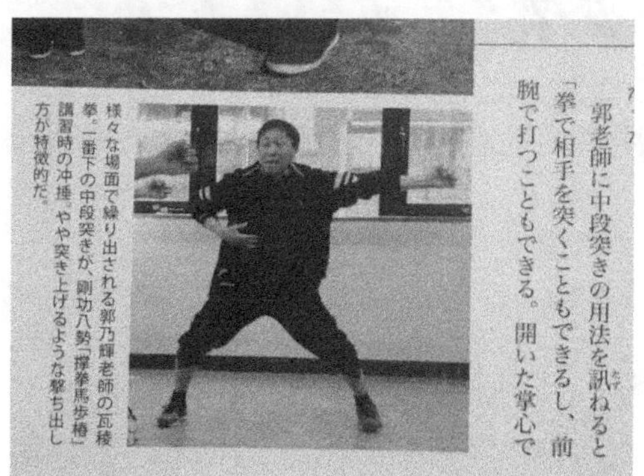

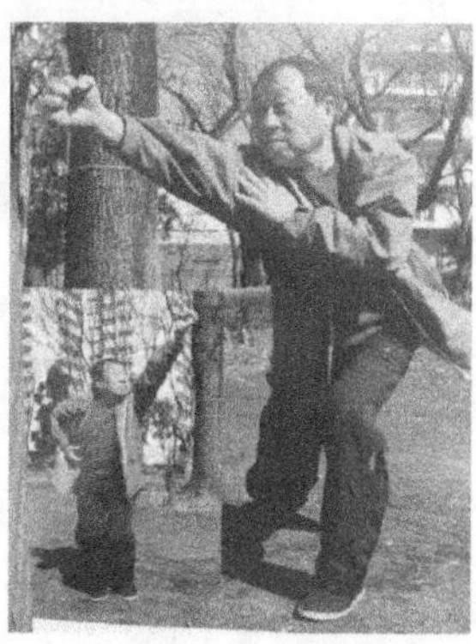

Even though the photos do not show how the fist is used, having reviewed their training videos, I can tell that they use a lot of arm-swinging techniques. If I ever meet a Tong Bei Quan practitioner, I would certainly like to discuss the use of this fist, which would be very interesting. If you are interested in viewing the techniques of this style of kung fu, here is the URL for a short video of Ma Style Tong Bei Quan: www.youtube.com/watch?v=ZRyk6hZ2lfQ.

Conclusion

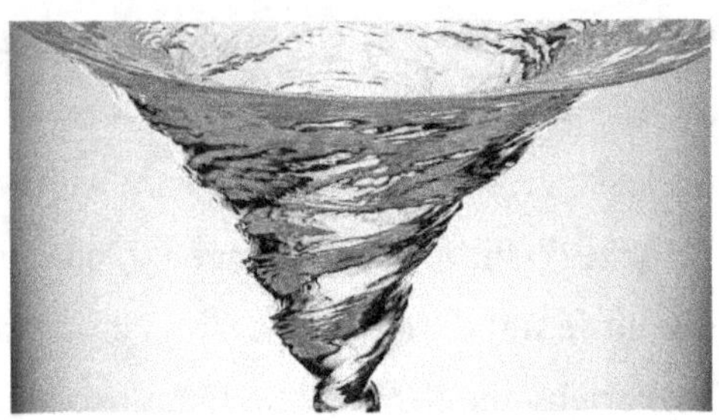

By practicing the two fist forms of *yo ken* and *in ken*, you may become skillful enough to swing and manage your arms in a spiraling and possibly vortex-type motion. By having this motion, you will be able to execute multiple circular punches in succession. I think it could be very effective in a *kumite* situation. You may want to try this out and see if it works for you. Good luck!

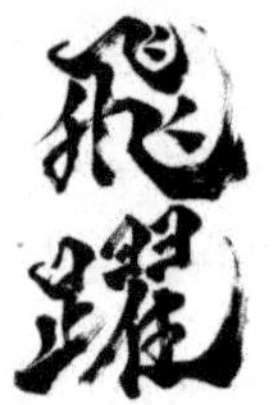

Chapter Sixteen
第十六章

Moving the Body vs. Using the Body
身体を動かすＶＳ身体を使う

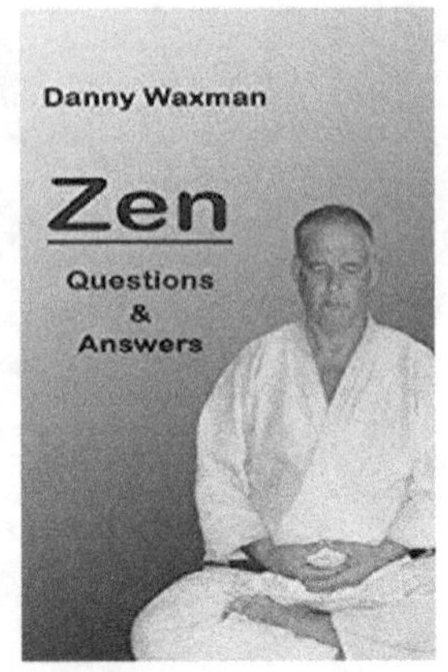

The title of this chapter may sound like a Zen puzzle. Just as it sounds, there is a deep meaning behind this concept, though you may consider it frivolous. But, I hope that, by finding the difference between these two terms, karate practitioners will have a better understanding of what is really required when they wish to develop their karate skills. Let's look at the meaning of these two terms.

The first one has to do with moving the parts of the body. Unless you have some kind of physical handicap or misalignment, you can certainly move most of your body parts without much effort. Of course, there are some parts, such as the ears, eyeballs, toes, etc., that are difficult for us to move freely. This is true for most of us but does not cause us any inconvenience in our daily lives. Other than that, we seem to have freedom of movement with our major limbs, such as the arms, legs, hands, and fingers. Thus, most of us have no problem moving our fingers, circling our arms, or lifting our feet. We need these movements in order for us to function normally in our daily lives.

When we get old and, say, are unable to lift our feet freely, it becomes a serious inconvenience to put our socks on. If we have a problem with any of our fingers, then we experience inconvenience in many different kinds of daily activities, such as writing, typing, holding a fork, etc. Let's look at writing as an easy example. Each person develops his own writing style, including how to hold a pen or pencil. Many people hold a pen with their right hand (first two photos below), but some use their left hand to write (third photo below).

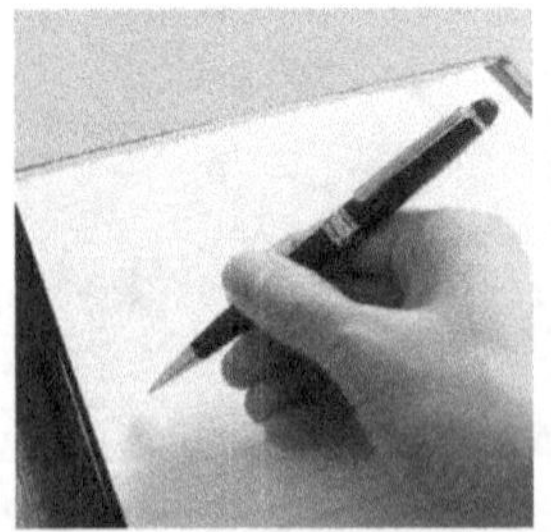

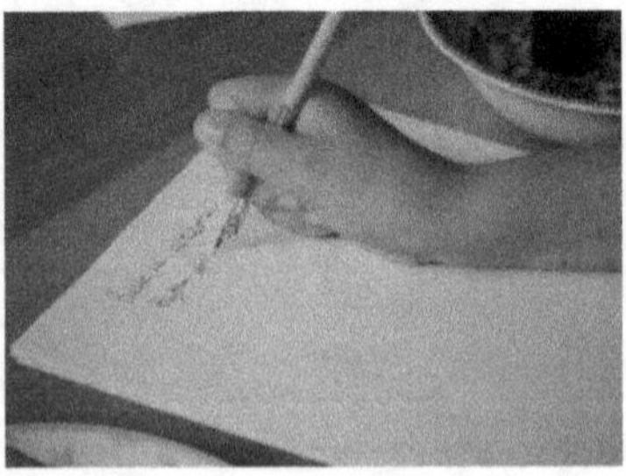

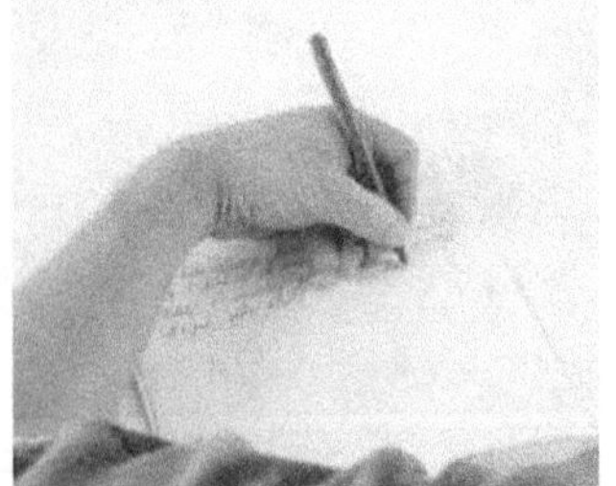

You cannot judge which one is right or wrong, or even determine which is better or worse. Each style is the individual's own developed way of writing, and it is OK as long as you can write adequately. So, provided you can write easily and naturally in your own way, then we must consider your style to be acceptable and proper. I am sure the reader will agree with this.

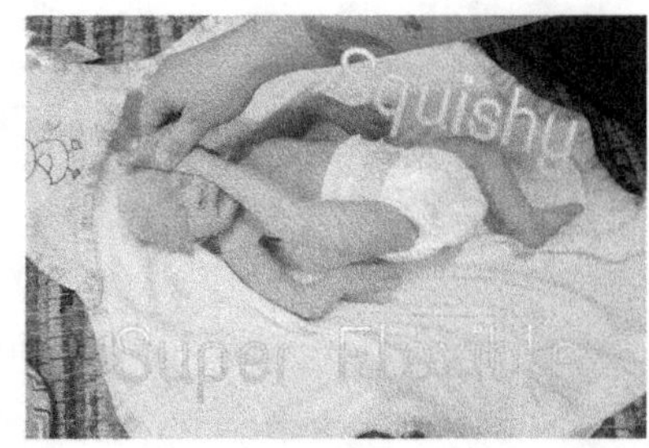

OK, let us go further into studying this. When we were born, though we do not remember, we came into this world with a tremendous (almost unbelievable) degree of physical freedom and possibilities. Our body has approximately 230 joints and between 550 and 650 muscles (depending on how you define them), which enable us to move our body parts to do thousands of different tasks. As we grow older, most of us lose some physical ability. Do you remember how flexible a baby is? Babies can do some amazing things with their bodies. For instance, a full split is so easy for them. All of us were flexible when we were babies. How many of us, as adults, can do a full split? Maybe not too many.

Though we may have lost some physical ability as we have grown older, we have gained many important and necessary skills, such as walking, speaking, writing, and driving, just to name a few. We learned these skills by initially failing many times before finding out how they were done. After that stage, we repeated the movements literally thousands of times to master them. We went through this process to learn all those necessary life skills, even though we do not quite remember the exact moments of the process that occurred while we were still babies.

So, we are now skillful at all these daily movements, such as walking. We walk every day, and walking is easy and feels very natural to us. Thus, these daily movements that we can carry out naturally are what we call *moving the body*. These are the physical movements that we have developed or learned in our life experience. They are certainly easy and natural. I hope the reader understands the concept up to this point.

OK, then what is using the body? Moving the body is a naturally acquired ability to move the parts of the body. On the other hand, when you need to change your body movements in order to learn a new skill, such as dance, sport, or a musical instrument, you need to pay close attention to how you must move your body parts.

Though our fingers have excellent dexterity, we find it challenging to move them correctly as we play piano or guitar. It takes training through thousands of repetitions to play a musical instrument right. Eventually, playing piano or guitar becomes natural.

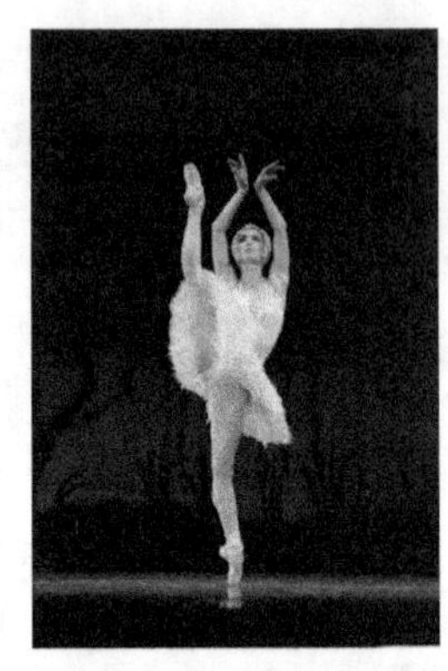

A similar situation occurs with other parts of the body when you perform other activities. If you are not a professional dancer, when you dance at a party, your actions are at the level of just moving the body. On the other hand, if you watch Fred Astaire (1899–1987) or Sylvie Guillem (1965– [photo right]) dance, you'll see that they are using their bodies. This is also true when you watch superathletes such as Michael Jordan (1963– [photo below left]) and Edson Arantes do Nascimento, more popularly known as *Pelé* (1940– [photo below right]). What they can do with their bodies seems to be so natural; however, neither nonprofessional athletes nor even their colleagues are able to imitate them.

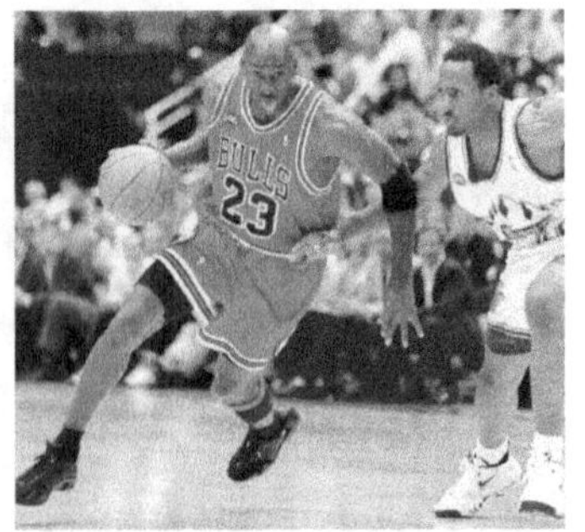

So, how do they do this? Are they geniuses? Maybe so, and we must agree that they are talented, but, at the same time, I can guarantee you that they practiced as hard as, if not harder than, their opponents. They also needed to ingrain their techniques into their bodies. These examples show what our body is capable of. This is what I call *using the body to its utmost*. These may be extreme examples of how to best use the body. We must remember that this does not mean that

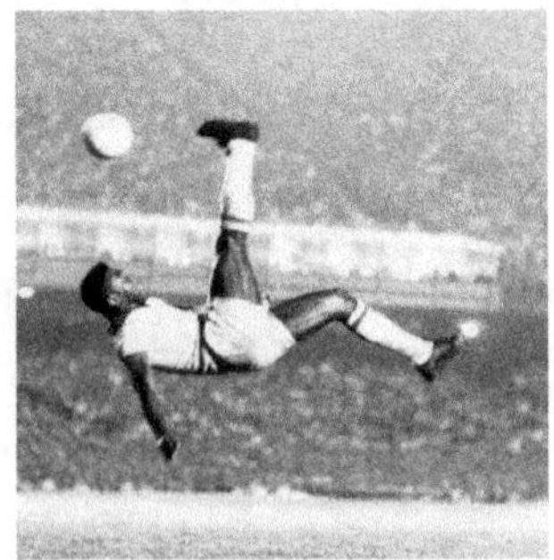

their expert moves came naturally. I bring this up to exemplify the clear difference between natural (untrained) body movements and skilled (trained) movements that are acquired after many hours of training.

Now, as you can imagine, this idea of hard training will lead us to the situation of karate. We can easily appreciate that learning karate techniques is acquiring skill and control of body movements. Though many of the movements are similar to natural body movements, such as striking, making a fist, kicking, etc., they are not the same. Often, knowing these natural movements stands in the way of executing the techniques correctly. For instance, you know that the natural way of making a fist that we see among those who are not karate practitioners is quite different from the fist that we make in karate. The surface of a natural nonkarate fist is often not flat, and you need to pound on a *makiwara* (photo right) to learn how to keep it flat.

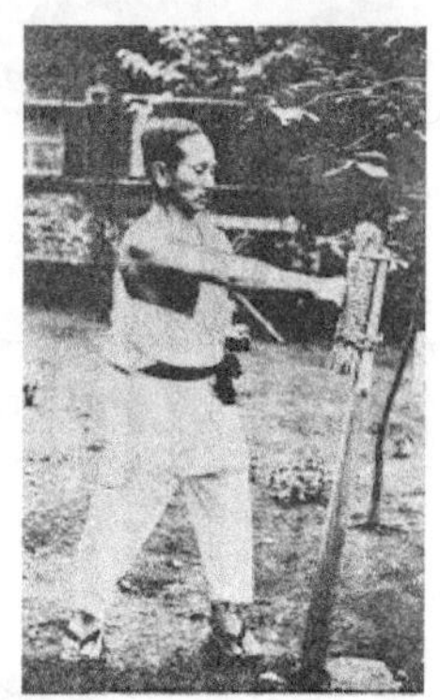

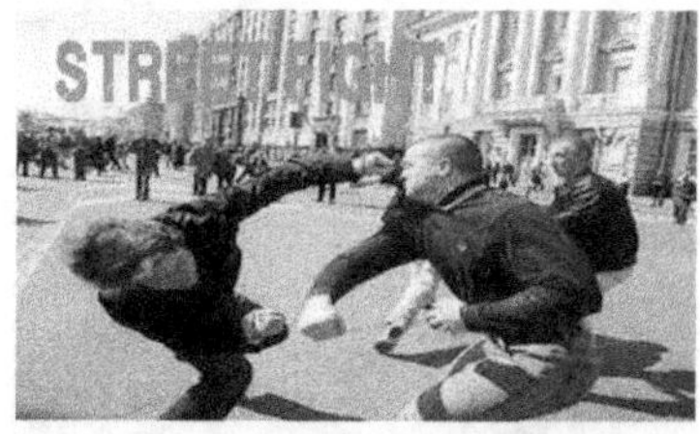

Another example is the punch itself. The natural nonkarate punch that you see in a street fight is the wide arm-swinging punch (photo left). The most popular, or most frequently used, punch in traditional karate, however, is *choku zuki* (photo right), which is a straight punch. I am sure your teacher had to tell you not to stick your elbow out as you punched. How many times did you have to punch this way before you began to feel comfortable with this punching method? Hundreds? Probably thousands, right?

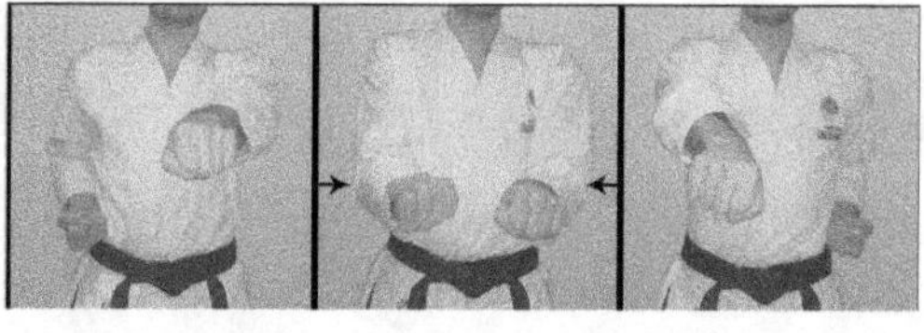

So, you agree that we need to acquire the use of these kinds of movements and develop our skill when we learn karate techniques. I do not think there is any problem with this concept. So, you will probably say, "We know all this. So, what is the point you are trying to make here?"

OK, let me explain my point. Our body is closely tied to our mind. As you

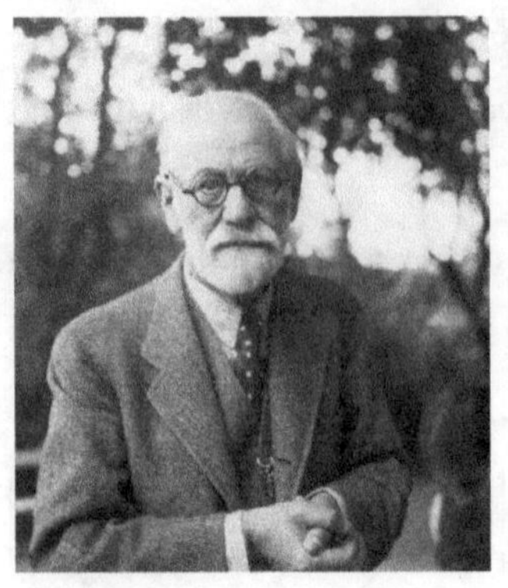

know, our mind consists of a conscious side and an unconscious side. Sigmund Freud (1856–1939) didn't exactly invent the idea of the conscious versus the unconscious mind, but he certainly was responsible for making this concept popular.

The conscious mind is your awareness at the present moment and consists of all the mental processes of which you are aware. Freud said this was the tip of the iceberg. With conscious behavior, you know why you are doing what you do. For example, you eat your food because you are hungry, and you go to bed because you feel sleepy. This is very straightforward, and not too many people have an issue with it.

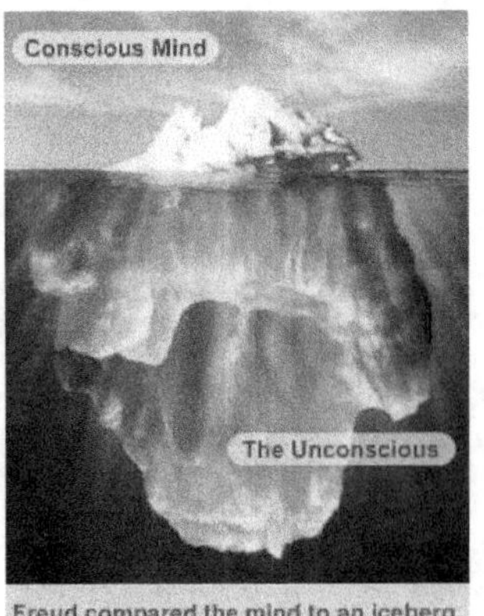

Freud compared the mind to an iceberg.

The unconscious mind, on the other hand, is almost invisible or is hidden behind your memory, and this is exactly why it is a bigger issue. It occupies a huge space in your mind, and Freud considered this to be the submerged part of the iceberg. Unconscious behavior would be the automatic responses of the human body, such as breathing, heartbeat, etc. (Note that breathing can also be done consciously.)

This is behavior that you carry out without being aware of it. In other words, as noted by Timothy D. Wilson in his book *Strangers to Ourselves* (Belknap Press, 2004), "the unconscious mind comprises mental processes that are inaccessible to consciousness but that influence judgments, feelings, or behavior." One example would be a phobic behavior such as screaming at the sight of a spider. Other popular examples would be your mannerisms, shaking your legs while sitting, biting your fingernails, doodling while listening to your teacher's lecture, or tapping your fingers when you are nervous or irritated, to name a few.

Many things we do in our daily lives, such as walking, sitting, writing, riding a bicycle, or driving a car, can be handled by the unconscious mind. Although our behaviors are driven by unconscious forces, we typically do not have access to the information stored in the unconscious mind. How can we do this? It is mainly because we did something so many times during our childhood. These are the countless memories and experiences we acquired, which formed who we are today; however, interestingly, we cannot recall most of these memories.

In addition, we also have one more layer of mind, the subconscious mind, which consists of accessible information. You can become aware of this information once you direct your attention to it. This is known as *recall*. You can walk or drive to your office or the neighborhood store without consciously needing to be alert to your surroundings. You can talk on your cell phone and still make it home without getting lost. You can easily bring to consciousness the subconscious information about the path to your home. You can also easily remember phone numbers that you frequently use.

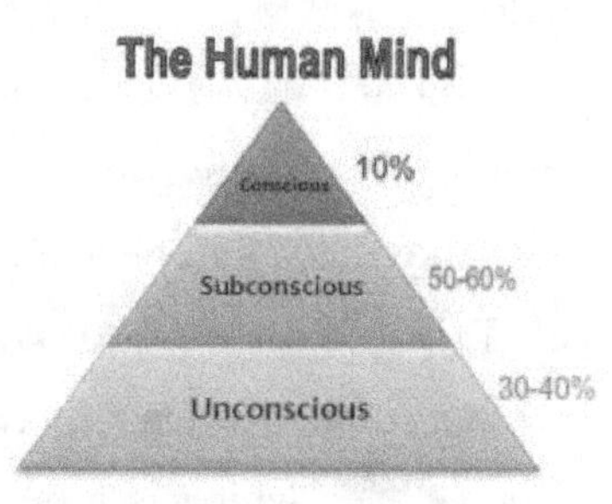

So, what does this mean? Many actions and techniques you find in karate seem to be similar to what you do in your daily life. For instance, the step you learn to take with *zenkutsu dachi* in a karate lesson is similar to your normal step, though a little greater in length. This is why the *zenkutsu dachi* executed by most beginners tends to be very high, and these practitioners have difficulty bending the front knee. It is not only because their legs are weaker than those of the senior students but also because they are so much more accustomed to standing with their knees straight rather than bent. Their actions are heavily influenced by unconscious direction. They have to pay much more attention (that is, apply much more consciousness) to their front leg so that they can keep it bent at the knee. After repeating this process thousands of times, deeply bending the front knee becomes natural, and they can perform this correctly with the subconscious mind.

So, if you depend on your karate technique before it reaches a skilled level or can be performed by the subconscious mind, you will only move your body according to unconscious direction or raw natural ability.

Then, beginners want to know how many times they have to repeat a technique before it becomes natural. This is the same as wanting to know how much training is required to change your movements from an unconscious state to a subconscious state. The famous samurai Musashi Miyamoto (宮本武蔵, c. 1584–1645) said that a thousand days (about three years) of training is required to complete the basics of kenjutsu and be at a beginner's level. This makes sense to us as we all know that it takes at least three years of continuous training before we can reach *shodan* (初段), which is a beginner's level according to Miyamoto. In addition, Miyamoto said that to reach a master's level, a minimum of ten thousand days (about thirty years) of continuous training is required.

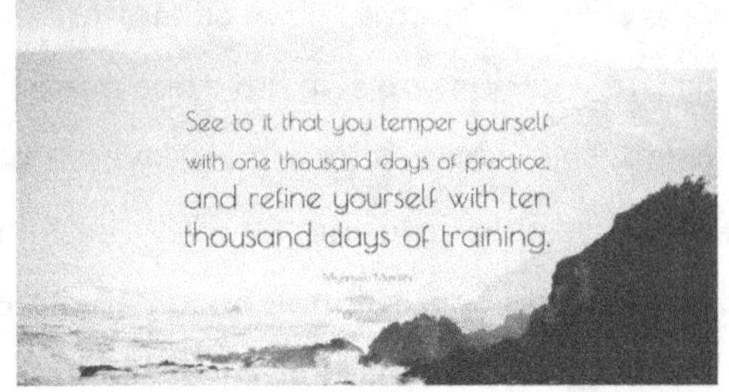

Miyamoto was saying that after a thousand days of training, a technique will be generated by the subconscious mind. However, it takes ten thousand days for that technique to become an unconscious-level movement. Many karate practitioners may boast that they have trained more than thirty years, but I doubt that any of them have trained every single day of that thirty years. If you trained regularly three days per week for thirty years, you would actually have trained only about thirteen years. At this pace, you would need to train a total of sixty-five years to reach a master's level. I suspect few karate practitioners train regularly more than three times per week. It is no wonder that only a few have been able to reach a master's level.

Most traditional Japanese instructors share this belief, and we emphasize repeating *kihon* not only hundreds but thousands of times. Yes, sometimes our training can be very boring and can seem to be a waste of time as we do the same thing over and over, but excellent instructors know how to make boring training into something more interesting.

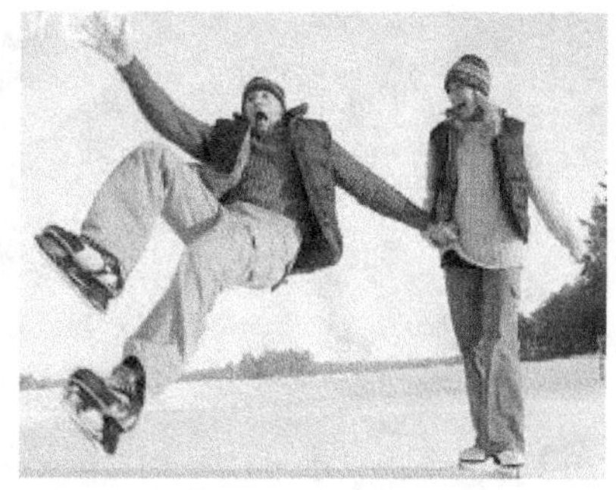

As they say, it is difficult to kick an old habit. In karate training, it is indeed, but you must learn how to kick your old habits. When you train to execute karate techniques such as *zenkutsu dachi*, an old habit may not be too obvious unless your instructor points out to you or taps your front knee. However, in a different situation, such as learning how to ski or ice-skate, your failure is very visible as you will fall if you just move your body according to your old walking technique. To avoid this, you must learn a new balancing skill so that you will be able to use your body to perform this new balancing technique in a new situation on ice or snow.

Relatively speaking, learning how to ski or ice-skate is much easier than learning karate techniques. The unfortunate thing for karate practitioners is that it is less likely to be recognized as such since it is much less noticeable. Most people who have just started karate training believe learning to develop a strong punch is the ultimate goal. They train at this by banging on either a *makiwara* or a punching bag. This is like trying to find a bigger stone or thicker stick to hit someone with. This is still at the level of moving the body or using raw action.

As you begin to understand the true meaning of karate skill, on the other hand, you realize that your techniques (both attacking and blocking) must be trained in such a way that a punch, kick, or block becomes sharp like a sword. This is at the level of using the body and requires continual training for ten thousand days, whether you like it or not.

Even though the exact number of repetitions will vary from one person to another, there is a turning point after thousands of repetitions where the quality of the body movements shows significant improvement. This is difficult to see in karate training. An easy example of this turning point in acquiring a technique can be seen in learning how to swim or ride a bike. Until you finally learn how to ride, you continue to fall. Since riding a bike is a much easier physical requirement, you

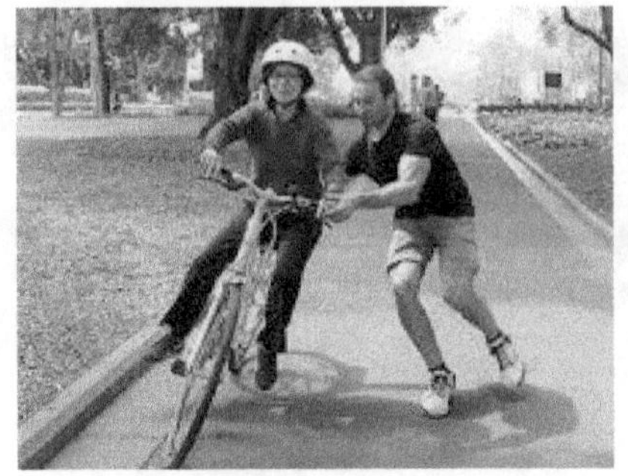

do not need to practice for a thousand days. However, if you are training for a professional championship or the Olympic Games, you will need at least that much training to condition yourself.

There are two key points in karate training that are often ignored. These two points must always be remembered as you continue your training.

The first point is that you must repeat the technique correctly. If you repeat a poor or incorrect technique, then that poor or incorrect technique becomes your fixed ability. Your aim must be for your techniques to be as sharp as a sword by repeating your training. You must never forget that these techniques may be used in a life-or-death situation. This is why we use the phrase *one punch, one kill* in karate.

Secondly, though physical skill is important and necessary, you must never forget the importance of training your mind. This includes not only fighting spirit but also *zanshin*, judgment, calmness, courage, and other mental requirements that can be found in Funakoshi's *Niju Kun*.

For your information, interestingly, Masutatsu Oyama (大山倍達, 1923–1994), the founder of Kyokushinkai (極真会), borrowed Miyamoto's concept. Here is his quote:

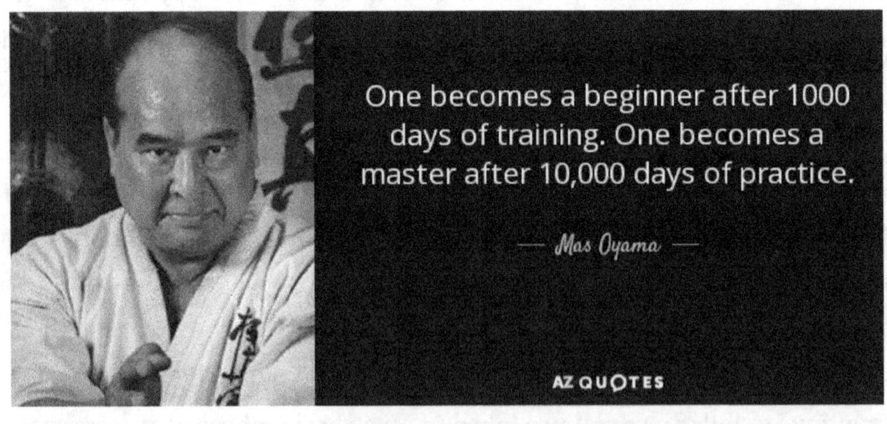

Conclusion

If you continue to train for ten thousand days and include the two important points that I mentioned earlier in your training, you will finally be able to graduate from just moving your body. No matter what dangerous situation you may be in, you will be able to use your body to defend not only your body but also your honor. Only then, perhaps, will you be able to say that your techniques are at a master's level.

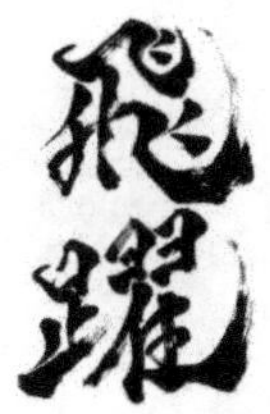

Chapter Seventeen
第十七章

Can Karate Be Mastered by Practicing Only Kata?
形稽古で空手の奥義が極めれるか

Can you master karate by practicing only *kata*? You may think this is an easy question. You certainly may believe that the correct answer is no. You are absolutely correct; however, I wish to present my opinion in this chapter that the essence of *kata* is surely the key that will assist you in achieving mastery of karate.

Before I present my ideas, I think it would be very beneficial to look at some quotes about *kata* by the karate masters of the past. I believe we can learn a lot from those who understood karate and thus have a much better understanding of the essence of *kata*.

The first master I want to introduce is Kenwa Mabuni (摩文仁賢和, 1889–1952 [photo below]), the founder of Shito Ryu. He was one of the first Okinawan masters who migrated to mainland Japan to teach karate in the early twentieth century.

> A *kata* is not fixed or immovable. Like water, it's ever changing and fits itself to the shape of the vessel containing it.
>
> —Kenwa Mabuni

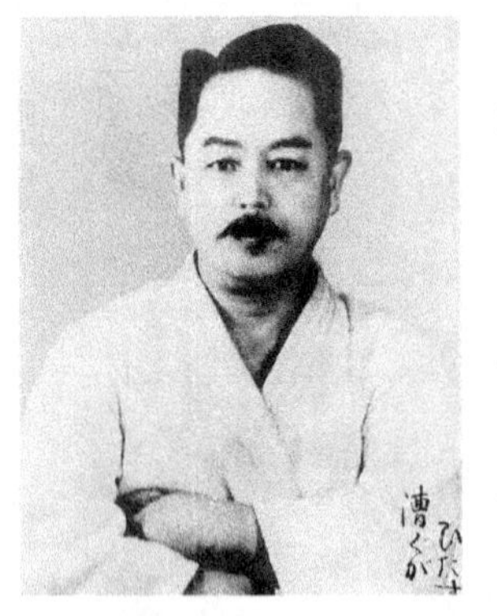

This is an interesting statement. I am also afraid that many people misunderstand his point. It is true that *kata* is like water as it is flexible and changes according to its container. Many people misunderstand this to mean that *kata* can be changed according to the practitioner (thinking that this is the container). However, I disagree with this interpretation. The container does not refer to the practitioner or the person performing the *kata*. Instead, it refers to the different situations and unpredictable environments in which the practitioner could be placed in a real fight. As far as I am concerned, Mabuni believed that the content and techniques within *kata* must not be changed.

> Do not fall into the trap of thinking that just because a *kata* begins to the left that the opponent is attacking from the left.
>
> —Kenwa Mabuni

I also like this quote. I feel that too many practitioners execute the *bunkai* in this manner with superficial understanding. An excellent example is the *bunkai* for the first step in all of the Heian/Pin'an *kata*. These begin to the left side, and many interpret this to mean that the opponent is coming from that side. I write about the reasons Master Anko Itosu (糸洲安恒, 1831–1915), the creator of these *kata*, wanted them to start to the left in Chapter 2: "The Mysteries of the Heian Kata" of my book *Shotokan Mysteries*. Heian/Pin'an and Tekki/Naihanchi are the best examples of the fact that the popular *bunkai* may not fit the ultimate purpose of the *kata*. I will explain what the ultimate purpose is later in this chapter.

Gichin Funakoshi (photo below right) was the founder of Shotokan karate. He migrated from Okinawa to Tokyo in 1922 to introduce mainland Japanese people to karate. He is considered to be the father of modern karate. I will share two of his quotes that are related to learning *kata*.

> In the past, it was expected that about three years were required to learn a single *kata*, and usually even an expert of considerable skill would only know three, or at most five, *kata*.
>
> —Gichin Funakoshi

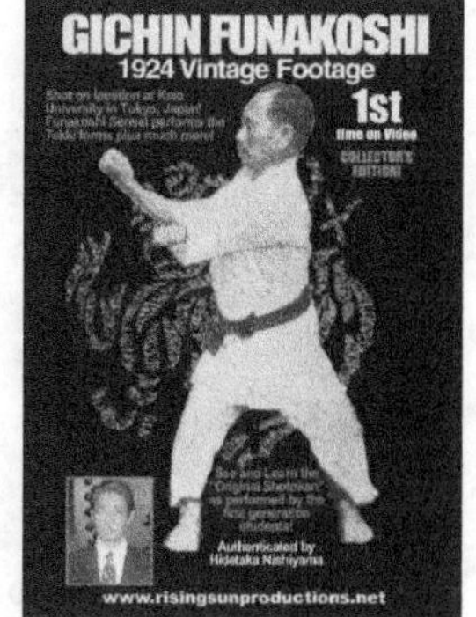

There are two major schools of thought regarding *kata*. One is to learn and practice only a few *kata*, the idea being that you learn those few *kata* in depth. The other is to learn and practice many *kata*, the idea being that you expand the training menu by having different *kata*, which increases training content. Both concepts have their own advantages, so I will not pass judgment regarding which is better or worse in this chapter.

By reading Funakoshi's quote above, we can easily see that he was from the school of few *kata*. Later on, I will explain the function of the *kata*, and you will see why Funakoshi said that a practitioner should spend three years or so to learn a single *kata*. Let's look at another quote by Funakoshi.

> Once a *kata* has been learned, it must be practiced repeatedly until it can be applied in an emergency, for knowledge of just the sequence of a form in karate is useless.
>
> —Gichin Funakoshi

What he is saying in this statement makes sense. A given *kata* must be learned to the point where the practitioner can utilize the knowledge in a real fight. Unfortunately, he stated only that it "must be practiced repeatedly" as the method for attaining a level at which one can use the *kata* techniques in a real fight. I say this statement is unfortunate because it lacks the reasoning as to why repeating a *kata* works. This is not his fault as it is only a quote, not a full essay.

In addition, a more detailed explanation on how *kata* training must be repeated is necessary as simply repeating a *kata* without knowing how to do it correctly is not sufficient. When I say, "how to do it correctly," I could easily be misunderstood as I am not referring to just performing the *kata* with the correct physical movements. There are other factors that become extremely important in the concept of "correctly." I will explain these factors later in this chapter.

Tsuyoshi Chitose (千歳強直, 1898–1984 [photo at top of following page]), from Naha, Okinawa Prefecture, founded Chito Ryu (千唐流) in 1946.

> Our teachers did not give us a clear explanation of the *kata* from old times. I must find the features and meaning of each form by my own study and effort, by repeating the exercises of form through training.
>
> —Tsuyoshi Chitose

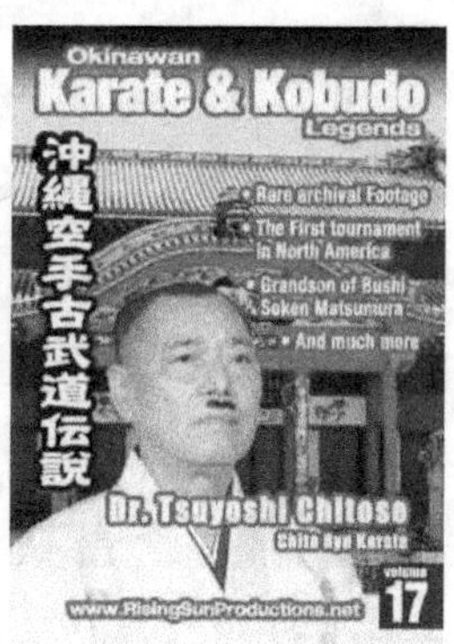

This is a surprising statement that could also be very controversial. In other words, Chitose, a karate master, "confessed" that his teachers had not taught him *bunkai* training. Isn't this shocking? Some people may doubt his words, believing that Chitose was hiding something. Others may disrespectfully believe his karate training was not thorough or comprehensive. I will explain later in this chapter why *bunkai* was not a part of karate training on Okinawa.

Shigeru Egami (江上茂, 1912–1981) was the founder of the Shotokai (松濤會), one of the two major organizations based on Funakoshi's style of karate, who was Egami's teacher from the time the latter was eighteen years old.

> Even in the forty years that I have been practicing karate, the changes have been many. It would be interesting to be able to go back in time, to the point when the *kata* were created, and study them.
>
> —Shigeru Egami

This is also an interesting "confession" by another master. It is supposedly an unwritten rule that we are not to change the content of *kata*. However, Egami admitted that there had been many changes in karate training. Even though he did not say the changes were specifically within the *kata*, the last sentence clearly states that he wanted to go back to the time when the *kata* were created. In addition, it is documented that the main training method used by his teacher, Gichin Funakoshi, was *kata* practice.

It is difficult to point out exactly when the changes were made in the wide time span of forty years. This may be an interesting subject to discuss further, but I will not do so here as I do not wish to deviate too much from the main subject of the relationship between *kata* training and the mastery of the art.

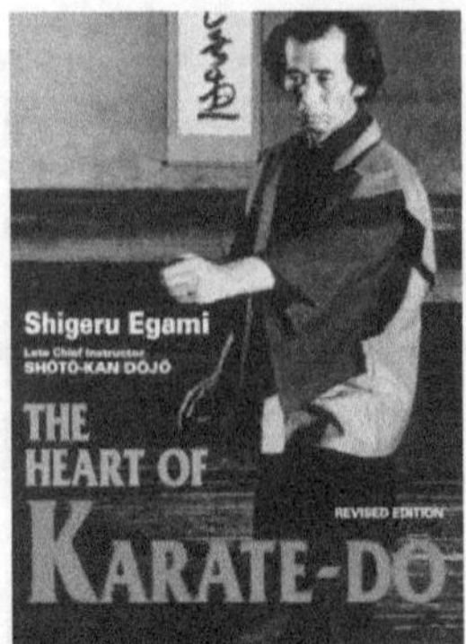

I would like to point out one thing from Egami's quote, however. It is obvious that he did not wish to go back to when he had started his karate training forty years prior. He wanted to go all the way back to the time when the *kata* were created. This means he correctly guessed that the *kata* he had learned even forty years earlier were not the same as when they had been created. It is very interesting how he changed the karate training after he created the Shotokai. If you are not from this style, I very strongly recommend that you read his famous book, *The Heart of Karate-Do* (posthumously published by Kodansha in 1986 and 2000 [photo above]).

Choki Motobu (photo right) was the founder of Motobu Ryu (本部流). He was born in Shuri, Okinawa Prefecture. As mentioned in Chapter 1, his nickname was *Saru* (猿, 'Monkey') because of his great agility.

> The techniques of *kata* have their limits and were never intended to be used against an opponent in an arena or on a battlefield.
>
> —Choki Motobu

This quote is extremely interesting and very understandable coming from Motobu. On the other hand, his words can also be misinterpreted. It is known that Motobu focused his training on *bunkai* and did not practice too many *kata*. Because of this, some Okinawan *karateka* have even mistakenly claimed that he knew only one *kata*, Tekki/Naihanchi. So, some people may think that he did not believe in the value of *kata*.

Motobu was known as a fighting man as he had great power and agility. In fact, his karate was marked by a series of two-person *kumite* drills, which was unique in the early twentieth century. His statement sounds as though he did not believe in the value of *kata* and thought that the techniques of *kata* were ineffective in a real fight. I do not agree with this understanding. I believe Motobu knew the importance of *kata*. At the same time, he also knew that there were two different ways of training: learning the techniques and using the techniques.

I will further explain this subject later in this chapter as I have written a separate work on *kata* that is related to the topic at hand. But, before getting into that, I would like to share another quote by Motobu that will better illustrate his clear understanding of the importance of using the techniques.

> All *kata* use the so-called postures [*kamae*]. In fact, there are many kinds of postures and many kinds of *kata*. While learning these postures should not be totally ignored, we must be careful not to overlook that they are just forms or templates of sort; it is the function of their application which needs to be mastered.
>
> —Choki Motobu

He wrote that we must not consider *kata* to be just a form or template but that we must know the application, or *bunkai*. By saying this, he was referring to both learning the techniques and using the techniques. Now you can see that he considered *kata* to be important and warned us not to practice it incorrectly.

Now that you have read all these quotes, I am sure you will agree that they are a treasure to us. We can easily see that all these masters considered *kata* to be an important tool in mastering karate. They said that the practitioner should repeat the *kata* and spend many years on all of them. So, many of us repeat the *kata* hundreds and thousands of times. Some feel their karate is improving, but I suspect many feel that just repeating the *kata* is not enough.

Unfortunately, these masters did not write down specifically how to practice the *kata*. This is something I would like to attempt here. Once you have read my explanation, I believe you will be able to understand what Motobu was trying to tell us in the second quote of his that was mentioned.

First, we need to understand what *kata* is. *Kata* is written in kanji as 型 or

形, which literally means 'form', 'shape', or 'cast'. We understand it to be a prearranged collection of detailed choreographed patterns of movements. This is a unique concept that is found mainly in Japan but also in the Chinese martial arts. In Japan, this concept exists not only in the martial arts but also in many other fields that require some type of physical skill, such as carpentry, dancing, cooking, etc.

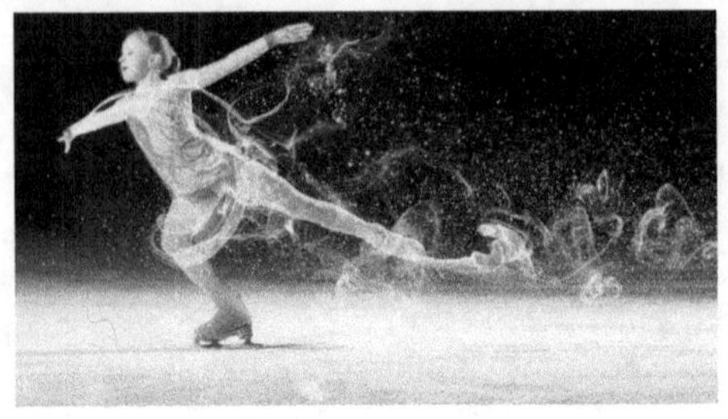

We do not find *kata* in sports, even though figure skating has some fixed requirements. There are seven required elements in the short program with mandatory deductions for failures on each element. However, the overall routine can be somewhat free within the required time (a maximum of two minutes fifty seconds), whereas in karate *kata*, all the steps and physical movements must be identical when performed by different people, which is a very unique requirement.

In addition, *kata* is not supposed to be augmented or changed at all. In fact, there has been debate over whether or not this requirement must really be adhered to. As a matter of fact, some instructors claim that *kata* should be augmented by the practitioners since they are all different in their body makeup and abilities. Even though I understand why they believe in their justification of this, I have to disagree with them. The reason I disagree is not based on any cultural aspect, such as respect for the creators of the *kata*. Please do not misunderstand; I do have a tremendous amount of respect for the creators. However, the real reason I believe we must not change the movements of the *kata* is different.

To master a karate skill, you have to meet two requirements. One is learning the karate techniques. Everyone understands this requirement, and this is why people are eager to learn *kata*. The other is learning how to use those techniques. This second requirement is often ignored because most instructors do not understand its value. Having read that second quote by Motobu, you can see that he knew the value of this requirement. I explain these two requirements in detail in Chapter 5: "The Reasons Why We Must Preserve Our Kata" of my book *Shotokan Transcen-*

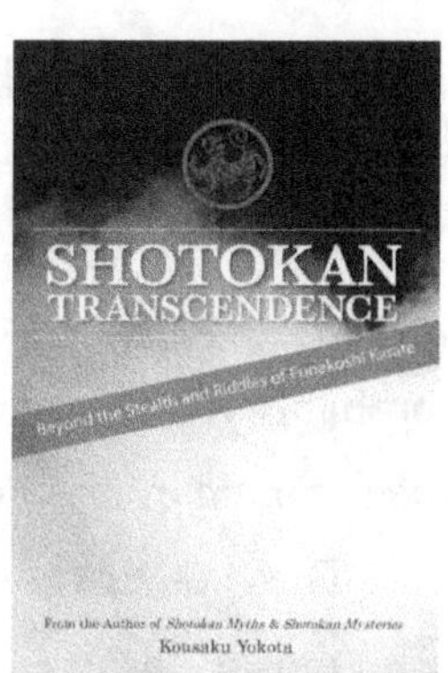

dence. Therefore, I will not repeat my full explanation here, but I will need to describe the key points as this is the core of this chapter.

Let me explain the important portion of these two requirements. *Kata* means 'form' or 'cast'. In other words, we need to think of a cast, which is an object that is made by pouring a hot liquid into a container and allowing it to become a solid. The reader can easily guess why the Japanese people chose the word *kata*. The *kata* function as a cast to take our uncertain body movements and make them solid, which means that our body knows how to do the techniques. If you do not know the karate punch, you will throw a street-fighting punch, which is typically a wide swinging punch.

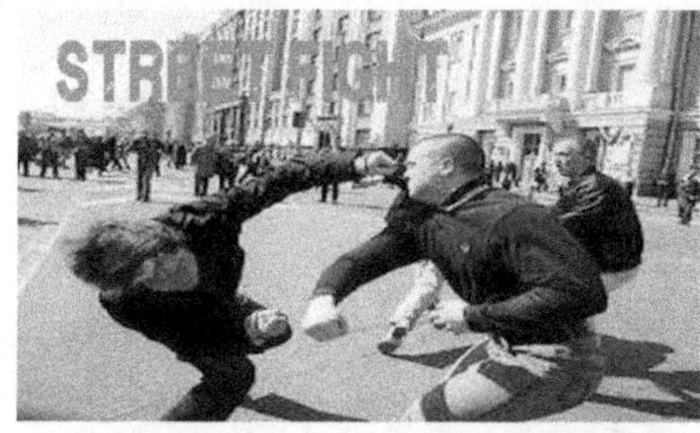

What's wrong with a street-fighting punch (photo left)? First, your fist typically starts from *jodan*, either near your chin or even from behind your head. This means your punch is much more visible than a punch that comes from *chudan* or from your hip. Secondly, it is a wide swinging punch, which is more visible and takes longer to reach the target than a karate *choku zuki* (photo below), which is a straight punch. A seasoned street fighter has a fast and effective punch, so he may not need to learn the karate punch. But, he typically has a crude kicking technique, so he should learn and master karate kicking techniques if he wishes to be able to defend himself better in a street fight.

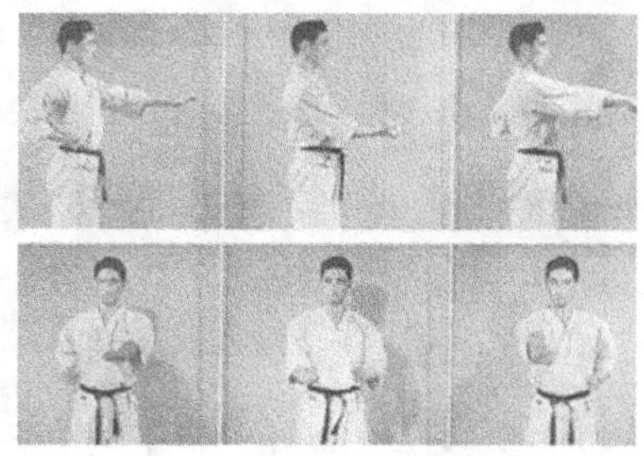

So, I believe we can all agree with the first requirement, which is learning the karate techniques. By understanding the purpose of a cast, you can easily understand why we must not change or augment *kata*. Can you imagine if you changed the cast size of the bricks used to build a wall? It would be like building a wall with rocks of various shapes.

I want you to remember your experience on the first day you began your karate training. I am sure you learned how to execute *choku zuki*. Did it feel natural to bring your fist to your hip and then punch straight out? Even before the punch, you probably felt unnatural making a karate fist. You felt unnatural because your body had learned other ways of doing things.

These other ways, or natural body movements, are called *kuse* in Japanese (as previously discussed in Chapter 13). Learning karate technique means that you first had to unlearn the *kuse* and then acquire new ways of doing things, which are the karate techniques. You must not adjust or augment the karate techniques (that is, the ideal textbook motions) just because it feels more comfortable or is easier to do them your way, which happens to be your *kuse*. In other words, you are being lazy about making an honest effort to drop your *kuse*.

Why do you have to acquire ideal textbook motions? The answer is simple. You are learning techniques to use in a life-or-death situation. Would you buy a gun with a bent barrel or a rusted trigger? This level of severity is not required if karate is being practiced for sport competition as the ultimate goal is quite different. Ideal textbook motions are not necessary to score points in a match.

Let us go on to the next requirement. This requirement is the ability to use the techniques. What does this mean? Many practitioners, including senior ones, ask this. Most practitioners falsely believe that once they learn the techniques, they can use them right away in a real fight. We karate instructors often see this false expectation in novices. Many of them operate on the wishful thinking that they can become karate experts in a few months. Most cannot even dream that it will take many years.

Even if you repeat the *kata* as accurately as possible, this will not be enough if you do not know how the techniques are used or applied as your precise techniques may be ineffective. It is as though you had a sword or a gun but did not know how to use it to cut or shoot. In this case, your techniques may not be able to help you in a life-or-death situation.

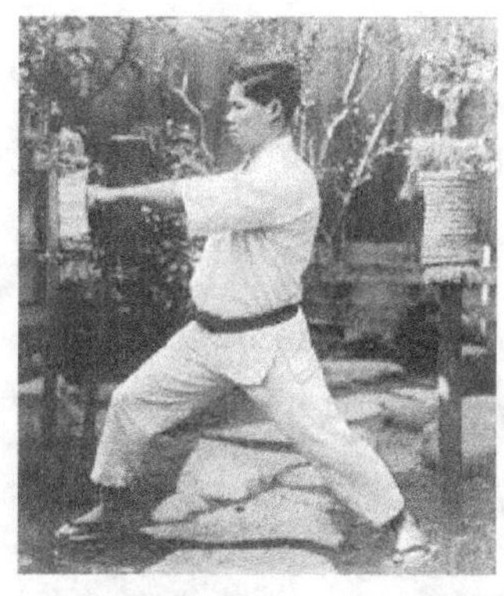

You practice the accuracy of the karate techniques through basic training, *kihon*. As you know, *kihon* is the repetitive training of certain key techniques taken out of the *kata*. *Kata* is great as it has turns, jumps, combinations, changes in direction, execution at different speeds, etc. I can see why Funakoshi believed that training in *kata* alone was sufficient. However, without an opponent, it is difficult to judge distance, timing, angle, power, direction of delivery, etc.

This is one of the reasons many practitioners punch a *makiwara*. Even though some people believe that the main purpose of *makiwara* training is to build up big knuckles, it is actually to check distance, build correct posture, align the arm correctly, etc. In kung fu, they practice with a wooden dummy, which is a more complex training tool, but it serves a similar purpose.

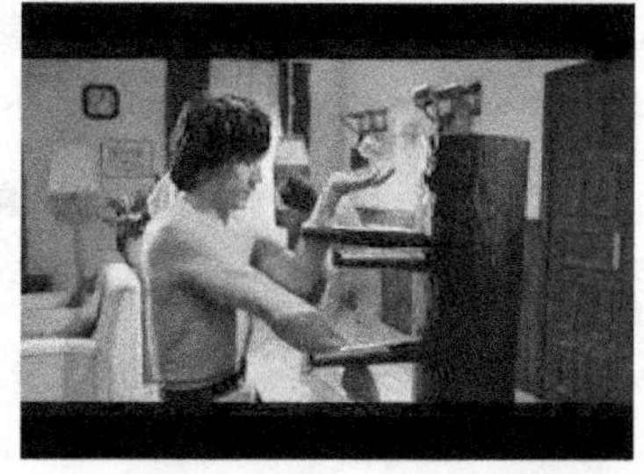

A lack of understanding regarding the true intention of the techniques in a *kata* such as Tekki causes many practitioners to have false beliefs about this *kata*'s true objectives. This *kata* is not limited to fighting in a small boat, in a narrow corridor, or with your back against a wall. Many people misjudge the *kata* based on their appearances, especially unique ones such as Tekki. Believe me, the ancient masters were more realistic and thus created *kata* that were more universal and useful. This is why Motobu promoted *kumite* and said that *bunkai* training with an opponent was necessary.

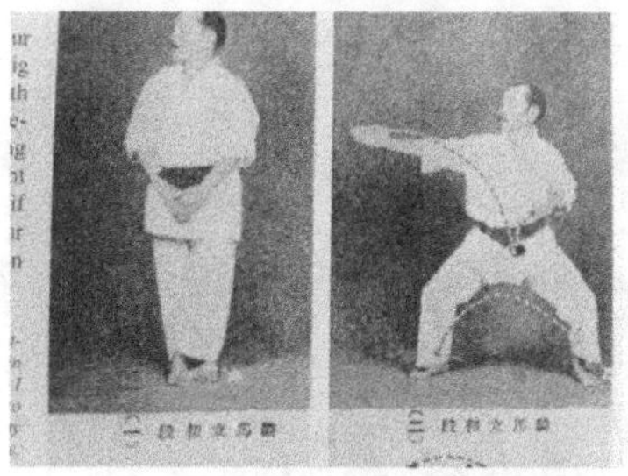

Then, am I saying it is impossible to master karate by practicing only *kata*? No, I truly believe it is very possible, although not at all easy. How can I say this confidently? Do you agree that there were many kenjutsu experts in the time of the samurai? Just think how difficult it would have been to practice kenjutsu with an opponent using a real sword. I cannot imagine they would have used free fighting in their training. One of the combatants surely would have died, or at least been maimed. That kind of training method was, and still is, impractical, if not impossible.

As you know, practitioners of iaido practice alone most of the time. In kenjutsu, they do *tameshigiri* (試し切り, 'test cutting'), where they cut a roll of straw mats. They also have *kata*; however, their *kata* are usually run with an opponent. This is like our *bunkai* training in karate. So, from this perspective, you could include *bunkai* as a part of *kata*.

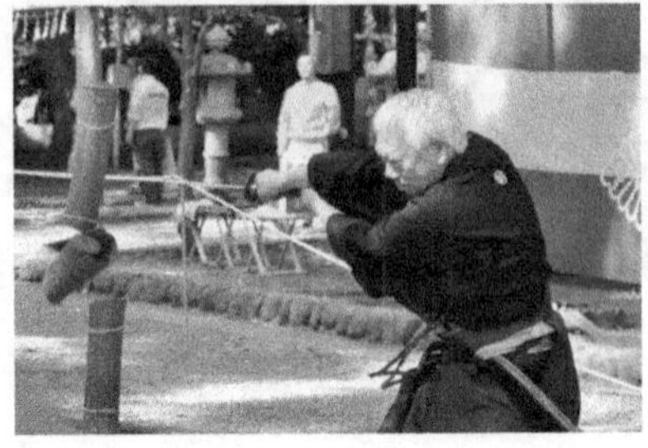

I know many kenjutsu practitioners use a *bokken* (木剣, 'wooden sword') and typically practice alone or against standing trees. My belief is that the ancient kenjutsu experts typically practiced alone but were able to improve their skill to an extremely high level. The key was, I think, that they imagined they were fighting against an opponent every time they swung their swords. This imagination technique is recognized as a useful training method in modern-day sports.

Well, we don't have to go too far back in history. Look at the *te* masters of the past. Those who were documented in the nineteenth, and even in the early twentieth, century became karate experts without doing *jiyu kumite*. They mainly practiced *kata*, and their teachers must have taught them the *bunkai* and applications.

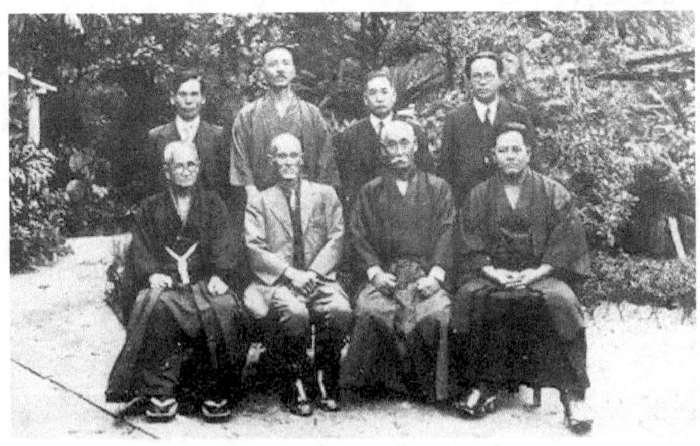

Conclusion

There are two requirements for mastering karate. First, learn the karate techniques as accurately as possible. Second, learn how to use the techniques, which is the *bunkai* and applications.

I need to add a word of caution here. You must not work on these two requirements at or around the same time. It depends on how frequently you practice, but you first need to spend at least a few years learning to execute the techniques accurately. If you practice *bunkai* before your techniques are solid, they will become modified or degraded. I write about this in Chapter 7: "Do Not Teach Bunkai" of my book *Karatedo Paradigm Shift*. The title can be puzzling, but I am writing about not teaching *bunkai* to beginners for the same reason I have explained above.

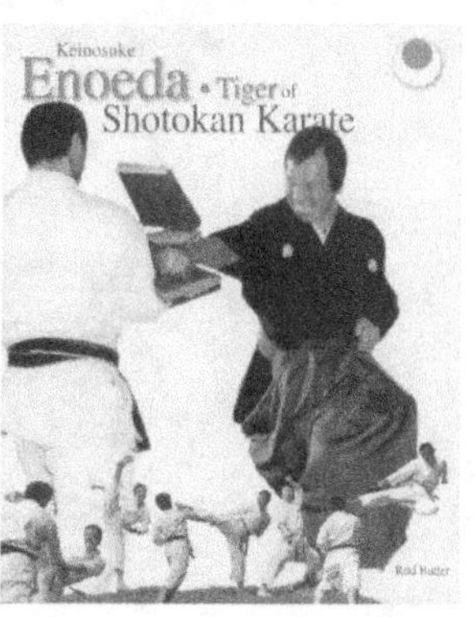

Here at the end of this chapter, I would like to share a quote by Keinosuke Enoeda (榎枝慶之輔, 1935–2003), who was a former chief instructor of the Karate Union of Great Britain (KUGB). He was widely renowned for his powerful karate. After his passing, he was awarded *kyudan* by the JKA. I am ending this chapter with these words not because he was from the same style as I am (Shotokan) but rather because his quote perfectly describes the essence of what I have written here.

> Whether you do sport karate or *budo* karate, remember that *kata* is the vehicle that will allow you to reach a true understanding of real karate.
>
> —Keinosuke Enoeda

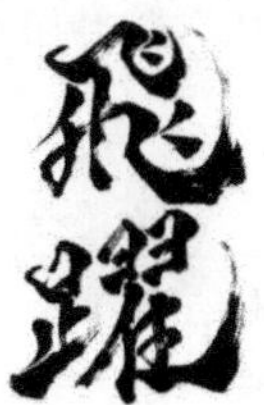

Chapter Eighteen
第十八章

What Is Hado?
波動とは何ぞや？

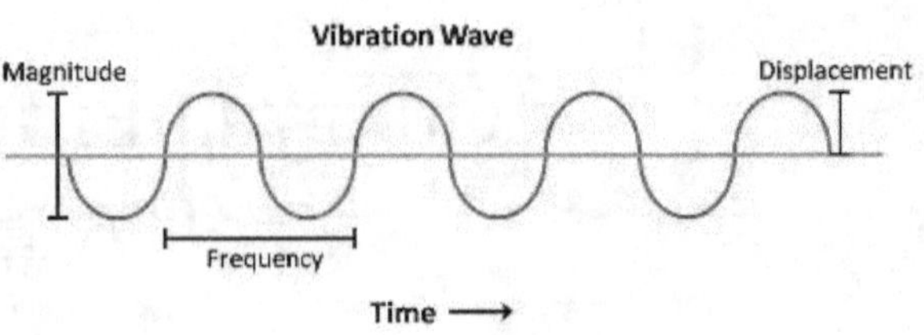

Have you ever heard of the Japanese term *hado*? I assume most readers have not. In fact, this is a concept that is not normally considered in karate. I am not an expert in kung fu, but I think it is in that art. I believe all senior karate practitioners should at least know the concept, even if they do not apply it in their karate training.

OK, so what is *hado* (波動)? *Ha* (波) means 'wave(s)', and *do* (動) means 'movement' in Japanese. This *do* is different from the *do* (道) used at the end of *karatedo* (空手道), which means 'way' or 'path'. So, the combined characters literally mean 'wave movement', and the word, of course, translates to 'vibration'. Most readers surely know the definition of the word *vibration*, but I will quote two relevant senses of the word (1 and 4) from *Merriam-Webster's Collegiate Dictionary, Eleventh Edition*, just to clarify.

1. a periodic motion of the particles of an elastic body or medium in alternately opposite directions from the position of equilibrium when that equilibrium has been disturbed (as when a stretched cord produces musical tones or molecules in the air transmit sounds to the ear)

4. a characteristic emanation, aura, or spirit that infuses or vitalizes someone or something and that can be instinctively sensed or experienced

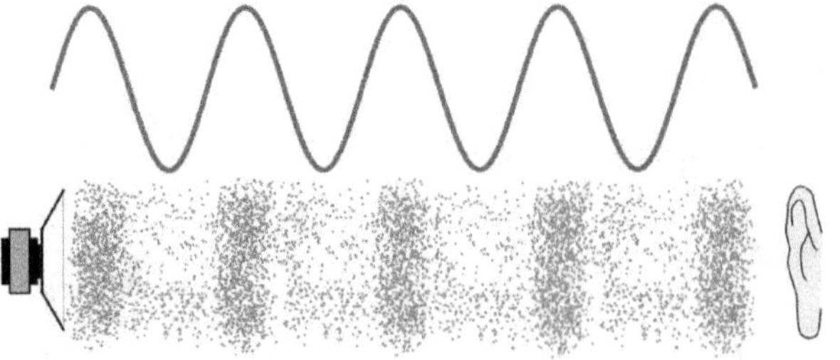

Probably the easiest context for you to sense the existence of vibration is sound. The waves in the air hit your eardrum, and you recognize this as sound. As you know, there are many different kinds of sounds: fast, slow, loud, quiet, high-pitched, low-pitched, etc. Different kinds of sounds have different wave patterns. Though you cannot see sound, you can see the different patterns of sound in the form of a musical score (illustration above).

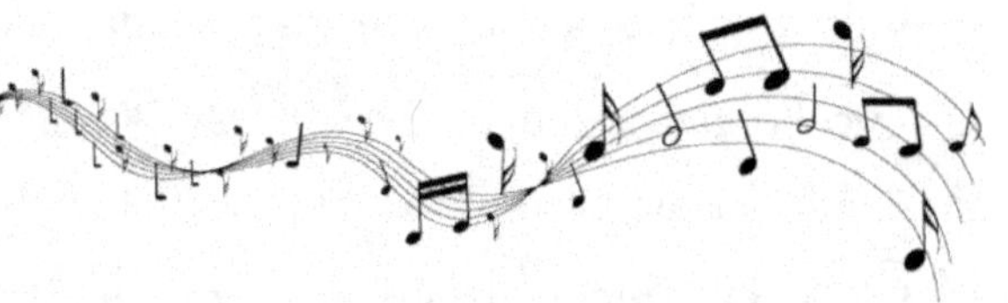

If you want to see waves with your eyes, the easiest way is to observe them in water. You can see them on the surface of a pond, a river, an ocean, or even a cup of tea. In fact, the reason you can see things is that light has different waves that are part of the visible spectrum of electromagnetic waves. You see these waves as the colors of the rainbow. Each color has a different wavelength. Red has the longest wavelength, and violet has the shortest (illustration left). Interestingly, when all the waves are seen together, they make white light.

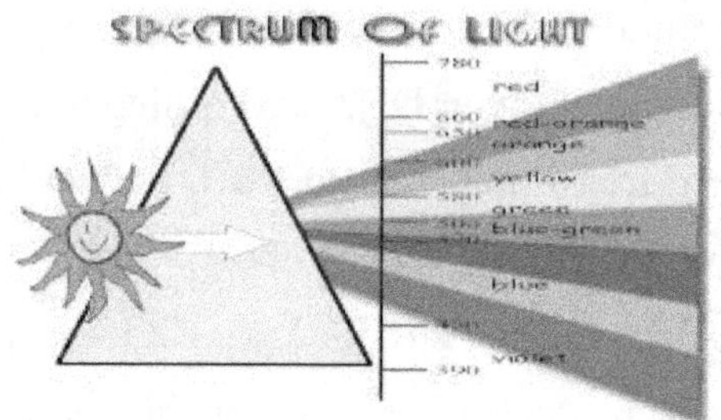

In fact, just about everything you can think of is actually made up of vibrations. Atoms are no exception. As you know, atoms make up the elements. With their protons, neutrons, and electrons, atoms are surprisingly not particles at all but pure waves of matter (illustration right).

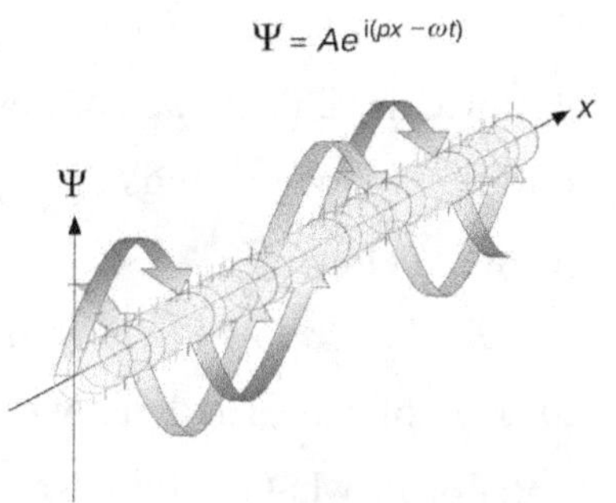

Now, let's look at our body and see where we can see waves there. We know that a normal resting heart rate for adults ranges from sixty to one hundred beats per minute. Depending on your physical condition, your heartbeat changes its vibration from fast to slow or vice versa. Regardless, as long as you can see or hear your heart beating, you know you are alive. When the vibration stops, you are most likely dead.

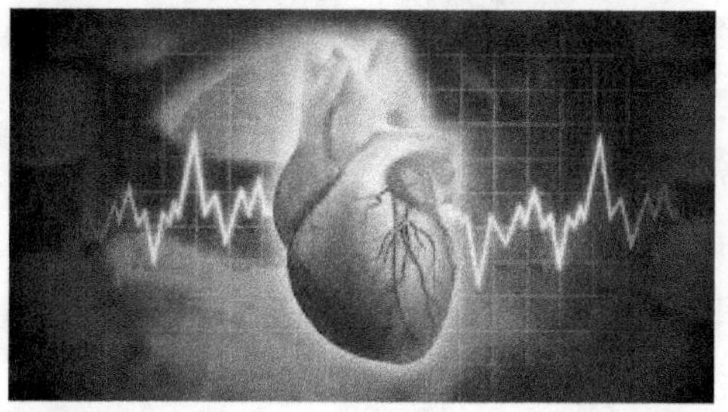

It is well known that the brain is an electrochemical organ. Believe it or not, a fully functioning brain can generate as much as ten watts of electrical power. Electrical activity in the brain is displayed in the form of brain waves, which are divided into four categories: beta, alpha, theta and delta (in order from highest to lowest frequency).

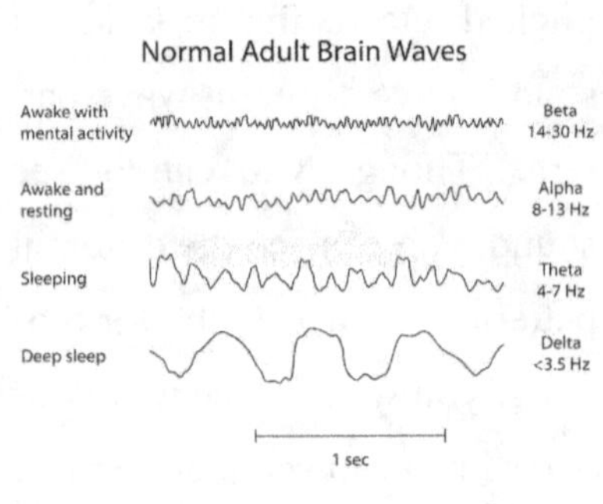

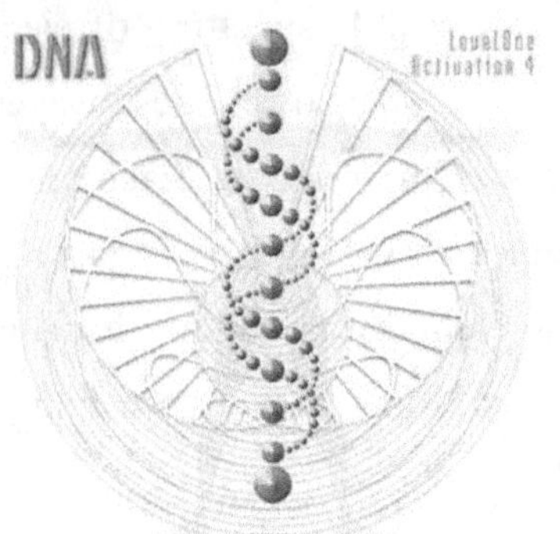

When you look even more closely at how we are made, you get into our DNA. According to the article "DNA: Definition, Structure & Discovery," published by Rachael Rettner on the *Live Science* website on December 7, 2017, "deoxyribonucleic acid, or DNA, is a molecule that contains the instructions an organism needs to develop, live and reproduce." She also states that "DNA is made up of molecules called *nucleotides*" and that these nucleotides are "attached together to form two long strands that spiral to create a structure called a *double helix*" (illustration above).

OK, I have spent enough time and space going over the fact that vibrations are made up of waves and that we are all vibrations. So, you may ask, "What does this vibration or what do these waves have to do with karate?" Let us get into the meat of the subject right now.

When you think of the power or effectiveness of karate, you often think of a devastating punch thrown at a *makiwara*. It is true that many karate practitioners develop large calluses on their fists to "prove" how strong and lethal their punches can be. With all due respect to these practitioners, there is little relationship between the size of their

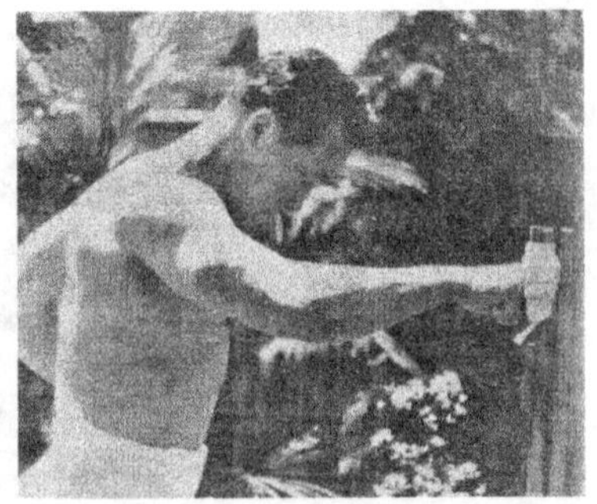

calluses and the effectiveness of their punch or the degree of their karate skill.

I do not mean to blame these people, but many of them tend to equate the skill level of a karate fighter with how hard he can punch a *makiwara*. I have to disagree with them as this is almost like equating karate skill with a baseball bat. Yes, if you swing a baseball bat and hit a person, you could kill that person. However, this action does not prove that you have a skilled fighting ability.

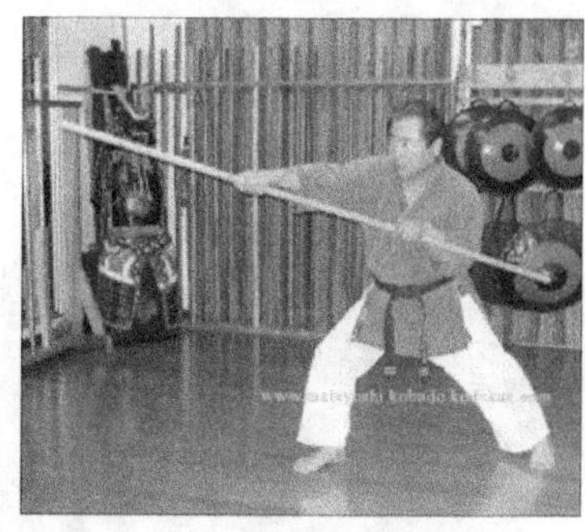

But, you may say that some of the *kobudo* weapons are the *jo* (杖) and the *bo* (photo right), which are stick-type weapons. This is true. If you have mastered the art of the *jo* or *bo*, you can say you are an expert in *kobudo*. However, that does not mean that you have mastered karate skills. Even though many karate masters are also experts in *kobudo*, mastering the ultimate skill of generating power in a karate punch is totally different from swinging a *bo*, for instance.

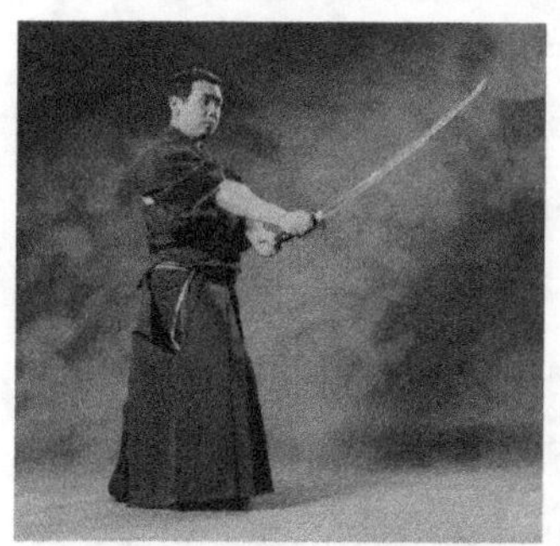

Some readers may say, "Yes, a karate attack should be like a samurai sword." It is very true that our karate technique should be as sharp as a katana and not like a baseball bat. On the other hand, we have to be honest with ourselves. Even though it is fun to imagine ourselves as modern-day samurai, we cannot lie about what we can or cannot do with our arms and legs. No matter how sharp our punches, strikes, or kicks may be, it is impossible for them to cut like a sword. The best we can expect is to break a nose, knock a tooth out, or crack a rib or two. In other words, our punches and kicks typically do damage the way a stick or a baseball bat does, which is ironic as I just wrote above that karate techniques are quite different from swinging a stick-type weapon such as a *bo*.

You might object to this by saying, "What's wrong with that? Who cares how I use my arms and legs as long as I can knock the opponent down?" Well, if you are

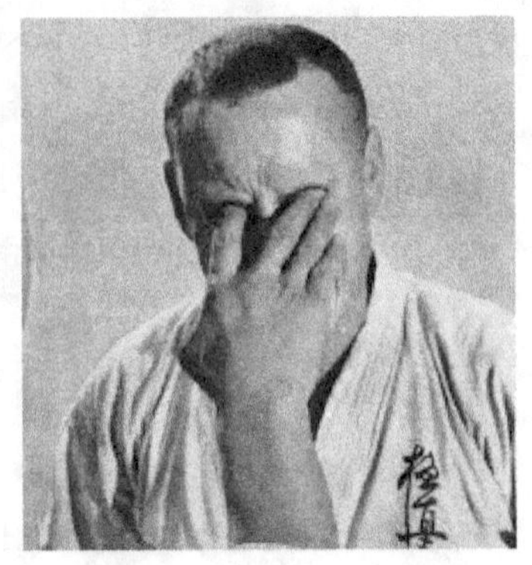

happy with just having a brutal punch or kick, then that is fine. However, if you are aiming at achieving *budo* karate, you must think about women, children, and seniors. You cannot expect most of these people to have enough brute force to break an arm or crack a jaw. Must these people be classified as unfit or inferior in the art of the empty hand? I hope not too many people think this way.

It is true that there are many karate techniques that women, children, and seniors can use in their self-defense strategy that do not require large, or even moderate, levels of brute force. Two good examples are eye jabs and groin kicks, which

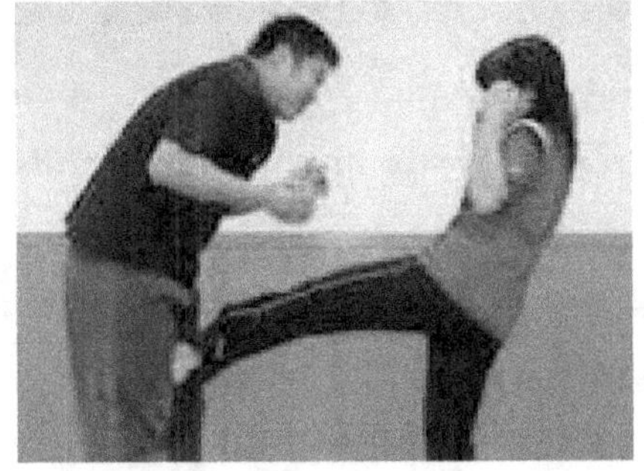

are very effective and do not require much power. Of course, there are many other self-defense techniques for women, children, and seniors. Regardless, is it possible for them to execute a powerful punch? My quick answer is yes, and this leads us into the main subject of this chapter, which is vibration, or *hado*.

If you are an advanced practitioner, you may have heard of hip vibration. Yes, the word *vibration* is used in karate. It is an advanced technique that is used to generate power by vibrating the hip region or twisting it quickly. This is used in Tekki/Naihanchi *kata*. For instance, it is difficult, as you know, to generate power with *kagi zuki* (鉤突き) while you are standing in *naihanchi dachi* (ナイハンチ立ち [photo right]) or *kiba dachi*. If you do not know how to vibrate your hips, your *kagi zuki* will depend mainly on the arm muscles and possibly on a leaning motion that you are not supposed to do. As you become familiar with the hip-vibration technique, you can generate this vibration in other stances, as well.

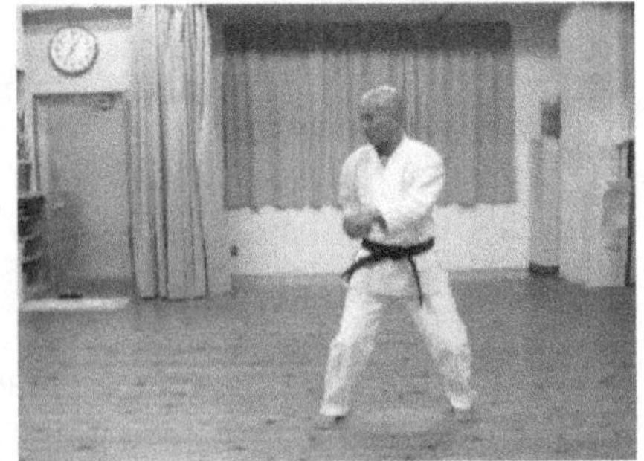

Though I consider this to be an important technique, it is not what I want to present in this chapter. What I would like to bring your attention to is the fact that you need to better understand your body. For example, did you know that most of your body, though it looks solid, is made up of water? According to Anne Marie Helmenstine, Ph.D., an author and consultant with a broad scientific and medical background, the amount of water in the human body ranges from fifty to seventy-five percent. The average adult body is fifty to sixty-five percent water, and the amount of water in the typical infant body is seventy-five to seventy-eight percent.

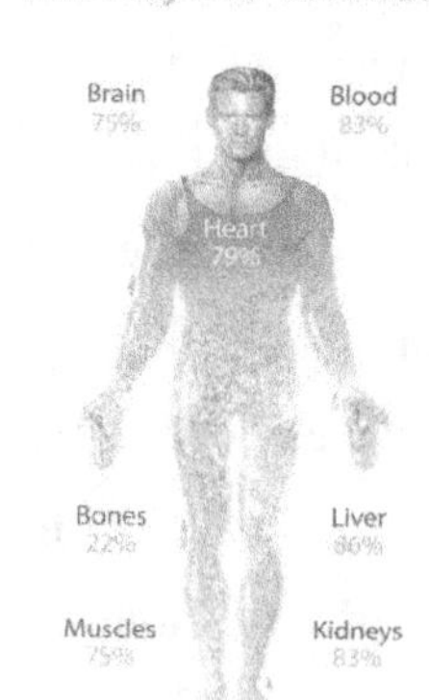

Isn't this interesting? I think it is amazing to find out that our body is not as much like a solid (like a *makiwara* or a board) as it is like a bag of water. This is an obvious condition of our body, yet we tend to consider it to be something solid. I believe this gap in our concept of our body is important as it determines how we train in our karate. In fact, aqua punching bags (photo left) are now commercially available. I think this equipment may still be expensive, but I definitely consider it to be much better than regular punching bags. Punching or kicking an aqua bag gives you better feedback in your fist or leg.

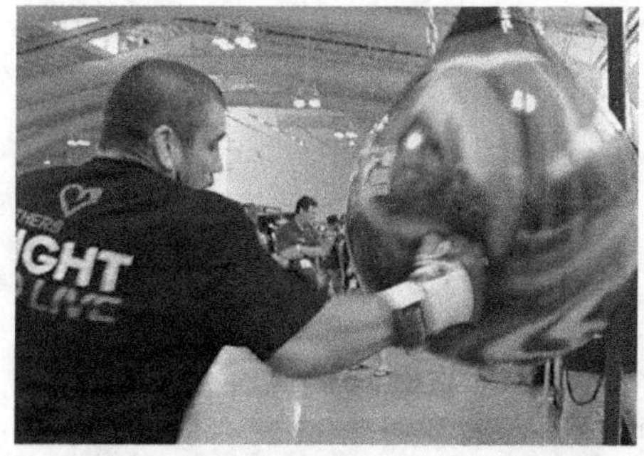

There is a memorable scene in the movie *Rocky* where the title character, played by Sylvester Stallone (1946–), goes into a meat freezer. He gets excited about the approaching boxing match and starts punching one of the large slabs of meat that are hanging there (photo right). Do you remember this scene? The intention of the director, or maybe Stallone himself as the

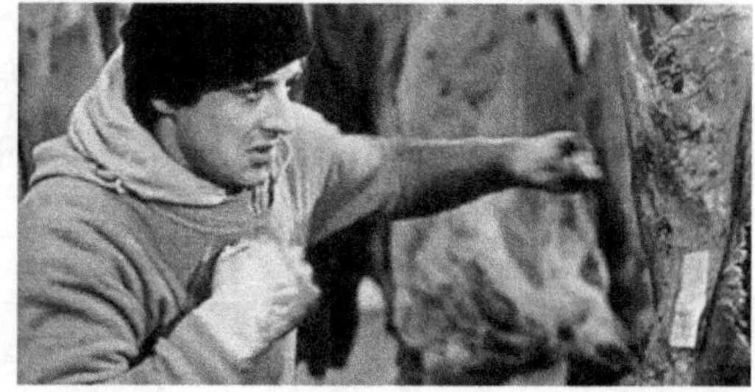

writer, was to project the idea that an unorthodox boxer was doing a crazy thing. However, it made a big impact on me. I was very impressed that he chose to hit that slab of meat. I got the impression that this was his regular training menu. Why was I so deeply impressed? I consider a slab of meat to be the best target for a boxer to simulate hitting a person.

Despite the above statement, I am not suggesting that karate practitioners pick up a side of beef to use as a punching target. The reason is that the punching mechanics of karate are fundamentally different from those of boxing. Even though boxing is a fighting system based on punching, the greatest difference between the two arts is that boxers use gloves. I do not mean that the gloves make the punches less damaging or effective. In fact, medical research has found that punching, especially to the head, is just as damaging with boxing gloves as without, if not more so. We all remember how Muhammad Ali suffered from Parkinson's disease resulting from head injury (photo above). So, the difference I am referring to has to do with the mechanics themselves.

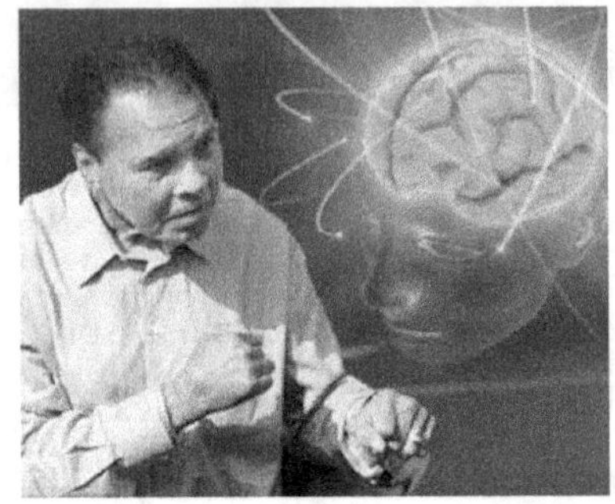

In other words, boxers must throw thrusting-type punches because they wear gloves. On the other hand, even though a karate punch can be a thrusting-type punch, most of the techniques that are considered to require a higher level of technical skill are impact punches (with or without a snapping motion). Some easy examples include *uraken uchi*, *shuto uchi*, *haito uchi* (背刀打ち), *nukite* (either *ippon* or *nihon*), etc. This can be debated, but these striking techniques in karate typically require a higher level of technical skill.

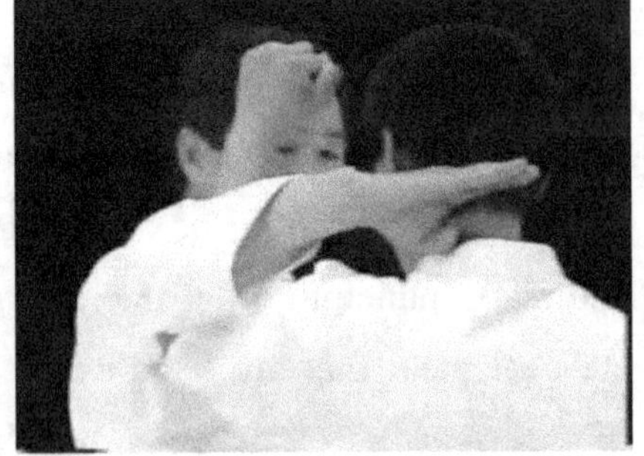

These techniques are mainly applied to the head or *jodan* but can also be thrown to the midsection (solar plexus or heart) and the lower area, especially the groin. I do not need to explain that a strike to the groin area does not require much power. The key point for a *nukite* to the eyes certainly is not the power of the technique but rather its accuracy. When striking the head, an expert *karateka* does not need to punch through to knock the opponent down. He would consider such a technique to be a waste of energy and thus unnecessary. He would rather hit in a way that creates a shock wave or vibration (*hado*) to the opponent's brain. This requires a precise strike to a certain point, such as the opponent's temple, but with much less power.

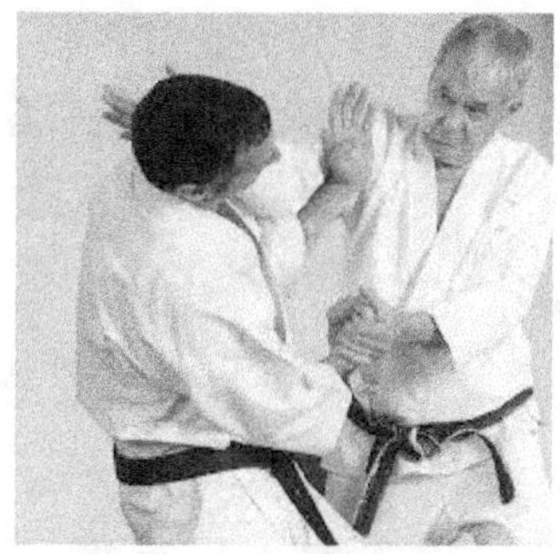

Why am I explaining this in such detail? My aim is to bring your attention to the essence of the martial arts. Power and speed are not that important. (Of course, this subject requires much explanation, which I have already done in the past.) On the contrary, what is more important in the martial arts is knowing how to deliver effective techniques to the correct targets with the least amount of power possible. This is because the martial arts were and are necessary not only for young men but also, and maybe even more so, for other people who may not be as strong, such as senior men, women, and even children.

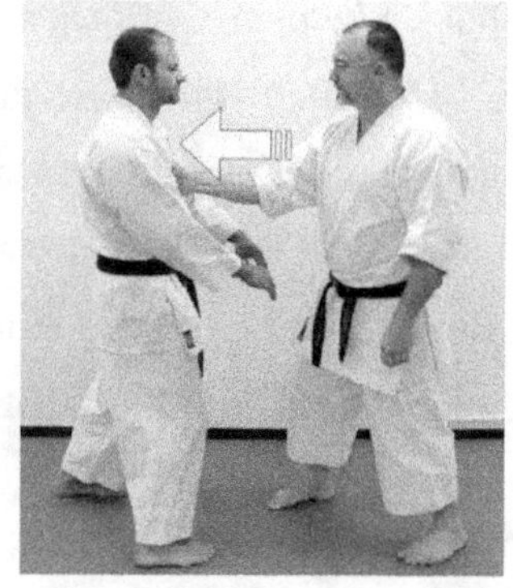

Now, let's go back to the main subject of *hado*. Knocking out an opponent with a punch powered by brute force is very possible, but you'll agree that this is not the ultimate aim of karate training. Earlier I touched on the fact that you can knock an opponent down with a punch or kick that may not be so hard but that can create *hado* to his brain. A karate expert also knows how to lightly punch or kick to the solar plexus and still cause enough shock to the diaphragm to knock the wind out of the opponent.

The techniques described above are important and can be mastered after training in karate for many years. In addition, I want to mention that *hado* is not only a physical technique; it also has a mental aspect. You are familiar with ki, which is also a wave of the mind. By having good, strong ki, you can sustain hard training. You can also build spirit or courage, and this positive wave (*hado*) will help you when you are facing a life problem or even being attacked by an assailant.

One thing I must add here is that there are many ki masters who claim they can knock their students down with their ki, a technique called *toate* (遠当て, 'hitting from afar'). Even though I am a full believer in the existence of ki, I do not believe these masters have the universal power to knock unsuspecting people down. Instead, I suspect they use some type of strong mental suggestion or hypnosis to control their students.

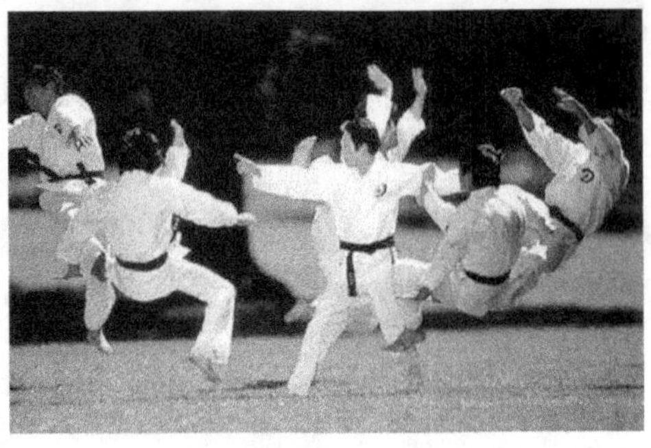

I can make this claim because I studied ki under one of the most famous ki experts in Japan, Master Kozo Nishino (西野皓三, 1926– [photo right]). He is known to possess *toate* ability and to be able to knock down more than a dozen students at one time. I wanted to learn this technique, so I joined his dojo in the nineties and trained there for two years. I write about the details of this experience in Chapter 13: "Tenketsu Jutsu" of my book *Shotokan Mysteries*, so I will give only a summary here.

Master Nishino was great. He could not only knock the students down but also control their movements, making them run, spin, etc. He had at least a few hundred students at that dojo alone, and he had several dojo across Japan. To make a long story short, he was not able to knock me down, or even move me. I was totally disappointed. I stood in front of him many times, but he was incapable of controlling me. More disappointingly, after a few months, he began to avoid me. Upon seeing this, I decided to quit training at his dojo. This does not mean that I can guarantee there is no ki master who can knock me down with his ki, but I will believe there is only when I experience it with my own body.

Regarding vibration in relation to the universe, I would like to share the wisdom of Nikola Tesla (Никола Тесла, 1856–1943), the famous Serbian American

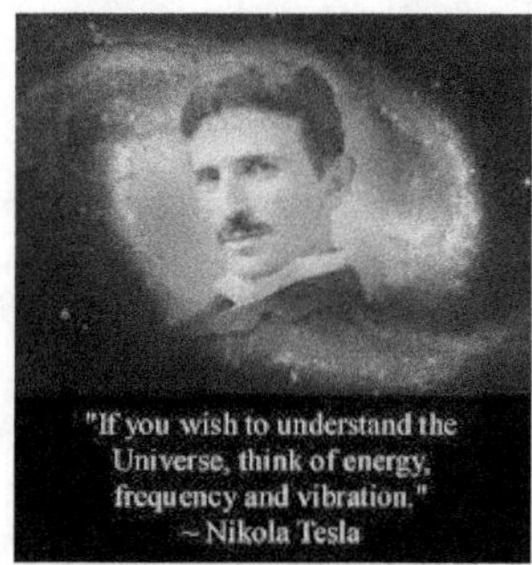

inventor, electrical and mechanical engineer, and physicist. He said, "If you want to find the secrets of the universe, think in terms of energy, frequency, and vibration" I find this idea coming from a genius such as him to be very interesting and educating. We can learn a lot from his findings and must examine his words closely. I believe Tesla, through the study of science, found the essence, or secret, of the universe. Maybe this is very close to the enlightenment a religious person or a martial artist searches for.

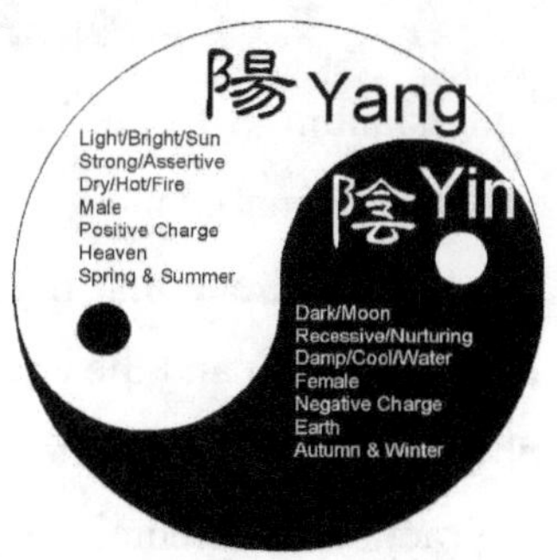

Western science may have discovered the secret of the universe in the twentieth century, but Asian wise men had discovered something similar many centuries prior. Our teachings say that this world is built on yin and yang. Everything in the universe is built with vibrations, or *hado*, and we need to train in *hado* in all three realms: physical, mental, and spiritual.

Self-defense may indeed be the most popular reason for people to start or maintain their martial arts training. However, believe it or not, defeating the opponent is not the most important aim of the martial arts. Many kenjutsu experts have come to realize this after having mastered their swordsmanship. But, for many of us, it is difficult to believe that victory in a fight is not the ultimate purpose of the martial arts.

Conclusion

You may be asking, "What is the ultimate purpose of the martial arts?" I have come to believe that the ultimate purpose of the martial arts is to learn how to achieve a pure form of *hado*. But, many readers may not agree with the concept I am about to share with you.

The ultimate stage of the martial arts, according to my understanding, is love as this is the purest form of the mind. If you learn how to love your life and the universe around you, I believe you have mastered the martial arts, as well. In other words, when you truly understand the martial arts, you will understand life. Even though this may sound like a nonsense statement, it is also the claim made by Morihei Ueshiba, the founder of aikido.

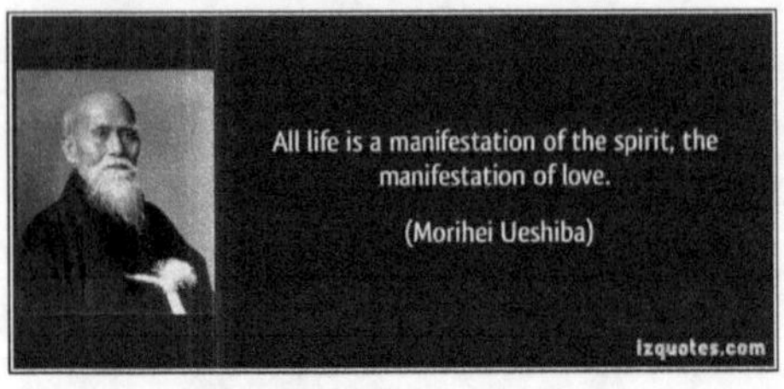

I still have not found or received such enlightenment as that which was found by Ueshiba, but at least I fully acknowledge that love is the ultimate goal of the martial arts. I am convinced that as I increase my understanding of love in my karate training, I will increase the *hado* within me, which will enable me to better understand karate.

I also believe that if you can love your enemy, then there is no need for self-defense as you and the enemy become one. This does not mean you do not need to physically train in karate. Of course, you must train your body, and you also need to practice the mental aspect of karate. If you train in and master both parts, then you can overcome the fear (small *hado*) that you have in your mind, and, at the same time, achieve a state of love (large *hado*).

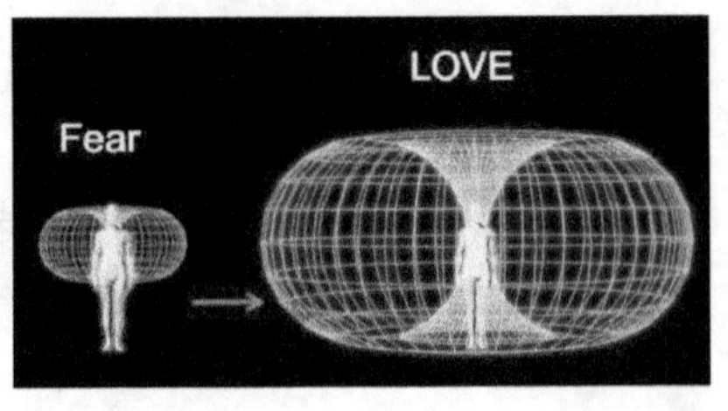

Therefore, I conclude that understanding this and being able to express it with your body must be the ultimate goal of the martial arts. At least, this is what I believe, and it is my life goal. What is the ultimate goal of your martial arts training?

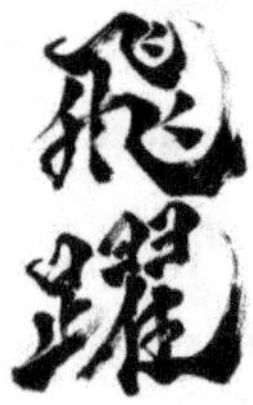

www.ingramcontent.com/pod-product-compliance
Lightning Source LLC
LaVergne TN
LVHW020710110826
845149LV00012B/2198

* 9 7 8 0 9 9 8 2 2 3 6 3 6 *